linux for human beings

Ubuntu 11.04
Ubuntu Server Guide

Fultus™ *Books*

ubuntu
linux for human beings

Ubuntu 11.04
Ubuntu Server Guide

ISBN-10: 1-59682-260-0
ISBN-13: 978-1-59682-260-3

Copyright © 2011 Canonical Ltd. and members of the Ubuntu Documentation Project

Cover design and book layout by Fultus Corporation

Published by Fultus Corporation

Publisher Web: *www.fultus.com*
Linbrary - Linux Library: *www.linbrary.com*
Online Bookstore: *store.fultus.com*
email: *production@fultus.com*

Table of Contents

List of Tables

Credits and License

The documents on this website are maintained by the *Ubuntu documentation team*[1]. For a list of contributors, see the *contributors page*[2].

This document is made available under the Creative Commons ShareAlike 2.5 License (CC-BY-SA).

You are free to modify, extend, and improve the Ubuntu documentation source code under the terms of this license. All derivative works must be released under this license.

This documentation is distributed in the hope that it will be useful, but WITHOUT ANY WARRANTY; without even the implied warranty of MERCHANTABILITY or FITNESS FOR A PARTICULAR PURPOSE AS DESCRIBED IN THE DISCLAIMER.

A copy of the license is available here: *Creative Commons ShareAlike License*[3].

[1] *https://wiki.ubuntu.com/DocumentationTeam*
[2] *https://help.ubuntu.com/11.04/serverguide/libs/C/contributors.html*
[3] *https://help.ubuntu.com/usr/share/ubuntu-docs/libs/C/ccbysa.xml*

Abstract

Welcome to the *Ubuntu Server Guide*! It contains information on how to install and configure various server applications on your Ubuntu system to fit your needs. It is a step-by-step, task-oriented guide for configuring and customizing your system.

Chapter 1.
Introduction

Welcome to the *Ubuntu Server Guide*!

Here you can find information on how to install and configure various server applications. It is a step-by-step, task-oriented guide for configuring and customizing your system.

This guide assumes you have a basic understanding of your Ubuntu system. Some installation details are covered in Chapter 2, *Installation*, but if you need detailed instructions installing Ubuntu please refer to the *Ubuntu Installation Guide* (ISBN-13: 978-1-59682-257-3).

A HTML version of the manual is available online at *the Ubuntu Documentation website*[1]. The HTML files are also available in the **ubuntu-serverguide** package. See Chapter 3, *Package Management* for details on installing packages.

If you choose to install the **ubuntu-serverguide** you can view this doc from a console by:

```
w3m /usr/share/ubuntu-serverguide/html/C/index.html
```

 Note

If you are using a localized version of Ubuntu, replace C with your language localization (e.g. *en_GB*).

1.1. Support

There are a couple of different ways that Ubuntu Server Edition is supported, commercial support and community support. The main commercial support (and development funding) is available from Canonical Ltd. They supply reasonably priced support contracts on a per desktop or per server basis. For more information see the *Canonical Services*[2] page.

Community support is also provided by dedicated individuals, and companies, that wish to make Ubuntu the best distribution possible. Support is provided through multiple mailing

---

[1] *https://help.ubuntu.com/*
[2] *http://www.canonical.com/services/support*

lists, IRC channels, forums, blogs, wikis, etc. The large amount of information available can be overwhelming, but a good search engine query can usually provide an answer to your questions. See the *Ubuntu Support*[3] page for more information.

---

[3] *http://www.ubuntu.com/support*

Chapter 2.
Installation

This chapter provides a quick overview of installing Ubuntu 11.04 Server Edition. For more detailed instructions, please refer to the *Ubuntu Installation Guide* (ISBN-13: 978-1-59682-257-3).

2.1. Preparing to Install

This section explains various aspects to consider before starting the installation.

2.1.1. System Requirements

Ubuntu 11.04 Server Edition supports two (2) major architectures: Intel x86 and AMD64. The table below lists recommended hardware specifications. Depending on your needs, you might manage with less than this. However, most users risk being frustrated if they ignore these suggestions.

Install Type	RAM	Hard Drive Space	
		Base System	All Tasks Installed
Server	128 megabytes	500 megabytes	1 gigabyte

Table 2.1. Recommended Minimum Requirements

The Server Edition provides a common base for all sorts of server applications. It is a minimalist design providing a platform for the desired services, such as file/print services, web hosting, email hosting, etc.

The requirements for UEC are slightly different for Front End requirements see the Section 19.3.2.1, *Front End Requirements*and for UEC Node requirements see the Section 19.3.2.2, *Node Requirements*.

2.1.2. Server and Desktop Differences

There are a few differences between the *Ubuntu Server Edition* and the *Ubuntu Desktop Edition*. It should be noted that both editions use the same **apt** repositories. Making it just as easy to install a server application on the Desktop Edition as it is on the Server Edition.

The differences between the two editions are the lack of an X window environment in the Server Edition, the installation process, and different Kernel options.

2.1.2.1. Kernel Differences

- The Server Edition uses the *Deadline* I/O scheduler instead of the *CFQ* scheduler used by the Desktop Edition.

- *Preemption* is turned off in the Server Edition.

- The timer interrupt is 100 Hz in the Server Edition and 250 Hz in the Desktop Edition.

 Note

When running a 64-bit version of Ubuntu on 64-bit processors you are not limited by memory addressing space.

To see all kernel configuration options you can look through `/boot/config-2.6.35-server`. Also, *Linux Kernel in a Nutshell*[1] is a great resource on the options available.

2.1.3. Backing Up

- Before installing **Ubuntu Server Edition** you should make sure all data on the system is backed up. See Chapter 18, *Backups* for backup options.

  If this is not the first time an operating system has been installed on your computer, it is likely you will need to re-partition your disk to make room for Ubuntu.

  Any time you partition your disk, you should be prepared to lose everything on the disk should you make a mistake or something goes wrong during partitioning. The programs used in installation are quite reliable, most have seen years of use, but they also perform destructive actions.

2.2. Installing from CD

The basic steps to install Ubuntu Server Edition from CD are the same for installing any operating system from CD. Unlike the *Desktop Edition* the *Server Edition* does not include a graphical installation program. Instead the Server Edition uses a console menu based process.

- First, download and burn the appropriate ISO file from the *Ubuntu web site*[2].
- Boot the system from the CD-ROM drive.

---

[1] *http://www.kroah.com/lkn/*
[2] *http://www.ubuntu.com/getubuntu/download*

- At the boot prompt you will be asked to select the language. Afterwards the installation process begins by asking for your keyboard layout.

- From the main boot menu there are some additional options to install Ubuntu Server Edition. You can install a basic Ubuntu Server, or install Ubuntu Server as part of a *Ubuntu Enterprise Cloud*. For more information on UEC see the Section 19.3, *UEC*. The rest of this section will cover the basic Ubuntu Server install.

- The installer then discovers your hardware configuration, and configures the network settings using DHCP. If you do not wish to use DHCP at the next screen choose "Go Back", and you have the option to "Configure the network manually".

- Next, the installer asks for the system's hostname and Time Zone.

- You can then choose from several options to configure the hard drive layout. For advanced disk options see the Section 2.4, *Advanced Installation*.

- The Ubuntu base system is then installed.

- A new user is setup, this user will have *root* access through the **sudo** utility.

- After the user is setup, you will be asked to encrypt your home directory.

- The next step in the installation process is to decide how you want to update the system. There are three options:

  - *No automatic updates*: this requires an administrator to log into the machine and manually install updates.

  - *Install security updates Automatically*: will install the **unattended-upgrades** package, which will install security updates without the intervention of an administrator. For more details see the Section 3.5, *Automatic Updates*.

  - *Manage the system with Landscape*: Landscape is a paid service provided by Canonical to help manage your Ubuntu machines. See the *Landscape*[3] site for details.

- You now have the option to install, or not install, several package tasks. See the Section 2.2.1, *Package Tasks* for details. Also, there is an option to launch **aptitude** to choose specific packages to install. For more information see the Section 3.4, *Aptitude*.

- Finally, the last step before rebooting is to set the clock to UTC.

 Note

If at any point during installation you are not satisfied by the default setting, use the "Go Back" function at any prompt to be brought to a detailed installation menu that will allow you to modify the default settings.

---

[3] *http://www.canonical.com/projects/landscape*

At some point during the installation process you may want to read the help screen provided by the installation system. To do this, press F1.

Once again, for detailed instructions see the *Ubuntu Installation Guide* (ISBN-13: 978-1-59682-257-3).

2.2.1. Package Tasks

During the Server Edition installation you have the option of installing additional packages from the CD. The packages are grouped by the type of service they provide.

- DNS server: Selects the BIND DNS server and its documentation.
- LAMP server: Selects a ready-made Linux/Apache/MySQL/PHP server.
- Mail server: This task selects a variety of package useful for a general purpose mail server system.
- OpenSSH server: Selects packages needed for an OpenSSH server.
- PostgreSQL database: This task selects client and server packages for the PostgreSQL database.
- Print server: This task sets up your system to be a print server.
- Samba File server: This task sets up your system to be a Samba file server, which is especially suitable in networks with both Windows and Linux systems.
- Tomcat Java server: Installs Apache Tomcat and needed dependencies.
- Virtual Machine host: Includes packages needed to run KVM virtual machines.
- Manually select packages: Executes **aptitude** allowing you to individually select packages.

Installing the package groups is accomplished using the **tasksel** utility. One of the important difference between Ubuntu (or Debian) and other GNU/Linux distribution is that, when installed, a package is also configured to reasonable defaults, eventually prompting you for additional required information. Likewise, when installing a task, the packages are not only installed, but also configured to provided a fully integrated service.

Once the installation process has finished you can view a list of available tasks by entering the following from a terminal prompt:

```
tasksel --list-tasks
```

Note

The output will list tasks from other Ubuntu based distributions such as Kubuntu and Edubuntu. Note that you can also invoke the **tasksel** command by itself, which will bring up a menu of the different tasks available.

You can view a list of which packages are installed with each task using the *--task-packages* option. For example, to list the packages installed with the *DNS Server* task enter the following:

```
tasksel --task-packages dns-server
```

The output of the command should list:

```
bind9-doc
bind9utils
bind9
```

Also, if you did not install one of the tasks during the installation process, but for example you decide to make your new LAMP server a DNS server as well. Simply insert the installation CD and from a terminal:

```
sudo tasksel install dns-server
```

2.3. Upgrading

There are several ways to upgrade from one Ubuntu release to another. This section gives an overview of the recommended upgrade method.

2.3.1. do-release-upgrade

The recommended way to upgrade a Server Edition installation is to use the **do-release-upgrade** utility. Part of the *update-manager-core* package, it does not have any graphical dependencies and is installed by default.

Debian based systems can also be upgraded by using **apt-get dist-upgrade**. However, using **do-release-upgrade** is recommended because it has the ability to handle system configuration changes sometimes needed between releases.

To upgrade to a newer release, from a terminal prompt enter:

```
do-release-upgrade
```

It is also possible to use **do-release-upgrade** to upgrade to a development version of Ubuntu. To accomplish this use the *-d* switch:

```
do-release-upgrade -d
```

Warning

Upgrading to a development release is *not* recommended for production environments.

2.4. Advanced Installation

2.4.1. Software RAID

RAID is a method of configuring multiple hard drives to act as one, reducing the probability of catastrophic data loss in case of drive failure. RAID is implemented in either software (where the operating system knows about both drives and actively maintains both of them) or hardware (where a special controller makes the OS think there's only one drive and maintains the drives 'invisibly').

The RAID software included with current versions of Linux (and Ubuntu) is based on the **'mdadm'** driver and works very well, better even than many so-called 'hardware' RAID controllers. This section will guide you through installing Ubuntu Server Edition using two RAID1 partitions on two physical hard drives, one for / and another for *swap*.

2.4.1.1. Partitioning

Follow the installation steps until you get to the *Partition disks* step, then:

1. Select *Manual* as the partition method.

2. Select the first hard drive, and agree to *"Create a new empty partition table on this device?"*.

    Repeat this step for each drive you wish to be part of the RAID array.

3. Select the *"FREE SPACE"* on the first drive then select *"Create a new partition"*.

4. Next, select the *Size* of the partition. This partition will be the *swap* partition, and a general rule for swap size is twice that of RAM. Enter the partition size, then choose *Primary*, then *Beginning*.

 Note

A swap partition size of twice the available RAM capacity may not always be desirable, especially on systems with large amounts of RAM. Calculating the swap partition size for servers is highly dependent on how the system is going to be used.

5. Select the *"Use as:"* line at the top. By default this is "Ext4 journaling file system", change that to *"physical volume for RAID"* then *"Done setting up partition"*.

6. For the / partition once again select *"Free Space"* on the first drive then *"Create a new partition"*.

7. Use the rest of the free space on the drive and choose *Continue*, then *Primary*.

8. As with the swap partition, select the *"Use as:"* line at the top, changing it to *"physical volume for RAID"*. Also select the *"Bootable flag:"* line to change the value to *"on"*. Then choose *"Done setting up partition"*.

9. Repeat steps three through eight for the other disk and partitions.

2.4.1.2. RAID Configuration

With the partitions setup the arrays are ready to be configured:

---

1. Back in the main "Partition Disks" page, select "*Configure Software RAID*" at the top.

2. Select "*yes*" to write the changes to disk.

3. Choose "*Create MD device* ".

4. For this example, select "*RAID1*", but if you are using a different setup choose the appropriate type (RAID0 RAID1 RAID5).

 Note

In order to use *RAID5* you need at least *three* drives. Using RAID0 or RAID1 only *two* drives are required.

5. Enter the number of active devices "*2*", or the amount of hard drives you have, for the array. Then select "*Continue*".

6. Next, enter the number of spare devices "*0*" by default, then choose "*Continue*".

7. Choose which partitions to use. Generally they will be sda1, sdb1, sdc1, etc. The numbers will usually match and the different letters correspond to different hard drives.

   For the *swap* partition choose *sda1* and *sdb1*. Select "*Continue*" to go to the next step.

8. Repeat steps *three* through *seven* for the / partition choosing *sda2* and *sdb2*.

9. Once done select "*Finish*".

2.4.1.3. Formatting

There should now be a list of hard drives and RAID devices. The next step is to format and set the mount point for the RAID devices. Treat the RAID device as a local hard drive, format and mount accordingly.

1. Select the *RAID1 device #0* partition.

2. Choose "*Use as:*". Then select "*swap area*", then "*Done setting up partition*".

3. Next, select the *RAID1 device #1* partition.

4. Choose "*Use as:*". Then select "*Ext3 journaling file system*".

5. Then select the "*Mount point*" and choose "*/ - the root file system*". Change any of the other options as appropriate, then select "*Done setting up partition*".

6. Finally, select "*Finish partitioning and write changes to disk*".

If you choose to place the root partition on a RAID array, the installer will then ask if you would like to boot in a *degraded* state. See the Section 2.4.1.4, *Degraded RAID* for further details.

The installation process will then continue normally.

2.4.1.4. Degraded RAID

At some point in the life of the computer a disk failure event may occur. When this happens, using Software RAID, the operating system will place the array into what is known as a *degraded* state.

If the array has become degraded, due to the chance of data corruption, by default Ubuntu Server Edition will boot to *initramfs* after thirty seconds. Once the initramfs has booted there is a fifteen second prompt giving you the option to go ahead and boot the system, or attempt manual recover. Booting to the initramfs prompt may or may not be the desired behavior, especially if the machine is in a remote location. Booting to a degraded array can be configured several ways:

- The **dpkg-reconfigure** utility can be used to configure the default behavior, and during the process you will be queried about additional settings related to the array. Such as monitoring, email alerts, etc. To reconfigure **mdadm** enter the following:

```
sudo dpkg-reconfigure mdadm
```

- The **dpkg-reconfigure mdadm** process will change the `/etc/initramfs-tools/conf.d/mdadm` configuration file. The file has the advantage of being able to pre-configure the system's behavior, and can also be manually edited:

```
BOOT_DEGRADED=true
```

 Note

The configuration file can be overridden by using a Kernel argument.

- Using a Kernel argument will allow the system to boot to a degraded array as well:

  - When the server is booting press **Shift** to open the **Grub** menu.
  - Press **e** to edit your kernel command options.
  - Press the **down** arrow to highlight the kernel line.
  - Add *"bootdegraded=true"* (without the quotes) to the end of the line.
  - Press **Ctrl+x** to boot the system.

Once the system has booted you can either repair the array see the Section 2.4.1.5, *RAID Maintenance* for details, or copy important data to another machine due to major hardware failure.

2.4.1.5. RAID Maintenance

The **mdadm** utility can be used to view the status of an array, add disks to an array, remove disks, etc:

- To view the status of an array, from a terminal prompt enter:

  ```
  sudo mdadm -D /dev/md0
  ```

  The *-D* tells **mdadm** to display *detailed* information about the /dev/md0 device. Replace /dev/md0 with the appropriate RAID device.

- To view the status of a disk in an array:

  ```
  sudo mdadm -E /dev/sda1
  ```

  The output if very similar to the **mdadm -D** command, adjust /dev/sda1 for each disk.

- If a disk fails and needs to be removed from an array enter:

  ```
  sudo mdadm --remove /dev/md0 /dev/sda1
  ```

  Change /dev/md0 and /dev/sda1 to the appropriate RAID device and disk.

- Similarly, to add a new disk:

  ```
  sudo mdadm --add /dev/md0 /dev/sda1
  ```

Sometimes a disk can change to a *faulty* state even though there is nothing physically wrong with the drive. It is usually worthwhile to remove the drive from the array then re-add it. This will cause the drive to re-sync with the array. If the drive will not sync with the array, it is a good indication of hardware failure.

The /proc/mdstat file also contains useful information about the system's RAID devices:

```
cat /proc/mdstat
Personalities : [linear] [multipath] [raid0] [raid1] [raid6] [raid5] [raid4] [raid10]
md0 : active raid1 sda1[0] sdb1[1]
      10016384 blocks [2/2] [UU]

unused devices: <none>
```

The following command is great for watching the status of a syncing drive:

```
watch -n1 cat /proc/mdstat
```

Press *Ctrl+c* to stop the **watch** command.

If you do need to replace a faulty drive, after the drive has been replaced and synced, **grub** will need to be installed. To install **grub** on the new drive, enter the following:

```
sudo grub-install /dev/md0
```

Replace /dev/md0 with the appropriate array device name.

2.4.1.6. Resources

The topic of RAID arrays is a complex one due to the plethora of ways RAID can be configured. Please see the following links for more information:

- *Ubuntu Wiki Articles on RAID*[4]

---

[4] *https://help.ubuntu.com/community/Installation#raid*

- *Software RAID HOWTO*[5]
- *Managing RAID on Linux*[6]

2.4.2. Logical Volume Manager (LVM)

Logical Volume Manger, or *LVM*, allows administrators to create *logical* volumes out of one or multiple physical hard disks. LVM volumes can be created on both software RAID partitions and standard partitions residing on a single disk. Volumes can also be extended, giving greater flexibility to systems as requirements change.

2.4.2.1. Overview

A side effect of LVM's power and flexibility is a greater degree of complication. Before diving into the LVM installation process, it is best to get familiar with some terms.

- *Volume Group (VG):* contains one or several Logical Volumes (LV).

- *Logical Volume (LV):* is similar to a partition in a non-LVM system. Multiple Physical Volumes (PV) can make up one LV, on top of which resides the actual EXT3, XFS, JFS, etc filesystem.

- *Physical Volume (PV):* physical hard disk or software RAID partition. The Volume Group can be extended by adding more PVs.

2.4.2.2. Installation

As an example this section covers installing Ubuntu Server Edition with /srv mounted on a LVM volume. During the initial install only one Physical Volume (PV) will be part of the Volume Group (VG). Another PV will be added after install to demonstrate how a VG can be extended.

There are several installation options for LVM, "*Guided - use the entire disk and setup LVM*" which will also allow you to assign a portion of the available space to LVM, "*Guided - use entire and setup encrypted LVM*", or *Manually* setup the partitions and configure LVM. At this time the only way to configure a system with both LVM and standard partitions, during installation, is to use the Manual approach.

1. Follow the installation steps until you get to the *Partition disks* step, then:

2. At the "*Partition Disks* screen choose "*Manual*".

3. Select the hard disk and on the next screen choose "yes" to "*Create a new empty partition table on this device*".

---

[5] *http://www.faqs.org/docs/Linux-HOWTO/Software-RAID-HOWTO.html*
[6] *http://oreilly.com/catalog/9781565927308/*

4. Next, create standard */boot*, *swap*, and */* partitions with whichever filesystem you prefer.

5. For the LVM */srv*, create a new *Logical* partition. Then change "*Use as*" to "*physical volume for LVM*" then "*Done setting up the partition*".

6. Now select "*Configure the Logical Volume Manager*" at the top, and choose "*Yes*" to write the changes to disk.

7. For the "*LVM configuration action*" on the next screen, choose "*Create volume group*". Enter a name for the VG such as *vg01*, or something more descriptive. After entering a name, select the partition configured for LVM, and choose "*Continue*".

8. Back at the "*LVM configuration action*" screen, select "*Create logical volume*". Select the newly created volume group, and enter a name for the new LV, for example *srv* since that is the intended mount point. Then choose a size, which may be the full partition because it can always be extended later. Choose "*Finish*" and you should be back at the main "*Partition Disks*" screen.

9. Now add a filesystem to the new LVM. Select the partition under "*LVM VG vg01, LV srv*", or whatever name you have chosen, the choose *Use as*. Setup a file system as normal selecting */srv* as the mount point. Once done, select "*Done setting up the partition*".

10. Finally, select "*Finish partitioning and write changes to disk*". Then confirm the changes and continue with the rest of the installation.

There are some useful utilities to view information about LVM:

*   *vgdisplay:* shows information about Volume Groups.
*   *lvdisplay:* has information about Logical Volumes.
*   *pvdisplay:* similarly displays information about Physical Volumes.

2.4.2.3. Extending Volume Groups

Continuing with *srv* as an LVM volume example, this section covers adding a second hard disk, creating a Physical Volume (PV), adding it to the volume group (VG), extending the logical volume `srv` and finally extending the filesystem. This example assumes a second hard disk has been added to the system. This hard disk will be named `/dev/sdb` in our example. BEWARE: make sure you don't already have an existing `/dev/sdb` before issuing the commands below. You could lose some data if you issue those commands on a non-empty disk. In our example we will use the entire disk as a physical volume (you could choose to create partitions and use them as different physical volumes).

1. First, create the physical volume, in a terminal execute:

```
sudo pvcreate /dev/sdb
```

2. Now extend the Volume Group (VG):

```
sudo vgextend vg01 /dev/sdb
```

3. Use **vgdisplay** to find out the free physical extents - Free PE / size (the size you can allocate). We will assume a free size of 511 PE (equivalent to 2GB with a PE size of 4MB) and we will use the whole free space available. Use your own PE and/or free space.

    The Logical Volume (LV) can now be extended by different methods, we will only see how to use the PE to extend the LV:

```
sudo lvextend /dev/vg01/srv -l +511
```

    The *-l* option allows the LV to be extended using PE. The *-L* option allows the LV to be extended using Meg, Gig, Tera, etc bytes.

4. Even though you are supposed to be able to *expand* an ext3 or ext4 filesystem without unmounting it first, it may be a good practice to unmount it anyway and check the filesystem, so that you don't mess up the day you want to reduce a logical volume (in that case unmounting first is compulsory).

    The following commands are for an *EXT3* or *EXT4* filesystem. If you are using another filesystem there may be other utilities available.

```
sudo umount /srv
sudo e2fsck -f /dev/vg01/srv
```

    The *-f* option of **e2fsck** forces checking even if the system seems clean.

5. Finally, resize the filesystem:

```
sudo resize2fs /dev/vg01/srv
```

6. Now mount the partition and check its size.

```
mount /dev/vg01/srv /srv && df -h /srv
```

2.4.2.4. Resources

- See the *Ubuntu Wiki LVM Articles*[7].
- See the *LVM HOWTO*[8] for more information.
- Another good article is *Managing Disk Space with LVM*[9] on O'Reilly's linuxdevcenter.com site.
- For more information on **fdisk** see the *fdisk man page*[10].

---

[7] *htttps://help.ubuntu.com/community/Installation#lvm*
[8] *http://tldp.org/HOWTO/LVM-HOWTO/index.html*
[9] *http://www.linuxdevcenter.com/pub/a/linux/2006/04/27/managing-disk-space-with-lvm.html*
[10] *http://manpages.ubuntu.com/manpages/natty/en/man8/fdisk.8.html*

Chapter 3.
Package Management

Ubuntu features a comprehensive package management system for the installation, upgrade, configuration, and removal of software. In addition to providing access to an organized base of over 24,000 software packages for your Ubuntu computer, the package management facilities also feature dependency resolution capabilities and software update checking.

Several tools are available for interacting with Ubuntu's package management system, from simple command-line utilities which may be easily automated by system administrators, to a simple graphical interface which is easy to use by those new to Ubuntu.

3.1. Introduction

Ubuntu's package management system is derived from the same system used by the Debian GNU/Linux distribution. The package files contain all of the necessary files, meta-data, and instructions to implement a particular functionality or software application on your Ubuntu computer.

Debian package files typically have the extension '.deb', and typically exist in repositories which are collections of packages found on various media, such as CD-ROM discs, or online. Packages are normally of the pre-compiled binary format; thus installation is quick and requires no compiling of software.

Many complex packages use the concept of dependencies. Dependencies are additional packages required by the principal package in order to function properly. For example, the speech synthesis package **Festival** depends upon the package **libasound2**, which is a package supplying the **ALSA** sound library needed for audio playback. In order for **Festival** to function, it and all of its dependencies must be installed. The software management tools in Ubuntu will do this automatically.

3.2. dpkg

dpkg is a package manager for *Debian* based systems. It can install, remove, and build packages, but unlike other package management system's, it can not automatically download and install packages or their dependencies. This section covers using **dpkg** to manage locally installed packages:

- To list all packages installed on the system, from a terminal prompt enter:
  ```
  dpkg -l
  ```
- Depending on the amount of packages on your system, this can generate a large amount of output. Pipe the output through **grep** to see if a specific package is installed:
  ```
  dpkg -l | grep apache2
  ```

  Replace *apache2* with any package name, part of a package name, or other regular expression.

- To list the files installed by a package, in this case the **ufw** package, enter:
  ```
  dpkg -L ufw
  ```
- If you are not sure which package installed a file, **dpkg -S** may be able to tell you. For example:
  ```
  dpkg -S /etc/host.conf
  base-files: /etc/host.conf
  ```

  The output shows that the /etc/host.conf belongs to the **base-files** package.

Note

Many files are automatically generated during the package install process, and even though they are on the filesystem **dpkg -S** may not know which package they belong to.

- You can install a local *.deb* file by entering:
  ```
  sudo dpkg -i zip_2.32-1_i386.deb
  ```

  Change `zip_2.32-1_i386.deb` to the actual file name of the local .deb file.

- Uninstalling a package can be accomplished by:
  ```
  sudo dpkg -r zip
  ```

Caution

Uninstalling packages using **dpkg**, in most cases, is *NOT* recommended. It is better to use a package manager that handles dependencies, to ensure that the system is in a consistent state. For example using **dpkg -r** you can remove the **zip** package, but any packages that depend on it will still be installed and may no longer function correctly.

For more **dpkg** options see the man page: **man dpkg**.

3.3. Apt-Get

The **apt-get** command is a powerful command-line tool used to work with Ubuntu's *Advanced Packaging Tool* (APT) performing such functions as installation of new software packages, upgrade of existing software packages, updating of the package list index, and even upgrading the entire Ubuntu system.

Being a simple command-line tool, **apt-get** has numerous advantages over other package management tools available in Ubuntu for server administrators. Some of these advantages include ease of use over simple terminal connections (SSH) and the ability to be used in system administration scripts, which can in turn be automated by the **cron** scheduling utility.

Some examples of popular uses for the **apt-get** utility:

- **Install a Package**: Installation of packages using the **apt-get** tool is quite simple. For example, to install the network scanner nmap, type the following:

```
sudo apt-get install nmap
```

- **Remove a Package**: Removal of a package or packages is also a straightforward and simple process. To remove the nmap package installed in the previous example, type the following:

```
sudo apt-get remove nmap
```

 Tip

> **Multiple Packages**: You may specify multiple packages to be installed or removed, separated by spaces.

- Also, adding the *--purge* options to **apt-get remove** will remove the package configuration files as well. This may or may not be the desired effect so use with caution.

- **Update the Package Index**: The APT package index is essentially a database of available packages from the repositories defined in the `/etc/apt/sources.list` file. To update the local package index with the latest changes made in repositories, type the following:

```
sudo apt-get update
```

- **Upgrade Packages**: Over time, updated versions of packages currently installed on your computer may become available from the package repositories (for example security updates). To upgrade your system, first update your package index as outlined above, and then type:

```
sudo apt-get upgrade
```

For information on upgrading to a new Ubuntu release see the Section 2.3, *Upgrading*.

Actions of the **apt-get** command, such as installation and removal of packages, are logged in the /var/log/dpkg.log log file.

For further information about the use of **APT**, read the comprehensive *Debian APT User Manual*[1] or type:

```
apt-get help
```

3.4. Aptitude

Aptitude is a menu-driven, text-based front-end to the *Advanced Packaging Tool* (APT) system. Many of the common package management functions, such as installation, removal, and upgrade, are performed in **Aptitude** with single-key commands, which are typically lowercase letters.

Aptitude is best suited for use in a non-graphical terminal environment to ensure proper functioning of the command keys. You may start **Aptitude** as a normal user with the following command at a terminal prompt:

```
sudo aptitude
```

When **Aptitude** starts, you will see a menu bar at the top of the screen and two panes below the menu bar. The top pane contains package categories, such as New Packages and Not Installed Packages. The bottom pane contains information related to the packages and package categories.

Using **Aptitude** for package management is relatively straightforward, and the user interface makes common tasks simple to perform. The following are examples of common package management functions as performed in **Aptitude**:

- **Install Packages**: To install a package, locate the package via the Not Installed Packages package category, for example, by using the keyboard arrow keys and the **ENTER** key, and highlight the package you wish to install. After highlighting the package you wish to install, press the **+** key, and the package entry should turn green, indicating it has been marked for installation. Now press **g** to be presented with a summary of package actions. Press **g** again, and you will be prompted to become root to complete the installation. Press **ENTER** which will result in a Password: prompt. Enter your user password to become root. Finally, press **g** once more and you'll be prompted to download the package. Press **ENTER** on the Continue prompt, and downloading and installation of the package will commence.

- **Remove Packages**: To remove a package, locate the package via the Installed Packages package category, for example, by using the keyboard arrow keys and the

---

[1] *http://www.debian.org/doc/user-manuals#apt-howto*

ENTER key, and highlight the package you wish to remove. After highlighting the package you wish to install, press the - key, and the package entry should turn pink, indicating it has been marked for removal. Now press **g** to be presented with a summary of package actions. Press **g** again, and you will be prompted to become root to complete the installation. Press **ENTER** which will result in a Password: prompt. Enter your user password to become root. Finally, press **g** once more, and you'll be prompted to download the package. Press **ENTER** on the Continue prompt, and removal of the package will commence.

- **Update Package Index**: To update the package index, simply press the **u** key and you will be prompted to become root to complete the update. Press **ENTER** which will result in a Password: prompt. Enter your user password to become root. Updating of the package index will commence. Press **ENTER** on the OK prompt when the download dialog is presented to complete the process.

- **Upgrade Packages**: To upgrade packages, perform the update of the package index as detailed above, and then press the **U** key to mark all packages with updates. Now press **g** whereby you'll be presented with a summary of package actions. Press **g** again, and you will be prompted to become root to complete the installation. Press **ENTER** which will result in a Password: prompt. Enter your user password to become root. Finally, press **g** once more, and you'll be prompted to download the packages. Press **ENTER** on the Continue prompt, and upgrade of the packages will commence.

The first column of information displayed in the package list in the top pane, when actually viewing packages lists the current state of the package, and uses the following key to describe the state of the package:

- **i**: Installed package
- **c**: Package not installed, but package configuration remains on system
- **p**: Purged from system
- **v**: Virtual package
- **B**: Broken package
- **u**: Unpacked files, but package not yet configured
- **C**: Half-configured - Configuration failed and requires fix
- **H**: Half-installed - Removal failed and requires fix

To exit Aptitude, simply press the **q** key and confirm you wish to exit. Many other functions are available from the Aptitude menu by pressing the **F10** key.

3.5. Automatic Updates

The **unattended-upgrades** package can be used to automatically install updated packages, and can be configured to update all packages or just install security updates. First, install the package by entering the following in a terminal:

```
sudo apt-get install unattended-upgrades
```

To configure **unattended-upgrades**, edit /etc/apt/apt.conf.d/50unattended-upgrades and adjust the following to fit your needs:

```
Unattended-Upgrade::Allowed-Origins {
        "Ubuntu natty-security";
//      "Ubuntu natty-updates";
};
```

Certain packages can also be *blacklisted* and therefore will not be automatically updated. To blacklist a package, add it to the list:

```
Unattended-Upgrade::Package-Blacklist {
//      "vim";
//      "libc6";
//      "libc6-dev";
//      "libc6-i686";
};
```

 Note

> The double "//" serve as comments, so whatever follows "//" will not be evaluated.

To enable automatic updates, edit /etc/apt/apt.conf.d/10periodic and set the appropriate **apt** configuration options:

```
APT::Periodic::Update-Package-Lists "1";
APT::Periodic::Download-Upgradeable-Packages "1";
APT::Periodic::AutocleanInterval "7";
APT::Periodic::Unattended-Upgrade "1";
```

The above configuration updates the package list, downloads, and installs available upgrades every day. The local download archive is cleaned every week.

 Note

> You can read more about **apt** Periodic configuration options in the /etc/cron.daily/apt script header.

The results of **unattended-upgrades** will be logged to /var/log/unattended-upgrades.

3.5.1. Notifications

Configuring *Unattended-Upgrade::Mail* in /etc/apt/apt.conf.d/50unattended-upgrades will enable **unattended-upgrades** to email an administrator detailing any packages that need upgrading or have problems.

Another useful package is **apticron**. **apticron** will configure a **cron** job to email an administrator information about any packages on the system that have updates available, as well as a summary of changes in each package.

To install the **apticron** package, in a terminal enter:

```
sudo apt-get install apticron
```

Once the package is installed edit /etc/apticron/apticron.conf, to set the email address and other options:

```
EMAIL="root@example.com"
```

3.6. Configuration

Configuration of the *Advanced Packaging Tool* (APT) system repositories is stored in the /etc/apt/sources.list configuration file. An example of this file is referenced here, along with information on adding or removing repository references from the file.

Here[2] is a simple example of a typical /etc/apt/sources.list file.

You may edit the file to enable repositories or disable them. For example, to disable the requirement of inserting the Ubuntu CD-ROM whenever package operations occur, simply comment out the appropriate line for the CD-ROM, which appears at the top of the file:

```
# no more prompting for CD-ROM please
# deb cdrom:[Ubuntu 11.04_Natty Narwhal_ - Release i386 (20070419.1)]/
                                        natty main restricted
```

3.6.1. Extra Repositories

In addition to the officially supported package repositories available for Ubuntu, there exist additional community-maintained repositories which add thousands more potential packages for installation. Two of the most popular are the *Universe* and *Multiverse* repositories. These repositories are not officially supported by Ubuntu, but because they are maintained by the community they generally provide packages which are safe for use with your Ubuntu computer.

 Note

> Packages in the *Multiverse* repository often have licensing issues that prevent them from being distributed with a free operating system, and they may be illegal in your locality.

---

[2] *https://help.ubuntu.com/9.10/serverguide/sample/sources.list*

Warning

Be advised that neither the *Universe* or *Multiverse* repositories contain officially supported packages. In particular, there may not be security updates for these packages.

Many other package sources are available, sometimes even offering only one package, as in the case of package sources provided by the developer of a single application. You should always be very careful and cautious when using non-standard package sources, however. Research the source and packages carefully before performing any installation, as some package sources and their packages could render your system unstable or non-functional in some respects.

By default, the *Universe* and *Multiverse* repositories are enabled but if you would like to disable them edit /etc/apt/sources.list and comment the following lines:

```
deb http://archive.ubuntu.com/ubuntu natty universe multiverse
deb-src http://archive.ubuntu.com/ubuntu natty universe multiverse

deb http://us.archive.ubuntu.com/ubuntu/ natty universe
deb-src http://us.archive.ubuntu.com/ubuntu/ natty universe
deb http://us.archive.ubuntu.com/ubuntu/ natty-updates universe
deb-src http://us.archive.ubuntu.com/ubuntu/ natty-updates universe

deb http://us.archive.ubuntu.com/ubuntu/ natty multiverse
deb-src http://us.archive.ubuntu.com/ubuntu/ natty multiverse
deb http://us.archive.ubuntu.com/ubuntu/ natty-updates multiverse
deb-src http://us.archive.ubuntu.com/ubuntu/ natty-updates multiverse

deb http://security.ubuntu.com/ubuntu natty-security universe
deb-src http://security.ubuntu.com/ubuntu natty-security universe
deb http://security.ubuntu.com/ubuntu natty-security multiverse
deb-src http://security.ubuntu.com/ubuntu natty-security multiverse
```

3.7. References

Most of the material covered in this chapter is available in **man** pages, many of which are available online.

- The *InstallingSoftware*[3] Ubuntu wiki page has more information.

- For more **dpkg** details see the *dpkg man page*[4].

- The *APT HOWTO*[5] and *apt-get man page*[6] contain useful information regarding **apt-get** usage.

---

[3] *https://help.ubuntu.com/community/InstallingSoftware*
[4] *http://manpages.ubuntu.com/manpages/natty/en/man1/dpkg.1.html*

- See the *aptitude man page*[7] for more **aptitude** options.

- The *Adding Repositories HOWTO (Ubuntu Wiki)*[8] page contains more details on adding repositories.

[5] *http://www.debian.org/doc/manuals/apt-howto/*
[6] *http://manpages.ubuntu.com/manpages/natty/en/man8/apt-get.8.html*
[7] *http://manpages.ubuntu.com/manpages/natty/man8/aptitude.8.html*
[8] *https://help.ubuntu.com/community/Repositories/Ubuntu*

Chapter 4.
Networking

Networks consist of two or more devices, such as computer systems, printers, and related equipment which are connected by either physical cabling or wireless links for the purpose of sharing and distributing information among the connected devices.

This section provides general and specific information pertaining to networking, including an overview of network concepts and detailed discussion of popular network protocols.

4.1. Network Configuration

Ubuntu ships with a number of graphical utilities to configure your network devices. This document is geared toward server administrators and will focus on managing your network on the command line.

4.1.1. Ethernet Interfaces

Ethernet interfaces are identified by the system using the naming convention of ethX, where X represents a numeric value. The first Ethernet interface is typically identified as eth0, the second as eth1, and all others should move up in numerical order.

4.1.1.1. Identify Ethernet Interfaces

To quickly identify all available Ethernet interfaces, you can use the **ifconfig** command as shown below.

```
ifconfig -a | grep eth
eth0      Link encap:Ethernet   HWaddr 00:15:c5:4a:16:5a
```

Another application that can help identify all network interfaces available to your system is the **lshw** command. In the example below, **lshw** shows a single Ethernet interface with the logical name of eth0 along with bus information, driver details and all supported capabilities.

```
sudo lshw -class network
  *-network
      description: Ethernet interface
      product: BCM4401-B0 100Base-TX
```

```
vendor: Broadcom Corporation
physical id: 0
bus info: pci@0000:03:00.0
logical name: eth0
version: 02
serial: 00:15:c5:4a:16:5a
size: 10MB/s
capacity: 100MB/s
width: 32 bits
clock: 33MHz
capabilities: (snipped for brevity)
configuration: (snipped for brevity)
resources: irq:17 memory:ef9fe000-ef9fffff
```

4.1.1.2. Ethernet Interface Logical Names

Interface logical names are configured in the file /etc/udev/rules.d/70-persistent-net.rules. If you would like control which interface receives a particular logical name, find the line matching the interfaces physical MAC address and modify the value of NAME=ethX to the desired logical name. Reboot the system to commit your changes.

```
SUBSYSTEM=="net", ACTION=="add", DRIVERS=="?*", ATTR{address}=="00:15:c5:4a:16:5a",
              ATTR{dev_id}=="0x0", ATTR{type}=="1", KERNEL=="eth*", NAME="eth0"
SUBSYSTEM=="net", ACTION=="add", DRIVERS=="?*", ATTR{address}=="00:15:c5:4a:16:5b",
              ATTR{dev_id}=="0x0", ATTR{type}=="1", KERNEL=="eth*", NAME="eth1"
```

4.1.1.3. Ethernet Interface Settings

ethtool is a program that displays and changes Ethernet card settings such as auto-negotiation, port speed, duplex mode, and Wake-on-LAN. It is not installed by default, but is available for installation in the repositories.

```
sudo apt-get install ethtool
```

The following is an example of how to view supported features and configured settings of an Ethernet interface.

```
sudo ethtool eth0
Settings for eth0:
        Supported ports: [ TP ]
        Supported link modes:   10baseT/Half 10baseT/Full
                                100baseT/Half 100baseT/Full
                                1000baseT/Half 1000baseT/Full
        Supports auto-negotiation: Yes
        Advertised link modes:  10baseT/Half 10baseT/Full
                                100baseT/Half 100baseT/Full
                                1000baseT/Half 1000baseT/Full
        Advertised auto-negotiation: Yes
        Speed: 1000Mb/s
        Duplex: Full
        Port: Twisted Pair
        PHYAD: 1
```

```
       Transceiver: internal
       Auto-negotiation: on
       Supports Wake-on: g
       Wake-on: d
       Current message level: 0x000000ff (255)
       Link detected: yes
```

Changes made with the **ethtool** command are temporary and will be lost after a reboot. If you would like to retain settings, simply add the desired **ethtool** command to a pre-up statement in the interface configuration file /etc/network/interfaces.

The following is an example of how the interface identified as eth0 could be permanently configured with a port speed of 1000Mb/s running in full duplex mode.

```
auto eth0
iface eth0 inet static
pre-up /usr/sbin/ethtool -s eth0 speed 1000 duplex full
```

 Note

> Although the example above shows the interface configured to use the static method, it actually works with other methods as well, such as DHCP. The example is meant to demonstrate only proper placement of the pre-up statement in relation to the rest of the interface configuration.

4.1.2. IP Addressing

The following section describes the process of configuring your systems IP address and default gateway needed for communicating on a local area network and the Internet.

4.1.2.1. Temporary IP Address Assignment

For temporary network configurations, you can use standard commands such as **ip**, **ifconfig** and **route**, which are also found on most other GNU/Linux operating systems. These commands allow you to configure settings which take effect immediately, however they are not persistent and will be lost after a reboot.

To temporarily configure an IP address, you can use the **ifconfig** command in the following manner. Just modify the IP address and subnet mask to match your network requirements.

```
sudo ifconfig eth0 10.0.0.100 netmask 255.255.255.0
```

To verify the IP address configuration of **eth0**, you can use the **ifconfig** command in the following manner.

```
ifconfig eth0
eth0      Link encap:Ethernet  HWaddr 00:15:c5:4a:16:5a
          inet addr:10.0.0.100  Bcast:10.0.0.255  Mask:255.255.255.0
          inet6 addr: fe80::215:c5ff:fe4a:165a/64 Scope:Link
          UP BROADCAST RUNNING MULTICAST  MTU:1500  Metric:1
```

```
RX packets:466475604 errors:0 dropped:0 overruns:0 frame:0
TX packets:403172654 errors:0 dropped:0 overruns:0 carrier:0
collisions:0 txqueuelen:1000
RX bytes:2574778386 (2.5 GB)  TX bytes:1618367329 (1.6 GB)
Interrupt:16
```

To configure a default gateway, you can use the **route** command in the following manner. Modify the default gateway address to match your network requirements.

```
sudo route add default gw 10.0.0.1 eth0
```

To verify your default gateway configuration, you can use the **route** command in the following manner.

```
route -n
Kernel IP routing table
Destination     Gateway         Genmask         Flags Metric Ref    Use Iface
10.0.0.0        0.0.0.0         255.255.255.0   U     1      0        0 eth0
0.0.0.0         10.0.0.1        0.0.0.0         UG    0      0        0 eth0
```

If you require DNS for your temporary network configuration, you can add DNS server IP addresses in the file /etc/resolv.conf. The example below shows how to enter two DNS servers to /etc/resolv.conf, which should be changed to servers appropriate for your network. A more lengthy description of DNS client configuration is in a following section.

```
nameserver 8.8.8.8
nameserver 8.8.4.4
```

If you no longer need this configuration and wish to purge all IP configuration from an interface, you can use the **ip** command with the flush option as shown below.

```
ip addr flush eth0
```

 Note

> Flushing the IP configuration using the **ip** command does not clear the contents of /etc/resolv.conf. You must remove or modify those entries manually.

4.1.2.2. Dynamic IP Address Assignment (DHCP Client)

To configure your server to use DHCP for dynamic address assignment, add the dhcp method to the inet address family statement for the appropriate interface in the file /etc/network/interfaces. The example below assumes you are configuring your first Ethernet interface identified as eth0.

```
auto eth0
iface eth0 inet dhcp
```

By adding an interface configuration as shown above, you can manually enable the interface through the **ifup** command which initiates the DHCP process via **dhclient**.

```
sudo ifup eth0
```

To manually disable the interface, you can use the **ifdown** command, which in turn will initiate the DHCP release process and shut down the interface.

```
sudo ifdown eth0
```

4.1.2.3. Static IP Address Assignment

To configure your system to use a static IP address assignment, add the static method to the inet address family statement for the appropriate interface in the file /etc/network/interfaces. The example below assumes you are configuring your first Ethernet interface identified as eth0. Change the address, netmask, and gateway values to meet the requirements of your network.

```
auto eth0
iface eth0 inet static
address 10.0.0.100
netmask 255.255.255.0
gateway 10.0.0.1
```

By adding an interface configuration as shown above, you can manually enable the interface through the **ifup** command.

```
sudo ifup eth0
```

To manually disable the interface, you can use the **ifdown** command.

```
sudo ifdown eth0
```

4.1.2.4. Loopback Interface

The loopback interface is identified by the system as lo and has a default IP address of 127.0.0.1. It can be viewed using the ifconfig command.

```
ifconfig lo
lo          Link encap:Local Loopback
            inet addr:127.0.0.1  Mask:255.0.0.0
            inet6 addr: ::1/128 Scope:Host
            UP LOOPBACK RUNNING  MTU:16436  Metric:1
            RX packets:2718 errors:0 dropped:0 overruns:0 frame:0
            TX packets:2718 errors:0 dropped:0 overruns:0 carrier:0
            collisions:0 txqueuelen:0
            RX bytes:183308 (183.3 KB)  TX bytes:183308 (183.3 KB)
```

By default, there should be two lines in /etc/network/interfaces responsible for automatically configuring your loopback interface. It is recommended that you keep the default settings unless you have a specific purpose for changing them. An example of the two default lines are shown below.

```
auto lo
iface lo inet loopback
```

4.1.3. Name Resolution

Name resolution as it relates to IP networking is the process of mapping IP addresses to hostnames, making it easier to identify resources on a network. The following section will explain how to properly configure your system for name resolution using DNS and static hostname records.

4.1.3.1. DNS Client Configuration

To configure your system to use DNS for name resolution, add the IP addresses of the DNS servers that are appropriate for your network in the file `/etc/resolv.conf`. You can also add an optional DNS suffix search-lists to match your network domain names.

Below is an example of a typical configuration of `/etc/resolv.conf` for a server on the domain "example.com" and using two public DNS servers.

```
search example.com
nameserver 8.8.8.8
nameserver 8.8.4.4
```

The search option can also be used with multiple domain names so that DNS queries will be appended in the order in which they are entered. For example, your network may have multiple sub-domains to search; a parent domain of example.com, and two sub-domains, sales.example.com and dev.example.com.

If you have multiple domains you wish to search, your configuration might look like the following.

```
search example.com sales.example.com dev.example.com
nameserver 8.8.8.8
nameserver 8.8.4.4
```

If you try to ping a host with the name of server1, your system will automatically query DNS for its Fully Qualified Domain Name (FQDN) in the following order:

1. server1.**example.com**
2. server1.**sales.example.com**
3. server1.**dev.example.com**

If no matches are found, the DNS server will provide a result of notfound and the DNS query will fail.

4.1.3.2. Static Hostnames

Static hostnames are locally defined hostname-to-IP mappings located in the file `/etc/hosts`. Entries in the `hosts` file will have precedence over DNS by default. This means that if your system tries to resolve a hostname and it matches an entry in /etc/hosts, it will not attempt to look up the record in DNS. In some configurations, especially when Internet access is not required, servers that communicate with a limited number of resources can be conveniently set to use static hostnames instead of DNS.

The following is an example of a `hosts` file where a number of local servers have been identified by simple hostnames, aliases and their equivalent Fully Qualified Domain Names (FQDN's).

```
127.0.0.1      localhost
127.0.1.1      ubuntu-server
10.0.0.11      server1 vpn server1.example.com
10.0.0.12      server2 mail server2.example.com
10.0.0.13      server3 www server3.example.com
10.0.0.14      server4 file server4.example.com
```

 Note

In the above example, notice that each of the servers have been given aliases in addition to their proper names and FQDN's. Server1 has been mapped to the name vpn, server2 is referred to as mail, server3 as www, and server4 as file.

4.1.3.3. Name Service Switch Configuration

The order in which your system selects a method of resolving hostnames to IP addresses is controlled by the Name Service Switch (NSS) configuration file `/etc/nsswitch.conf`. As mentioned in the previous section, typically static hostnames defined in the systems `/etc/hosts` file have precedence over names resolved from DNS. The following is an example of the line responsible for this order of hostname lookups in the file `/etc/nsswitch.conf`.

```
hosts:          files mdns4_minimal [NOTFOUND=return] dns mdns4
```

- **files** first tries to resolve static hostnames located in `/etc/hosts`.
- **mdns4_minimal** attempts to resolve the name using Multicast DNS.
- **[NOTFOUND=return]** means that any response of notfound by the preceding mdns4_minimal process should be treated as authoritative and that the system should not try to continue hunting for an answer.
- **dns** represents a legacy unicast DNS query.
- **mdns4** represents a Multicast DNS query.

To modify the order of the above mentioned name resolution methods, you can simply change the hosts: string to the value of your choosing. For example, if you prefer to use legacy Unicast DNS versus Multicast DNS, you can change the string in `/etc/nsswitch.conf` as shown below.

```
hosts:          files dns [NOTFOUND=return] mdns4_minimal mdns4
```

4.1.4. Bridging

Bridging multiple interfaces is a more advanced configuration, but is very useful in multiple scenarios. One scenario is setting up a bridge with multiple network interfaces, then using a firewall to filter traffic between two network segments. Another scenario is using bridge on a system with one interface to allow virtual machines direct access to the outside network. The following example covers the latter scenario.

Before configuring a bridge you will need to install the **bridge-utils** package. To install the package, in a terminal enter:

```
sudo apt-get install bridge-utils
```

Next, configure the bridge by editing /etc/network/interfaces:

```
auto lo
iface lo inet loopback

auto br0
iface br0 inet static
        address 192.168.0.10
        network 192.168.0.0
        netmask 255.255.255.0
        broadcast 192.168.0.255
        gateway 192.168.0.1
        bridge_ports eth0
        bridge_fd 9
        bridge_hello 2
        bridge_maxage 12
        bridge_stp off
```

 Note

Enter the appropriate values for your physical interface and network.

Now restart networking to enable the bridge interface:

```
sudo /etc/init.d/networking restart
```

The new bridge interface should now be up and running. The **brctl** provides useful information about the state of the bridge, controls which interfaces are part of the bridge, etc. See **man brctl** for more information.

4.1.5. Resources

- The *Ubuntu Wiki Network page*[1] has links to articles covering more advanced network configuration.

---

[1] *https://help.ubuntu.com/community/Network*

- The *interafaces man page*[2] has details on more options for
  `/etc/network/interfaces`.
- The *dhclient man page*[3] has details on more options for configuring DHCP client
  settings.
- For more information on DNS client configuration see the *resolver man page*[4]. Also,
  Chapter 6 of O'Reilly's *Linux Network Administrator's Guide*[5] is a good source of
  resolver and name service configuration information.
- For more information on *bridging* see the *brctl man page*[6] and the Linux Foundation's
  Net:Bridge[7] page.

4.2. TCP/IP

The Transmission Control Protocol and Internet Protocol (TCP/IP) is a standard set of
protocols developed in the late 1970s by the Defense Advanced Research Projects Agency
(DARPA) as a means of communication between different types of computers and computer
networks. TCP/IP is the driving force of the Internet, and thus it is the most popular set of
network protocols on Earth.

4.2.1. TCP/IP Introduction

The two protocol components of TCP/IP deal with different aspects of computer
networking. *Internet Protocol,* the "IP" of TCP/IP is a connectionless protocol which deals
only with network packet routing using the IP Datagram as the basic unit of networking
information. The IP Datagram consists of a header followed by a message. The *Transmission
Control Protocol* is the "TCP" of TCP/IP and enables network hosts to establish connections
which may be used to exchange data streams. TCP also guarantees that the data between
connections is delivered and that it arrives at one network host in the same order as sent
from another network host.

4.2.2. TCP/IP Configuration

The TCP/IP protocol configuration consists of several elements which must be set by
editing the appropriate configuration files, or deploying solutions such as the Dynamic Host
Configuration Protocol (DHCP) server which in turn, can be configured to provide the

---

[2] *http://manpages.ubuntu.com/manpages/natty/en/man5/interfaces.5.html*
[3] *http://manpages.ubuntu.com/manpages/natty/en/man8/dhclient.8.html*
[4] *http://manpages.ubuntu.com/manpages/natty/en/man5/resolver.5.html*
[5] *http://oreilly.com/catalog/linag2/book/ch06.html*
[6] *http://manpages.ubuntu.com/manpages/natty/en/man8/brctl.8.html*
[7] *http://www.linuxfoundation.org/en/Net:Bridge*

proper TCP/IP configuration settings to network clients automatically. These configuration values must be set correctly in order to facilitate the proper network operation of your Ubuntu system.

The common configuration elements of TCP/IP and their purposes are as follows:

- **IP address** The IP address is a unique identifying string expressed as four decimal numbers ranging from zero (0) to two-hundred and fifty-five (255), separated by periods, with each of the four numbers representing eight (8) bits of the address for a total length of thirty-two (32) bits for the whole address. This format is called *dotted quad notation*.

- **Netmask** The Subnet Mask (or simply, *netmask*) is a local bit mask, or set of flags which separate the portions of an IP address significant to the network from the bits significant to the *subnetwork*. For example, in a Class C network, the standard netmask is 255.255.255.0 which masks the first three bytes of the IP address and allows the last byte of the IP address to remain available for specifying hosts on the subnetwork.

- **Network Address** The Network Address represents the bytes comprising the network portion of an IP address. For example, the host 12.128.1.2 in a Class A network would use 12.0.0.0 as the network address, where twelve (12) represents the first byte of the IP address, (the network part) and zeroes (0) in all of the remaining three bytes to represent the potential host values. A network host using the private IP address 192.168.1.100 would in turn use a Network Address of 192.168.1.0, which specifies the first three bytes of the Class C 192.168.1 network and a zero (0) for all the possible hosts on the network.

- **Broadcast Address** The Broadcast Address is an IP address which allows network data to be sent simultaneously to all hosts on a given subnetwork rather than specifying a particular host. The standard general broadcast address for IP networks is 255.255.255.255, but this broadcast address cannot be used to send a broadcast message to every host on the Internet because routers block it. A more appropriate broadcast address is set to match a specific subnetwork. For example, on the private Class C IP network, 192.168.1.0, the broadcast address is 192.168.1.255. Broadcast messages are typically produced by network protocols such as the Address Resolution Protocol (ARP) and the Routing Information Protocol (RIP).

- **Gateway Address** A Gateway Address is the IP address through which a particular network, or host on a network, may be reached. If one network host wishes to communicate with another network host, and that host is not located on the same network, then a *gateway* must be used. In many cases, the Gateway Address will be that of a router on the same network, which will in turn pass traffic on to other networks or hosts, such as Internet hosts. The value of the Gateway Address setting must be correct, or your system will not be able to reach any hosts beyond those on the same network.

- **Nameserver Address** Nameserver Addresses represent the IP addresses of Domain Name Service (DNS) systems, which resolve network hostnames into IP addresses. There are three levels of Nameserver Addresses, which may be specified in order of precedence: The *Primary* Nameserver, the *Secondary* Nameserver, and the *Tertiary* Nameserver. In order for your system to be able to resolve network hostnames into their corresponding IP addresses, you must specify valid Nameserver Addresses which you are authorized to use in your system's TCP/IP configuration. In many cases these addresses can and will be provided by your network service provider, but many free and publicly accessible nameservers are available for use, such as the Level3 (Verizon) servers with IP addresses from 4.2.2.1 to 4.2.2.6.

Tip

The IP address, Netmask, Network Address, Broadcast Address, and Gateway Address are typically specified via the appropriate directives in the file `/etc/network/interfaces`. The Nameserver Addresses are typically specified via *nameserver* directives in the file `/etc/resolv.conf`. For more information, view the system manual page for `interfaces` or `resolv.conf` respectively, with the following commands typed at a terminal prompt:

- Access the system manual page for `interfaces` with the following command:
  ```
  man interfaces
  ```
- Access the system manual page for `resolv.conf` with the following command:
  ```
  man resolv.conf
  ```

4.2.3. IP Routing

IP routing is a means of specifying and discovering paths in a TCP/IP network along which network data may be sent. Routing uses a set of *routing tables* to direct the forwarding of network data packets from their source to the destination, often via many intermediary network nodes known as *routers*. There are two primary forms of IP routing: *Static Routing* and *Dynamic Routing*.

Static routing involves manually adding IP routes to the system's routing table, and this is usually done by manipulating the routing table with the **route** command. Static routing enjoys many advantages over dynamic routing, such as simplicity of implementation on smaller networks, predictability (the routing table is always computed in advance, and thus the route is precisely the same each time it is used), and low overhead on other routers and network links due to the lack of a dynamic routing protocol. However, static routing does present some disadvantages as well. For example, static routing is limited to small networks and does not scale well. Static routing also fails completely to adapt to network outages and failures along the route due to the fixed nature of the route.

Dynamic routing depends on large networks with multiple possible IP routes from a source to a destination and makes use of special routing protocols, such as the Router Information Protocol (RIP), which handle the automatic adjustments in routing tables that make dynamic routing possible. Dynamic routing has several advantages over static routing, such as superior scalability and the ability to adapt to failures and outages along network routes. Additionally, there is less manual configuration of the routing tables, since routers learn from one another about their existence and available routes. This trait also eliminates the possibility of introducing mistakes in the routing tables via human error. Dynamic routing is not perfect, however, and presents disadvantages such as heightened complexity and additional network overhead from router communications, which does not immediately benefit the end users, but still consumes network bandwidth.

4.2.4. TCP and UDP

TCP is a connection-based protocol, offering error correction and guaranteed delivery of data via what is known as *flow control*. Flow control determines when the flow of a data stream needs to be stopped, and previously sent data packets should to be re-sent due to problems such as *collisions*, for example, thus ensuring complete and accurate delivery of the data. TCP is typically used in the exchange of important information such as database transactions.

The User Datagram Protocol (UDP), on the other hand, is a *connectionless* protocol which seldom deals with the transmission of important data because it lacks flow control or any other method to ensure reliable delivery of the data. UDP is commonly used in such applications as audio and video streaming, where it is considerably faster than TCP due to the lack of error correction and flow control, and where the loss of a few packets is not generally catastrophic.

4.2.5. ICMP

The Internet Control Messaging Protocol (ICMP) is an extension to the Internet Protocol (IP) as defined in the Request For Comments (RFC) #792 and supports network packets containing control, error, and informational messages. ICMP is used by such network applications as the **ping** utility, which can determine the availability of a network host or device. Examples of some error messages returned by ICMP which are useful to both network hosts and devices such as routers, include *Destination Unreachable* and *Time Exceeded*.

4.2.6. Daemons

Daemons are special system applications which typically execute continuously in the background and await requests for the functions they provide from other applications. Many daemons are network-centric; that is, a large number of daemons executing in the background on an Ubuntu system may provide network-related functionality. Some examples of such network daemons include the *Hyper Text Transport Protocol Daemon* (httpd), which provides web server functionality; the *Secure SHell Daemon* (sshd), which provides secure remote login shell and file transfer capabilities; and the *Internet Message Access Protocol Daemon* (imapd), which provides E-Mail services.

4.2.7. Resources

- There are man pages for *TCP*[8] and *IP*[9] that contain more useful information.
- Also, see the *TCP/IP Tutorial and Technical Overview*[10] IBM Redbook.
- Another resource is O'Reilly's *TCP/IP Network Administration*[11].

4.3. Dynamic Host Configuration Protocol (DHCP)

The Dynamic Host Configuration Protocol (DHCP) is a network service that enables host computers to be automatically assigned settings from a server as opposed to manually configuring each network host. Computers configured to be DHCP clients have no control over the settings they receive from the DHCP server, and the configuration is transparent to the computer's user.

The most common settings provided by a DHCP server to DHCP clients include:

- IP-Address and Netmask
- DNS
- WINS

However, a DHCP server can also supply configuration properties such as:

- Host Name
- Domain Name
- Default Gateway
- Time Server
- Print Server

---

[8] *http://manpages.ubuntu.com/manpages/natty/en/man7/tcp.7.html*
[9] *http://manpages.ubuntu.com/manpages/natty/man7/ip.7.html*
[10] *http://www.redbooks.ibm.com/abstracts/gg243376.html*
[11] *http://oreilly.com/catalog/9780596002978/*

The advantage of using DHCP is that changes to the network, for example a change in the address of the DNS server, need only be changed at the DHCP server, and all network hosts will be reconfigured the next time their DHCP clients poll the DHCP server. As an added advantage, it is also easier to integrate new computers into the network, as there is no need to check for the availability of an IP address. Conflicts in IP address allocation are also reduced.

A DHCP server can provide configuration settings using two methods:

MAC Address

> This method entails using DHCP to identify the unique hardware address of each network card connected to the network and then continually supplying a constant configuration each time the DHCP client makes a request to the DHCP server using that network device.

Address Pool

> This method entails defining a pool (sometimes also called a range or scope) of IP addresses from which DHCP clients are supplied their configuration properties dynamically and on a "first come, first served" basis. When a DHCP client is no longer on the network for a specified period, the configuration is expired and released back to the address pool for use by other DHCP Clients.

Ubuntu is shipped with both DHCP server and client. The server is **dhcpd** (dynamic host configuration protocol daemon). The client provided with Ubuntu is **dhclient** and should be installed on all computers required to be automatically configured. Both programs are easy to install and configure and will be automatically started at system boot.

4.3.1. Installation

At a terminal prompt, enter the following command to install **dhcpd**:

```
sudo apt-get install dhcp3-server
```

You will probably need to change the default configuration by editing /etc/dhcp3/dhcpd.conf to suit your needs and particular configuration.

You also need to edit /etc/default/dhcp3-server to specify the interfaces dhcpd should listen to. By default it listens to eth0.

 Note

> dhcpd's messages are being sent to syslog. Look there for diagnostics messages.

4.3.2. Configuration

The error message the installation ends with might be a little confusing, but the following steps will help you configure the service.

Most commonly, what you want to do is assign an IP address randomly. This can be done with settings as follows:

```
# Sample /etc/dhcpd.conf
# (add your comments here)
default-lease-time 600;
max-lease-time 7200;
option subnet-mask 255.255.255.0;
option broadcast-address 192.168.1.255;
option routers 192.168.1.254;
option domain-name-servers 192.168.1.1, 192.168.1.2;
option domain-name "mydomain.example";

subnet 192.168.1.0 netmask 255.255.255.0 {
range 192.168.1.10 192.168.1.100;
range 192.168.1.150 192.168.1.200;
}
```

This will result in the DHCP server giving a client an IP address from the range 192.168.1.10-192.168.1.100 or 192.168.1.150-192.168.1.200. It will lease an IP address for 600 seconds if the client doesn't ask for a specific time frame. Otherwise the maximum (allowed) lease will be 7200 seconds. The server will also "advise" the client that it should use 255.255.255.0 as its subnet mask, 192.168.1.255 as its broadcast address, 192.168.1.254 as the router/gateway and 192.168.1.1 and 192.168.1.2 as its DNS servers.

If you need to specify a WINS server for your Windows clients, you will need to include the netbios-name-servers option, e.g.

```
option netbios-name-servers 192.168.1.1;
```

Dhcpd configuration settings are taken from the DHCP mini-HOWTO, which can be found here[12].

4.3.3. References

- The *dhcp3-server Ubuntu Wiki*[13] page has more information.
- For more `/etc/dhcp3/dchpd.conf` options see the *dhcpd.conf man page*[14].
- Also see the *DHCP FAQ*[15]

4.4. Time Synchronisation with NTP

This page describes methods for keeping your computer's time accurate. This is useful for servers, but is not necessary (or desirable) for desktop machines.

---

[12] *http://www.tldp.org/HOWTO/DHCP/index.html*

[13] *https://help.ubuntu.com/community/dhcp3-server*

[14] *http://manpages.ubuntu.com/manpages/natty/en/man5/dhcpd.conf.5.html*

[15] *http://www.dhcp-handbook.com/dhcp_faq.html*

NTP is a TCP/IP protocol for synchronising time over a network. Basically a client requests the current time from a server, and uses it to set its own clock.

Behind this simple description, there is a lot of complexity - there are tiers of NTP servers, with the tier one NTP servers connected to atomic clocks (often via GPS), and tier two and three servers spreading the load of actually handling requests across the Internet. Also the client software is a lot more complex than you might think - it has to factor out communication delays, and adjust the time in a way that does not upset all the other processes that run on the server. But luckily all that complexity is hidden from you!

Ubuntu has two ways of automatically setting your time: ntpdate and ntpd.

4.4.1. ntpdate

Ubuntu comes with ntpdate as standard, and will run it once at boot time to set up your time according to Ubuntu's NTP server. However, a server's clock is likely to drift considerably between reboots, so it makes sense to correct the time occasionally. The easiest way to do this is to get cron to run ntpdate every day. With your favorite editor, as root, create a file `/etc/cron.daily/ntpdate` containing:

```
ntpdate -s ntp.ubuntu.com
```

The file `/etc/cron.daily/ntpdate` must also be executable.

```
sudo chmod 755 /etc/cron.daily/ntpdate
```

4.4.2. ntpd

ntpdate is a bit of a blunt instrument - it can only adjust the time once a day, in one big correction. The ntp daemon ntpd is far more subtle. It calculates the drift of your system clock and continuously adjusts it, so there are no large corrections that could lead to inconsistent logs for instance. The cost is a little processing power and memory, but for a modern server this is negligible.

To install ntpd, from a terminal prompt enter:

```
sudo apt-get install ntp
```

4.4.3. Changing Time Servers

In both cases above, your system will use Ubuntu's NTP server at *ntp.ubuntu.com* by default. This is OK, but you might want to use several servers to increase accuracy and resilience, and you may want to use time servers that are geographically closer to you. to do this for ntpdate, change the contents of `/etc/cron.daily/ntpdate` to:

```
ntpdate -s ntp.ubuntu.com pool.ntp.org
```

And for ntpd edit `/etc/ntp.conf` to include additional server lines:

```
server ntp.ubuntu.com
```

```
server pool.ntp.org
```

You may notice *pool.ntp.org* in the examples above. This is a really good idea which uses round-robin DNS to return an NTP server from a pool, spreading the load between several different servers. Even better, they have pools for different regions - for instance, if you are in New Zealand, so you could use *nz.pool.ntp.org* instead of *pool.ntp.org*. Look at *http://www.pool.ntp.org/* for more details.

You can also Google for NTP servers in your region, and add these to your configuration. To test that a server works, just type:

```
sudo ntpdate ntp.server.name
```

4.4.4. References

- See the *Ubuntu Time*[16] wiki page for more information.
- *NTP Support*[17]
- *The NTP FAQ and HOWTO*[18]

---

[16] *https://help.ubuntu.com/community/UbuntuTime*
[17] *http://support.ntp.org/bin/view/Support/WebHome*
[18] *http://www.ntp.org/ntpfaq/NTP-a-faq.htm*

Chapter 5.
Remote Administration

There are many ways to remotely administer a Linux server. This chapter will cover one of the most popular **OpenSSH**.

5.1. OpenSSH Server

5.1.1. Introduction

This section of the Ubuntu Server Guide introduces a powerful collection of tools for the remote control of networked computers and transfer of data between networked computers, called *OpenSSH*. You will also learn about some of the configuration settings possible with the OpenSSH server application and how to change them on your Ubuntu system.

OpenSSH is a freely available version of the Secure Shell (SSH) protocol family of tools for remotely controlling a computer or transferring files between computers. Traditional tools used to accomplish these functions, such as **telnet** or **rcp**, are insecure and transmit the user's password in cleartext when used. OpenSSH provides a server daemon and client tools to facilitate secure, encrypted remote control and file transfer operations, effectively replacing the legacy tools.

The OpenSSH server component, **sshd**, listens continuously for client connections from any of the client tools. When a connection request occurs, **sshd** sets up the correct connection depending on the type of client tool connecting. For example, if the remote computer is connecting with the **ssh** client application, the OpenSSH server sets up a remote control session after authentication. If a remote user connects to an OpenSSH server with **scp**, the OpenSSH server daemon initiates a secure copy of files between the server and client after authentication. OpenSSH can use many authentication methods, including plain password, public key, and **Kerberos** tickets.

5.1.2. Installation

Installation of the OpenSSH client and server applications is simple. To install the OpenSSH client applications on your Ubuntu system, use this command at a terminal prompt:

```
sudo apt-get install openssh-client
```

To install the OpenSSH server application, and related support files, use this command at a terminal prompt:

```
sudo apt-get install openssh-server
```

The **openssh-server** package can also be selected to install during the Server Edition installation process.

5.1.3. Configuration

You may configure the default behavior of the OpenSSH server application, **sshd**, by editing the file /etc/ssh/sshd_config. For information about the configuration directives used in this file, you may view the appropriate manual page with the following command, issued at a terminal prompt:

```
man sshd_config
```

There are many directives in the **sshd** configuration file controlling such things as communication settings and authentication modes. The following are examples of configuration directives that can be changed by editing the /etc/ssh/sshd_config file.

 Tip

Prior to editing the configuration file, you should make a copy of the original file and protect it from writing so you will have the original settings as a reference and to reuse as necessary.

Copy the /etc/ssh/sshd_config file and protect it from writing with the following commands, issued at a terminal prompt:

```
sudo cp /etc/ssh/sshd_config /etc/ssh/sshd_config.original
sudo chmod a-w /etc/ssh/sshd_config.original
```

The following are examples of configuration directives you may change:

- To set your OpenSSH to listen on TCP port 2222 instead of the default TCP port 22, change the Port directive as such:

  Port 2222

- To have **sshd** allow public key-based login credentials, simply add or modify the line:

  PubkeyAuthentication yes

  In the /etc/ssh/sshd_config file, or if already present, ensure the line is not commented out.

- To make your OpenSSH server display the contents of the `/etc/issue.net` file as a pre-login banner, simply add or modify the line:

Banner /etc/issue.net

In the `/etc/ssh/sshd_config` file.

After making changes to the `/etc/ssh/sshd_config` file, save the file, and restart the **sshd** server application to effect the changes using the following command at a terminal prompt:

```
sudo /etc/init.d/ssh restart
```

Warning

Many other configuration directives for **sshd** are available for changing the server application's behavior to fit your needs. Be advised, however, if your only method of access to a server is **ssh**, and you make a mistake in configuring **sshd** via the `/etc/ssh/sshd_config` file, you may find you are locked out of the server upon restarting it, or that the **sshd** server refuses to start due to an incorrect configuration directive, so be extra careful when editing this file on a remote server.

5.1.4. SSH Keys

SSH *keys* allow authentication between two hosts without the need of a password. SSH key authentication uses two keys a *private* key and a *public* key.

To generate the keys, from a terminal prompt enter:

```
ssh-keygen -t dsa
```

This will generate the keys using a *DSA* authentication identity of the user. During the process you will be prompted for a password. Simply hit *Enter* when prompted to create the key.

By default the *public* key is saved in the file `~/.ssh/id_dsa.pub`, while `~/.ssh/id_dsa` is the *private* key. Now copy the `id_dsa.pub` file to the remote host and append it to `~/.ssh/authorized_keys` by entering:

```
ssh-copy-id username@remotehost
```

Finally, double check the permissions on the `authorized_keys` file, only the authenticated user should have read and write permissions. If the permissions are not correct change them by:

```
chmod 600 .ssh/authorized_keys
```

You should now be able to SSH to the host without being prompted for a password.

5.1.5. References

- *Ubuntu Wiki SSH[1] page*
- *OpenSSH Website[2]*
- *Advanced OpenSSH Wiki Page[3]*

5.2. Puppet

Puppet is a cross platform framework enabling system administrators to perform common tasks using code. The code can do a variety of tasks from installing new software, to checking file permissions, or updating user accounts. Puppet is great not only during the initial installation of a system, but also throughout the system's entire life cycle. In most circumstances **puppet** will be used in a client/server configuration.

This section will cover installing and configuring **puppet** in a client/server configuration. This simple example will demonstrate how to install **Apache** using **Puppet**.

5.2.1. Installation

To install **puppet**, in a terminal on the *server* enter:

```
sudo apt-get install puppetmaster
```

On the *client* machine, or machines, enter:

```
sudo apt-get install puppet
```

5.2.2. Configuration

Prior to configuring **puppet** you may want to add a DNS *CNAME* record for *puppet.example.com*, where *example.com* is your domain. By default **puppet** clients check DNS for puppet.example.com as the puppet server name, or *Puppet Master*. See Chapter 7, *Domain Name Service (DNS)* for more DNS details.

If you do not wish to use DNS, you can add entries to the server and client /etc/hosts file. For example, in the **puppet** server's /etc/hosts file add:

```
127.0.0.1 localhost.localdomain localhost puppet
192.168.1.17 meercat02.example.com meercat02
```

On each **puppet** client, add an entry for the server:

```
192.168.1.16 meercat.example.com meercat puppet
```

---

[1] *https://help.ubuntu.com/community/SSH*
[2] *http://www.openssh.org/*
[3] *https://wiki.ubuntu.com/AdvancedOpenSSH*

Note

Replace the example IP addresses and domain names above with your actual server and client addresses and domain names.

Now setup some resources for **apache2**. Create a file /etc/puppet/manifests/site.pp containing the following:

```
package {
    'apache2':
        ensure => installed
}

service {
    'apache2':
        ensure => true,
        enable => true,
        require => Package['apache2']
}
```

Next, create a node file /etc/puppet/manifests/nodes.pp with:

```
node 'meercat02.example.com' {
    include apache2
}
```

Note

Replace *meercat02.example.com* with your actual puppet client's host name.

The final step for this simple **puppet** server is to restart the daemon:

```
sudo /etc/init.d/puppetmaster restart
```

Now everything is configured on the **puppet** server, it is time to configure the client.

First, configure the **puppet agent** daemon to start. Edit /etc/default/puppet, changing *START* to yes:

```
START=yes
```

Then start the service:

```
sudo /etc/init.d/puppet start
```

Back on the **puppet** server sign the client certificate by entering:

```
sudo puppetca --sign meercat02.example.com
```

Check /var/log/syslog for any errors with the configuration. If all goes well the **apache2** package and it's dependencies will be installed on the **puppet** client.

Note

This example is *very* simple, and does not highlight many of **Puppet's** features and benefits. For more information see Section 5.2.3, *Resources*.

5.2.3. Resources

- See the *Official Puppet Documentation*[4] web site.
- Also see *Pulling Strings with Puppet*[5].
- Another source of additional information is the *Ubuntu Wiki Puppet Page*[6].

---

[4] *http://docs.puppetlabs.com/*
[5] *http://apress.com/book/view/1590599780*
[6] *https://help.ubuntu.com/community/Puppet*

Chapter 6.
Network Authentication

This section explains various Network Authentication protocols.

6.1. OpenLDAP Server

LDAP is an acronym for Lightweight Directory Access Protocol, it is a simplified version of the X.500 protocol. The directory setup in this section will be used for authentication. Nevertheless, LDAP can be used in numerous ways: authentication, shared directory (for mail clients), address book, etc.

To describe LDAP quickly, all information is stored in a tree structure. With **OpenLDAP** you have freedom to determine the directory arborescence (the Directory Information Tree: the DIT) yourself. We will begin with a basic tree containing two nodes below the root:

- "People" node where your users will be stored
- "Groups" node where your groups will be stored

Before beginning, you should determine what the root of your LDAP directory will be. By default, your tree will be determined by your Fully Qualified Domain Name (FQDN). If your domain is example.com (which we will use in this example), your root node will be dc=example,dc=com.

6.1.1. Installation

First, install the **OpenLDAP** server daemon **slapd** and **ldap-utils**, a package containing LDAP management utilities:

```
sudo apt-get install slapd ldap-utils
```

By default **slapd** is configured with minimal options needed to run the **slapd** daemon.

The configuration example in the following sections will match the domain name of the server. For example, if the machine's Fully Qualified Domain Name (FQDN) is ldap.example.com, the default suffix will be *dc=example,dc=com*.

6.1.2. Populating LDAP

OpenLDAP uses a separate directory which contains the *cn=config* Directory Information Tree (DIT). The *cn=config* DIT is used to dynamically configure the **slapd** daemon, allowing the modification of schema definitions, indexes, ACLs, etc without stopping the service.

The backend *cn=config* directory has only a minimal configuration and will need additional configuration options in order to populate the frontend directory. The frontend will be populated with a "classical" scheme that will be compatible with address book applications and with Unix Posix accounts. Posix accounts will allow authentication to various applications, such as web applications, email Mail Transfer Agent (MTA) applications, etc.

Note

For external applications to authenticate using LDAP they will each need to be specifically configured to do so. Refer to the individual application documentation for details.

Note

Remember to change *dc=example,dc=com* in the following examples to match your LDAP configuration.

First, some additional schema files need to be loaded. In a terminal enter:

```
sudo ldapadd -Y EXTERNAL -H ldapi:/// -f /etc/ldap/schema/cosine.ldif
sudo ldapadd -Y EXTERNAL -H ldapi:/// -f /etc/ldap/schema/nis.ldif
sudo ldapadd -Y EXTERNAL -H ldapi:/// -f /etc/ldap/schema/inetorgperson.ldif
```

Next, copy the following example LDIF file, naming it `backend.example.com.ldif`, somewhere on your system:

```
# Load dynamic backend modules
dn: cn=module,cn=config
objectClass: olcModuleList
cn: module
olcModulepath: /usr/lib/ldap
olcModuleload: back_hdb.la

# Database settings
dn: olcDatabase=hdb,cn=config
objectClass: olcDatabaseConfig
objectClass: olcHdbConfig
olcDatabase: {1}hdb
olcSuffix: dc=example,dc=com
olcDbDirectory: /var/lib/ldap
olcRootDN: cn=admin,dc=example,dc=com
olcRootPW: secret
olcDbConfig: set_cachesize 0 2097152 0
olcDbConfig: set_lk_max_objects 1500
olcDbConfig: set_lk_max_locks 1500
olcDbConfig: set_lk_max_lockers 1500
olcDbIndex: objectClass eq
olcLastMod: TRUE
olcDbCheckpoint: 512 30
olcAccess: to attrs=userPassword by dn="cn=admin,dc=example,dc=com" write by
anonymous auth by self write by * none
```

```
olcAccess: to attrs=shadowLastChange by self write by * read
olcAccess: to dn.base="" by * read
olcAccess: to * by dn="cn=admin,dc=example,dc=com" write by * read
```

 Note

Change *olcRootPW: secret* to a password of your choosing.

Now add the LDIF to the directory:

```
sudo ldapadd -Y EXTERNAL -H ldapi:/// -f backend.example.com.ldif
```

The frontend directory is now ready to be populated. Create a
`frontend.example.com.ldif` with the following contents:

```
# Create top-level object in domain
dn: dc=example,dc=com
objectClass: top
objectClass: dcObject
objectclass: organization
o: Example Organization
dc: Example
description: LDAP Example

# Admin user.
dn: cn=admin,dc=example,dc=com
objectClass: simpleSecurityObject
objectClass: organizationalRole
cn: admin
description: LDAP administrator
userPassword: secret

dn: ou=people,dc=example,dc=com
objectClass: organizationalUnit
ou: people

dn: ou=groups,dc=example,dc=com
objectClass: organizationalUnit
ou: groups

dn: uid=john,ou=people,dc=example,dc=com
objectClass: inetOrgPerson
objectClass: posixAccount
objectClass: shadowAccount
uid: john
sn: Doe
givenName: John
cn: John Doe
displayName: John Doe
uidNumber: 1000
gidNumber: 10000
userPassword: password
gecos: John Doe
```

```
loginShell: /bin/bash
homeDirectory: /home/john
shadowExpire: -1
shadowFlag: 0
shadowWarning: 7
shadowMin: 8
shadowMax: 999999
shadowLastChange: 10877
mail: john.doe@example.com
postalCode: 31000
l: Toulouse
o: Example
mobile: +33 (0)6 xx xx xx xx
homePhone: +33 (0)5 xx xx xx xx
title: System Administrator
postalAddress:
initials: JD

dn: cn=example,ou=groups,dc=example,dc=com
objectClass: posixGroup
cn: example
gidNumber: 10000
```

In this example the directory structure, a user, and a group have been setup. In other examples you might see the *objectClass: top* added in every entry, but that is the default behaviour so you do not have to add it explicitly.

Add the entries to the LDAP directory:

```
sudo ldapadd -x -D cn=admin,dc=example,dc=com -W -f frontend.example.com.ldif
```

We can check that the content has been correctly added with the **ldapsearch** utility. Execute a search of the LDAP directory:

```
ldapsearch -xLLL -b "dc=example,dc=com" uid=john sn givenName cn

dn: uid=john,ou=people,dc=example,dc=com
cn: John Doe
sn: Doe
givenName: John
```

Just a quick explanation:

- -*x:* will not use SASL authentication method, which is the default.
- -*LLL:* disable printing LDIF schema information.

6.1.3. Further Configuration

The *cn=config* tree can be manipulated using the utilities in the **ldap-utils** package. For example:

- Use **ldapsearch** to view the tree, entering the admin password set during installation or reconfiguration:

```
sudo ldapsearch -LLL -Y EXTERNAL -H ldapi:/// -b cn=config dn

SASL/EXTERNAL authentication started
SASL username: gidNumber=0+uidNumber=0,cn=peercred,cn=external,cn=auth
SASL SSF: 0
dn: cn=config

dn: cn=module{0},cn=config

dn: cn=schema,cn=config

dn: cn={0}core,cn=schema,cn=config

dn: cn={1}cosine,cn=schema,cn=config

dn: cn={2}nis,cn=schema,cn=config

dn: cn={3}inetorgperson,cn=schema,cn=config

dn: olcDatabase={-1}frontend,cn=config

dn: olcDatabase={0}config,cn=config

dn: olcDatabase={1}hdb,cn=config
```

The output above is the current configuration options for the *cn=config* backend database. Your output may be vary.

- As an example of modifying the *cn=config* tree, add another attribute to the index list using **ldapmodify**:

```
sudo ldapmodify -Y EXTERNAL -H ldapi:///

SASL/EXTERNAL authentication started
SASL username: gidNumber=0+uidNumber=0,cn=peercred,cn=external,cn=auth
SASL SSF: 0
dn: olcDatabase={1}hdb,cn=config
add: olcDbIndex
olcDbIndex: uidNumber eq

modifying entry "olcDatabase={1}hdb,cn=config"
```

Once the modification has completed, press *Ctrl+D* to exit the utility.

- **ldapmodify** can also read the changes from a file. Copy and paste the following into a file named `uid_index.ldif`:

```
dn: olcDatabase={1}hdb,cn=config
add: olcDbIndex
olcDbIndex: uid eq,pres,sub
```

Then execute **ldapmodify**:

```
sudo ldapmodify -Y EXTERNAL -H ldapi:/// -f uid_index.ldif

SASL/EXTERNAL authentication started
SASL username: gidNumber=0+uidNumber=0,cn=peercred,cn=external,cn=auth
SASL SSF: 0
modifying entry "olcDatabase={1}hdb,cn=config"
```

The file method is very useful for large changes.

- Adding additional *schemas* to **slapd** requires the schema to be converted to LDIF format. The /etc/ldap/schema directory contains some schema files already converted to LDIF format as demonstrated in the previous section. Fortunately, the **slapd** program can be used to automate the conversion. The following example will add the *dyngroup.schema*:

  1. First, create a conversion schema_convert.conf file containing the following lines:

     ```
     include /etc/ldap/schema/core.schema
     include /etc/ldap/schema/collective.schema
     include /etc/ldap/schema/corba.schema
     include /etc/ldap/schema/cosine.schema
     include /etc/ldap/schema/duaconf.schema
     include /etc/ldap/schema/dyngroup.schema
     include /etc/ldap/schema/inetorgperson.schema
     include /etc/ldap/schema/java.schema
     include /etc/ldap/schema/misc.schema
     include /etc/ldap/schema/nis.schema
     include /etc/ldap/schema/openldap.schema
     include /etc/ldap/schema/ppolicy.schema
     ```

  2. Next, create a temporary directory to hold the output:

     ```
     mkdir /tmp/ldif_output
     ```

  3. Now using **slapcat** convert the schema files to LDIF:

     ```
     slapcat -f schema_convert.conf -F /tmp/ldif_output -n0 -s
     "cn={5}dyngroup,cn=schema,cn=config" > /tmp/cn=dyngroup.ldif
     ```

     Adjust the configuration file name and temporary directory names if yours are different. It may be worthwhile to keep the ldif_output directory around in case you want to add additional schemas in the future.

     Note

     The "*cn={5}*" index number may change according to the configuration ordering. To find out the correct number execute the following:

     ```
     slapcat -f schema_convert.conf -F /tmp/ldif_output -n 0 | grep dyngroup
     ```

     Replace *dyngroup* with the appropriate schema name.

  4. Edit the /tmp/cn\=dyngroup.ldif file, changing the following attributes:

     ```
     dn: cn=dyngroup,cn=schema,cn=config
     ...
     cn: dyngroup
     ```

     And remove the following lines from the bottom of the file:

```
structuralObjectClass: olcSchemaConfig
entryUUID: 10dae0ea-0760-102d-80d3-f9366b7f7757
creatorsName: cn=config
createTimestamp: 20080826021140Z
entryCSN: 20080826021140.791425Z#000000#000#000000
modifiersName: cn=config
modifyTimestamp: 20080826021140Z
```

Note

The attribute values will vary, just be sure the attributes are removed.

5. Finally, using the **ldapadd** utility, add the new schema to the directory:

```
sudo ldapadd -Y EXTERNAL -H ldapi:/// -f /tmp/cn\=dyngroup.ldif
```

There should now be a *dn: cn={4}dyngroup,cn=schema,cn=config* entry in the cn=config tree.

6.1.4. LDAP Replication

LDAP often quickly becomes a highly critical service to the network. Multiple systems will come to depend on LDAP for authentication, authorization, configuration, etc. It is a good idea to setup a redundant system through replication.

Replication is achieved using the *Syncrepl* engine. Syncrepl allows the changes to be synced using a *consumer, provider* model. A provider sends directory changes to consumers.

6.1.4.1. Provider Configuration

The following is an example of a *Single-Master* configuration. In this configuration one OpenLDAP server is configured as a *provider* and another as a *consumer*.

1. First, configure the provider server. Copy the following to a file named `provider_sync.ldif`:

```
# Add indexes to the frontend db.
dn: olcDatabase={1}hdb,cn=config
changetype: modify
add: olcDbIndex
olcDbIndex: entryCSN eq
-
add: olcDbIndex
olcDbIndex: entryUUID eq

#Load the syncprov and accesslog modules.
dn: cn=module{0},cn=config
changetype: modify
add: olcModuleLoad
olcModuleLoad: syncprov
-
```

```
add: olcModuleLoad
olcModuleLoad: accesslog

# Accesslog database definitions
dn: olcDatabase={2}hdb,cn=config
objectClass: olcDatabaseConfig
objectClass: olcHdbConfig
olcDatabase: {2}hdb
olcDbDirectory: /var/lib/ldap/accesslog
olcSuffix: cn=accesslog
olcRootDN: cn=admin,dc=example,dc=com
olcDbIndex: default eq
olcDbIndex: entryCSN,objectClass,reqEnd,reqResult,reqStart

# Accesslog db syncprov.
dn: olcOverlay=syncprov,olcDatabase={2}hdb,cn=config
changetype: add
objectClass: olcOverlayConfig
objectClass: olcSyncProvConfig
olcOverlay: syncprov
olcSpNoPresent: TRUE
olcSpReloadHint: TRUE

# syncrepl Provider for primary db
dn: olcOverlay=syncprov,olcDatabase={1}hdb,cn=config
changetype: add
objectClass: olcOverlayConfig
objectClass: olcSyncProvConfig
olcOverlay: syncprov
olcSpNoPresent: TRUE

# accesslog overlay definitions for primary db
dn: olcOverlay=accesslog,olcDatabase={1}hdb,cn=config
objectClass: olcOverlayConfig
objectClass: olcAccessLogConfig
olcOverlay: accesslog
olcAccessLogDB: cn=accesslog
olcAccessLogOps: writes
olcAccessLogSuccess: TRUE
# scan the accesslog DB every day, and purge entries older than 7 days
olcAccessLogPurge: 07+00:00 01+00:00
```

2. The **AppArmor** profile for **slapd** will need to be adjusted for the accesslog database
    location. Edit /etc/apparmor.d/usr.sbin.slapd adding:

```
  /var/lib/ldap/accesslog/ r,
  /var/lib/ldap/accesslog/** rwk,
```

Then create the directory, reload the **apparmor** profile, and copy the DB_CONFIG file:

```
sudo -u openldap mkdir /var/lib/ldap/accesslog
sudo -u openldap cp /var/lib/ldap/DB_CONFIG /var/lib/ldap/accesslog/
sudo /etc/init.d/apparmor reload
```

Note

Using the *-u openldap* option with the **sudo** commands above removes the need to adjust permissions for the new directory later.

3. Edit the file and change the *olcRootDN* to match your directory:

```
olcRootDN: cn=admin,dc=example,dc=com
```

4. Next, add the LDIF file using the **ldapadd** utility:

```
sudo ldapadd -Y EXTERNAL -H ldapi:/// -f provider_sync.ldif
```

5. Restart **slapd**:

```
sudo /etc/init.d/slapd restart
```

The *Provider* server is now configured, and it is time to configure a *Consumer* server.

6.1.4.2. Consumer Configuration

1. On the *Consumer* server configure it the same as the *Provider* except for the *Syncrepl* configuration steps.

   Add the additional schema files:

```
sudo ldapadd -Y EXTERNAL -H ldapi:/// -f /etc/ldap/schema/cosine.ldif
sudo ldapadd -Y EXTERNAL -H ldapi:/// -f /etc/ldap/schema/nis.ldif
sudo ldapadd -Y EXTERNAL -H ldapi:/// -f /etc/ldap/schema/inetorgperson.ldif
```

   Also, create, or copy from the provider server, the `backend.example.com.ldif`

```
# Load dynamic backend modules
dn: cn=module,cn=config
objectClass: olcModuleList
cn: module
olcModulepath: /usr/lib/ldap
olcModuleload: back_hdb.la

# Database settings
dn: olcDatabase=hdb,cn=config
objectClass: olcDatabaseConfig
objectClass: olcHdbConfig
olcDatabase: {1}hdb
olcSuffix: dc=example,dc=com
olcDbDirectory: /var/lib/ldap
olcRootDN: cn=admin,dc=example,dc=com
olcRootPW: secret
olcDbConfig: set_cachesize 0 2097152 0
olcDbConfig: set_lk_max_objects 1500
olcDbConfig: set_lk_max_locks 1500
olcDbConfig: set_lk_max_lockers 1500
olcDbIndex: objectClass eq
olcLastMod: TRUE
olcDbCheckpoint: 512 30
olcAccess: to attrs=userPassword by dn="cn=admin,dc=example,dc=com" write by
anonymous auth by self write by * none
```

```
olcAccess: to attrs=shadowLastChange by self write by * read
olcAccess: to dn.base="" by * read
olcAccess: to * by dn="cn=admin,dc=example,dc=com" write by * read
```

And add the LDIF by entering:

```
sudo ldapadd -Y EXTERNAL -H ldapi:/// -f backend.example.com.ldif
```

2. Do the same with the `frontend.example.com.ldif` file listed above, and add it:

```
sudo ldapadd -x -D cn=admin,dc=example,dc=com -W -f
frontend.example.com.ldif
```

The two severs should now have the same configuration except for the *Syncrepl* options.

3. Now create a file named `consumer_sync.ldif` containing:

```
#Load the syncprov module.
dn: cn=module{0},cn=config
changetype: modify
add: olcModuleLoad
olcModuleLoad: syncprov

# syncrepl specific indices
dn: olcDatabase={1}hdb,cn=config
changetype: modify
add: olcDbIndex
olcDbIndex: entryUUID eq
-
add: olcSyncRepl
olcSyncRepl: rid=0 provider=ldap://ldap01.example.com bindmethod=simple
binddn="cn=admin,dc=example,dc=com"
 credentials=secret searchbase="dc=example,dc=com" logbase="cn=accesslog"
 logfilter="(&(objectClass=auditWriteObject)(reqResult=0))"
schemachecking=on
 type=refreshAndPersist retry="60 +" syncdata=accesslog
-
add: olcUpdateRef
olcUpdateRef: ldap://ldap01.example.com
```

You will probably want to change the following attributes:

- *ldap01.example.com* to your server's hostname.
- *binddn*
- *credentials*
- *searchbase*
- *olcUpdateRef:*

4. Add the LDIF file to the configuration tree:

```
sudo ldapadd -c -Y EXTERNAL -H ldapi:/// -f consumer_sync.ldif
```

The frontend database should now sync between servers. You can add additional servers using the steps above as the need arises.

 Note

The **slapd** daemon will send log information to /var/log/syslog by default. So if all does *not* go well check there for errors and other troubleshooting information. Also, be sure that each server knows it's Fully Qualified Domain Name (FQDN). This is configured in /etc/hosts with a line similar to:

```
127.0.0.1  ldap01.example.com ldap01
```

6.1.5. Setting up ACL

Authentication requires access to the password field, that should be not accessible by default. Also, in order for users to change their own password, using **passwd** or other utilities, *shadowLastChange* needs to be accessible once a user has authenticated.

To view the Access Control List (ACL) for the *cn=config* tree, use the **ldapsearch** utility:

```
sudo ldapsearch -c -Y EXTERNAL -H ldapi:///  -LLL -b cn=config olcDatabase=config olcAccess
SASL/EXTERNAL authentication started
SASL username: gidNumber=0+uidNumber=0,cn=peercred,cn=external,cn=auth
SASL SSF: 0
dn: olcDatabase={0}config,cn=config
olcAccess: {0}to * by dn.exact=gidNumber=0+uidNumber=0,cn=peercred,cn=external
 ,cn=auth manage by * break
```

To see the ACL for the frontend tree enter:

```
sudo ldapsearch -c -Y EXTERNAL -H ldapi:///  -LLL -b cn=config olcDatabase={1}hdb olcAccess
```

6.1.6. TLS and SSL

When authenticating to an OpenLDAP server it is best to do so using an encrypted session. This can be accomplished using Transport Layer Security (TLS) and/or Secure Sockets Layer (SSL).

The first step in the process is to obtain or create a *certificate*. Because **slapd** is compiled using the **gnutls** library, the **certtool** utility will be used to create certificates.

1. First, install **gnutls-bin** by entering the following in a terminal:

    ```
    sudo apt-get install gnutls-bin
    ```

2. Next, create a private key for the *Certificate Authority* (CA):

    ```
    sudo sh -c "certtool --generate-privkey > /etc/ssl/private/cakey.pem"
    ```

3. Create a /etc/ssl/ca.info details file to self-sign the CA certificate containing:

    ```
    cn = Example Company
    ca
    ```

```
cert_signing_key
```

4. Now create the self-signed CA certificate:

```
sudo certtool --generate-self-signed --load-privkey
/etc/ssl/private/cakey.pem \
 --template /etc/ssl/ca.info --outfile /etc/ssl/certs/cacert.pem
```

5. Make a private key for the server:

```
sudo sh -c "certtool --generate-privkey >
/etc/ssl/private/ldap01_slapd_key.pem"
```

 Note

Replace *ldap01* in the filename with your server's hostname. Naming the certificate and key for the host and service that will be using them will help keep filenames and paths straight.

6. To sign the server's certificate with the CA, create the /etc/ssl/ldap01.info info file containing:

```
organization = Example Company
cn = ldap01.example.com
tls_www_server
encryption_key
signing_key
```

7. Create the server's certificate:

```
sudo certtool --generate-certificate --load-privkey /etc/ssl/private/
                                          ldap01_slapd_key.pem \
 --load-ca-certificate /etc/ssl/certs/cacert.pem --load-ca-privkey
                                          /etc/ssl/private/cakey.pem \
 --template /etc/ssl/ldap01.info --outfile /etc/ssl/certs/
                                          ldap01_slapd_cert.pem
```

Once you have a certificate, key, and CA cert installed, use **ldapmodify** to add the new configuration options:

```
sudo ldapmodify -Y EXTERNAL -H ldapi:///

Enter LDAP Password:
dn: cn=config
add: olcTLSCACertificateFile
olcTLSCACertificateFile: /etc/ssl/certs/cacert.pem
-
add: olcTLSCertificateFile
olcTLSCertificateFile: /etc/ssl/certs/ldap01_slapd_cert.pem
-
add: olcTLSCertificateKeyFile
olcTLSCertificateKeyFile: /etc/ssl/private/ldap01_slapd_key.pem

modifying entry "cn=config"
```

Note

Adjust the `ldap01_slapd_cert.pem`, `ldap01_slapd_key.pem`, and `cacert.pem` names if yours are different.

Next, edit `/etc/default/slapd` uncomment the *SLAPD_SERVICES* option:

```
SLAPD_SERVICES="ldap:/// ldapi:/// ldaps:///"
```

Now the *openldap* user needs access to the certificate:

```
sudo adduser openldap ssl-cert
sudo chgrp ssl-cert /etc/ssl/private/ldap01_slapd_key.pem
sudo chmod g+r /etc/ssl/private/ldap01_slapd_key.pem
```

Note

If the `/etc/ssl/private` and `/etc/ssl/private/server.key` have different permissions, adjust the commands appropriately.

Finally, restart **slapd**:

```
sudo /etc/init.d/slapd restart
```

The **slapd** daemon should now be listening for LDAPS connections and be able to use STARTTLS during authentication.

Note

If you run into troubles with the server not starting, check the /var/log/syslog. If you see errors like main: TLS init def ctx failed: -1, it is likely there is a configuration problem. Check that the certificate is signed by the authority from in the files configured, and that the ssl-cert group has read permissions on the private key.

6.1.6.1. TLS Replication

If you have setup **Syncrepl** between servers, it is prudent to encrypt the replication traffic using *Transport Layer Security (TLS)*. For details on setting up replication see the Section 6.1.4, *LDAP Replication*.

Assuming you have followed the above instructions and created a CA certificate and server certificate on the *Provider* server. Follow the following instructions to create a certificate and key for the *Consumer* server.

1. Create a new key for the Consumer server:

   ```
   mkdir ldap02-ssl
   cd ldap02-ssl
   certtool --generate-privkey > ldap02_slapd_key.pem
   ```

Note

Creating a new directory is not strictly necessary, but it will help keep things organized and make it easier to copy the files to the Consumer server.

2. Next, create an info file, `ldap02.info` for the Consumer server, changing the attributes to match your locality and server:

```
country = US
state = North Carolina
locality = Winston-Salem
organization = Example Company
cn = ldap02.salem.edu
tls_www_client
encryption_key
signing_key
```

3. Create the certificate:

```
sudo certtool --generate-certificate --load-privkey ldap02_slapd_key.pem \
 --load-ca-certificate /etc/ssl/certs/cacert.pem --load-ca-privkey
/etc/ssl/private/cakey.pem \
 --template ldap02.info --outfile ldap02_slapd_cert.pem
```

4. Copy the `cacert.pem` to the directory:

```
cp /etc/ssl/certs/cacert.pem .
```

5. The only thing left is to copy the `ldap02-ssl` directory to the Consumer server, then copy `ldap02_slapd_cert.pem` and `cacert.pem` to `/etc/ssl/certs`, and copy `ldap02_slapd_key.pem` to `/etc/ssl/private`.

6. Once the files are in place adjust the *cn=config* tree by entering:

```
sudo ldapmodify -Y EXTERNAL -H ldapi:///

Enter LDAP Password:
dn: cn=config
add: olcTLSCACertificateFile
olcTLSCACertificateFile: /etc/ssl/certs/cacert.pem
-
add: olcTLSCertificateFile
olcTLSCertificateFile: /etc/ssl/certs/ldap02_slapd_cert.pem
-
add: olcTLSCertificateKeyFile
olcTLSCertificateKeyFile: /etc/ssl/private/ldap02_slapd_key.pem

modifying entry "cn=config"
```

7. As with the Provider you can now edit `/etc/default/slapd` and add the *ldaps:///* parameter to the *SLAPD_SERVICES* option.

Now that *TLS* has been setup on each server, once again modify the *Consumer* server's *cn=config* tree by entering the following in a terminal:

```
sudo ldapmodify -Y EXTERNAL -H ldapi:///
SASL/EXTERNAL authentication started
SASL username: gidNumber=0+uidNumber=0,cn=peercred,cn=external,cn=auth
SASL SSF: 0

dn: olcDatabase={1}hdb,cn=config
replace: olcSyncrepl
olcSyncrepl: {0}rid=0 provider=ldap://ldap01.example.com bindmethod=simple binddn="cn=ad
 min,dc=example,dc=com" credentials=secret searchbase="dc=example,dc=com" logbas
 e="cn=accesslog" logfilter="(&(objectClass=auditWriteObject)(reqResult=0))" s
 chemachecking=on type=refreshAndPersist retry="60 +" syncdata=accesslog starttls=yes

modifying entry "olcDatabase={1}hdb,cn=config"
```

If the LDAP server hostname does not match the Fully Qualified Domain Name (FQDN) in the certificate, you may have to edit `/etc/ldap/ldap.conf` and add the following TLS options:

```
TLS_CERT /etc/ssl/certs/ldap02_slapd_cert.pem
TLS_KEY /etc/ssl/private/ldap02_slapd_key.pem
TLS_CACERT /etc/ssl/certs/cacert.pem
```

Finally, restart **slapd** on each of the servers:

```
sudo /etc/init.d/slapd restart
```

6.1.7. LDAP Authentication

Once you have a working LDAP server, the **auth-client-config** and **libnss-ldap** packages take the pain out of configuring an Ubuntu client to authenticate using LDAP. To install the packages from, a terminal prompt enter:

```
sudo apt-get install libnss-ldap
```

During the install a menu dialog will ask you connection details about your LDAP server.

If you make a mistake when entering your information you can execute the dialog again using:

```
sudo dpkg-reconfigure ldap-auth-config
```

The results of the dialog can be seen in `/etc/ldap.conf`. If your server requires options not covered in the menu edit this file accordingly.

Now that **libnss-ldap** is configured enable the **auth-client-config** LDAP profile by entering:

```
sudo auth-client-config -t nss -p lac_ldap
```

- *-t:* only modifies `/etc/nsswitch.conf`.
- *-p:* name of the profile to enable, disable, etc.
- *lac_ldap:* the **auth-client-config** profile that is part of the **ldap-auth-config** package.

Using the **pam-auth-update** utility, configure the system to use LDAP for authentication:

```
sudo pam-auth-update
```

From the **pam-auth-update** menu, choose LDAP and any other authentication mechanisms you need.

You should now be able to login using user credentials stored in the LDAP directory.

 Note

> If you are going to use LDAP to store Samba users you will need to configure the server to authenticate using LDAP. See the Section 6.2, *Samba and LDAP* for details.

6.1.8. User and Group Management

The **ldap-utils** package comes with multiple utilities to manage the directory, but the long string of options needed, can make them a burden to use. The **ldapscripts** package contains configurable scripts to easily manage LDAP users and groups.

To install the package, from a terminal enter:

```
sudo apt-get install ldapscripts
```

Next, edit the config file `/etc/ldapscripts/ldapscripts.conf` uncommenting and changing the following to match your environment:

```
SERVER=localhost
BINDDN='cn=admin,dc=example,dc=com'
BINDPWDFILE="/etc/ldapscripts/ldapscripts.passwd"
SUFFIX='dc=example,dc=com'
GSUFFIX='ou=Groups'
USUFFIX='ou=People'
MSUFFIX='ou=Computers'
GIDSTART=10000
UIDSTART=10000
MIDSTART=10000
```

Now, create the `ldapscripts.passwd` file to allow authenticated access to the directory:

```
sudo sh -c "echo -n 'secret' > /etc/ldapscripts/ldapscripts.passwd"
sudo chmod 400 /etc/ldapscripts/ldapscripts.passwd
```

 Note

> Replace "secret" with the actual password for your LDAP admin user.

The **ldapscripts** are now ready to help manage your directory. The following are some examples of how to use the scripts:

- Create a new user:

  ```
  sudo ldapadduser george example
  ```

This will create a user with uid george and set the user's primary group (gid) to example

- Change a user's password:

```
sudo ldapsetpasswd george
Changing password for user uid=george,ou=People,dc=example,dc=com
New Password:
New Password (verify):
```

- Delete a user:

```
sudo ldapdeleteuser george
```

- Add a group:

```
sudo ldapaddgroup qa
```

- Delete a group:

```
sudo ldapdeletegroup qa
```

- Add a user to a group:

```
sudo ldapaddusertogroup george qa
```

You should now see a *memberUid* attribute for the qa group with a value of george.

- Remove a user from a group:

```
sudo ldapdeleteuserfromgroup george qa
```

The *memberUid* attribute should now be removed from the qa group.

- The **ldapmodifyuser** script allows you to add, remove, or replace a user's attributes. The script uses the same syntax as the **ldapmodify** utility. For example:

```
sudo ldapmodifyuser george
# About to modify the following entry :
dn: uid=george,ou=People,dc=example,dc=com
objectClass: account
objectClass: posixAccount
cn: george
uid: george
uidNumber: 1001
gidNumber: 1001
homeDirectory: /home/george
loginShell: /bin/bash
gecos: george
description: User account
userPassword:: e1NTSEF9eXFsTFcyWlhwWkF1eGUybVddFWHZKRzJVMjFTSG9vcHk=

# Enter your modifications here, end with CTRL-D.
dn: uid=george,ou=People,dc=example,dc=com
replace: gecos
gecos: George Carlin
```

The user's *gecos* should now be "George Carlin".

- Another great feature of **ldapscripts**, is the template system. Templates allow you to customize the attributes of user, group, and machine objectes. For example, to enable the *user* template edit `/etc/ldapscripts/ldapscripts.conf` changing:

```
UTEMPLATE="/etc/ldapscripts/ldapadduser.template"
```

There are sample templates in the `/etc/ldapscripts` directory. Copy or rename the `ldapadduser.template.sample` file to `/etc/ldapscripts/ldapadduser.template`:

```
sudo cp /usr/share/doc/ldapscripts/examples/ldapadduser.template.sample /
                              etc/ldapscripts/ldapadduser.template
```

Edit the new template to add the desired attributes. The following will create new user's as with an *objectClass* of *inetOrgPerson*:

```
dn: uid=<user>,<usuffix>,<suffix>
objectClass: inetOrgPerson
objectClass: posixAccount
cn: <user>
sn: <ask>
uid: <user>
uidNumber: <uid>
gidNumber: <gid>
homeDirectory: <home>
loginShell: <shell>
gecos: <user>
description: User account
title: Employee
```

Notice the *<ask>* option used for the *ssn* value. Using <ask> will configure **ldapadduser** to prompt you for the attribute value during user creation.

There are more useful scripts in the package, to see a full list enter: **dpkg -L ldapscripts | grep bin**

6.1.9. Resources

- The *OpenLDAP Ubuntu Wiki*[1] page has more details.
- For more information see *OpenLDAP Home Page*[2]
- Though starting to show it's age, a great source for in depth LDAP information is O'Reilly's *LDAP System Administration*[3]
- Packt's *Mastering OpenLDAP*[4] is a great reference covering newer versions of OpenLDAP.

---

[1] *https://help.ubuntu.com/community/OpenLDAPServer*

[2] *http://www.openldap.org/*

[3] *http://www.oreilly.com/catalog/ldapsa/*

[4] *http://www.packtpub.com/OpenLDAP-Developers-Server-Open-Source-Linux/book*

- For more information on **auth-client-config** see the man page: **man auth-client-config**.

- For more details regarding the **ldapscripts** package see the man pages: **man ldapscripts**, **man ldapadduser**, **man ldapaddgroup**, etc.

6.2. Samba and LDAP

This section covers configuring Samba to use LDAP for user, group, and machine account information and authentication. The assumption is, you already have a working OpenLDAP directory installed and the server is configured to use it for authentication. See the Section 6.1, *OpenLDAP Server* and the Section 6.1.7, *LDAP Authentication* for details on setting up OpenLDAP. For more information on installing and configuring Samba see Chapter 17, *Windows Networking*.

6.2.1. Installation

There are three packages needed when integrating Samba with LDAP. **samba**, **samba-doc**, and **smbldap-tools** packages . To install the packages, from a terminal enter:

```
sudo apt-get install samba samba-doc smbldap-tools
```

Strictly speaking the **smbldap-tools** package isn't needed, but unless you have another package or custom scripts, a method of managing users, groups, and computer accounts is needed.

6.2.2. OpenLDAP Configuration

In order for Samba to use OpenLDAP as a *passdb backend*, the user objects in the directory will need additional attributes. This section assumes you want Samba to be configured as a Windows NT domain controller, and will add the necessary LDAP objects and attributes.

- The Samba attributes are defined in the `samba.schema` file which is part of the **samba-doc** package. The schema file needs to be unzipped and copied to `/etc/ldap/schema`. From a terminal prompt enter:

```
sudo cp /usr/share/doc/samba-doc/examples/LDAP/samba.schema.gz /etc/ldap/schema/
sudo gzip -d /etc/ldap/schema/samba.schema.gz
```

- The *samba* schema needs to be added to the *cn=config* tree. The procedure to add a new schema to **slapd** is also detailed in the Section 6.1.3, *Further Configuration*

  1. First, create a configuration file named `schema_convert.conf`, or a similar descriptive name, containing the following lines:

```
include /etc/ldap/schema/core.schema
include /etc/ldap/schema/collective.schema
include /etc/ldap/schema/corba.schema
```

```
include /etc/ldap/schema/cosine.schema
include /etc/ldap/schema/duaconf.schema
include /etc/ldap/schema/dyngroup.schema
include /etc/ldap/schema/inetorgperson.schema
include /etc/ldap/schema/java.schema
include /etc/ldap/schema/misc.schema
include /etc/ldap/schema/nis.schema
include /etc/ldap/schema/openldap.schema
include /etc/ldap/schema/ppolicy.schema
include /etc/ldap/schema/samba.schema
```

2. Next, create a temporary directory to hold the output:

```
mkdir /tmp/ldif_output
```

3. Now use **slapcat** to convert the schema files:

```
slapcat -f schema_convert.conf -F /tmp/ldif_output -n0 -s "cn={12}samba,
                        cn=schema,cn=config" > /tmp/cn=samba.ldif
```

Change the above file and path names to match your own if they are different.

4. Edit the generated /tmp/cn\=samba.ldif file by removing *{XX}* at the top of the file, where "*{XX}*" is the index number in curly braces:

```
dn: cn=samba,cn=schema,cn=config
...
cn: samba
```

And remove the following lines from the bottom of the file:

```
structuralObjectClass: olcSchemaConfig
entryUUID: b53b75ca-083f-102d-9fff-2f64fd123c95
creatorsName: cn=config
createTimestamp: 20080827045234Z
entryCSN: 20080827045234.341425Z#000000#000#000000
modifiersName: cn=config
modifyTimestamp: 20080827045234Z
```

Note

The attribute values will vary, just be sure the attributes are removed.

5. Finally, using the **ldapadd** utility, add the new schema to the directory:

```
ldapadd -x -D cn=admin,cn=config -W -f /tmp/cn\=samba.ldif
```

If you have not followed the Section 6.1 *OpenLDAP Server*, you can add the schema by entering:

```
sudo ldapadd -Y EXTERNAL -H ldapi:/// -f /tmp/cn\=samba.ldif
```

There should now be a *dn: cn={X}misc,cn=schema,cn=config*, where "X" is the next sequential schema, entry in the cn=config tree.

- Copy and paste the following into a file named `samba_indexes.ldif`:

```
dn: olcDatabase={1}hdb,cn=config
changetype: modify
add: olcDbIndex
olcDbIndex: uidNumber eq
olcDbIndex: gidNumber eq
olcDbIndex: loginShell eq
olcDbIndex: uid eq,pres,sub
olcDbIndex: memberUid eq,pres,sub
olcDbIndex: uniqueMember eq,pres
olcDbIndex: sambaSID eq
olcDbIndex: sambaPrimaryGroupSID eq
olcDbIndex: sambaGroupType eq
olcDbIndex: sambaSIDList eq
olcDbIndex: sambaDomainName eq
olcDbIndex: default sub
```

Using the **ldapmodify** utility load the new indexes:

```
ldapmodify -x -D cn=admin,cn=config -W -f samba_indexes.ldif
```

If all went well you should see the new indexes using **ldapsearch**:

```
ldapsearch -xLLL -D cn=admin,cn=config -x -b cn=config -W olcDatabase={1}hdb
```

- Next, configure the **smbldap-tools** package to match your environment. The package comes with a configuration script that will ask questions about the needed options. To run the script enter:

```
sudo gzip -d /usr/share/doc/smbldap-tools/configure.pl.gz
sudo perl /usr/share/doc/smbldap-tools/configure.pl
```

Once you have answered the questions, there should be `/etc/smbldap-tools/smbldap.conf` and `/etc/smbldap-tools/smbldap_bind.conf` files. These files are generated by the configure script, so if you made any mistakes while executing the script it may be simpler to edit the file appropriately.

- The **smbldap-populate** script will add the necessary users, groups, and LDAP objects required for Samba. It is a good idea to make a backup LDAP Data Interchange Format (LDIF) file with **slapcat** before executing the command:

```
sudo slapcat -l backup.ldif
```

Once you have a current backup execute **smbldap-populate** by entering:

```
sudo smbldap-populate
```

 Note

You can create an LDIF file containing the new Samba objects by executing **sudo smbldap-populate -e samba.ldif**. This allows you to look over the changes making sure everything is correct.

Your LDAP directory now has the necessary domain information to authenticate Samba users.

6.2.3. Samba Configuration

There a multiple ways to configure Samba for details on some common configurations see Chapter 17, *Windows Networking*. To configure Samba to use LDAP, edit the main Samba configuration file `/etc/samba/smb.conf` commenting the *passdb backend* option and adding the following:

```
#    passdb backend = tdbsam

# LDAP Settings
    passdb backend = ldapsam:ldap://hostname
    ldap suffix = dc=example,dc=com
    ldap user suffix = ou=People
    ldap group suffix = ou=Groups
    ldap machine suffix = ou=Computers
    ldap idmap suffix = ou=Idmap
    ldap admin dn = cn=admin,dc=example,dc=com
    ldap ssl = start tls
    ldap passwd sync = yes
...
    add machine script = sudo /usr/sbin/smbldap-useradd -t 0 -w "%u"
```

Restart **samba** to enable the new settings:

```
sudo restart smbd
sudo restart nmbd
```

Now Samba needs to know the LDAP admin password. From a terminal prompt enter:

```
sudo smbpasswd -w secret
```

 Note

Replacing secret with your LDAP admin password.

If you currently have users in LDAP, and you want them to authenticate using Samba, they will need some Samba attributes defined in the `samba.schema` file. Add the Samba attributes to existing users using the **smbpasswd** utility, replacing username with an actual user:

```
sudo smbpasswd -a username
```

You will then be asked to enter the user's password.

To add new user, group, and machine accounts use the utilities from the **smbldap-tools** package. Here are some examples:

- To add a new user to LDAP with Samba attributes enter the following, replacing username with an actual username:

```
sudo smbldap-useradd -a -P username
```

The *-a* option adds the Samba attributes, and the *-P* options calls the **smbldap-passwd** utility after the user is created allowing you to enter a password for the user.

- To remove a user from the directory enter:

```
sudo smbldap-userdel username
```

The **smbldap-userdel** utility also has a *-r* option to remove the user's home directory.

- Use **smbldap-groupadd** to add a group, replacing groupname with an appropriate group:

```
sudo smbldap-groupadd -a groupname
```

Similar to **smbldap-useradd**, the *-a* adds the Samba attributes.

- To add a user to a group use **smbldap-groupmod**:

```
sudo smbldap-groupmod -m username groupname
```

Be sure to replace *username* with a real user. Also, the *-m* option can add more than one user at a time by listing them in *comma separated* format.

- **smbldap-groupmod** can also be used to remove a user from a group:

```
sudo smbldap-groupmod -x username groupname
```

- Additionally, the **smbldap-useradd** utility can add Samba machine accounts:

```
sudo smbldap-useradd -t 0 -w username
```

Replace *username* with the name of the workstation. The *-t 0* option creates the machine account without a delay, while the *-w* option specifies the user as a machine account. Also, note the *add machine script* option in /etc/samba/smb.conf was changed to use **smbldap-useradd**.

There are more useful utilities and options in the **smbldap-tools** package. The man page for each utility provides more details.

6.2.4. Resources

- There are multiple places where LDAP and Samba is documented in the *Samba HOWTO Collection*[5].
- Specifically see the *passdb section*[6].
- Another good site is *Samba OpenLDAP HOWTO*[7].

---

[5] *http://samba.org/samba/docs/man/Samba-HOWTO-Collection/*

[6] *http://samba.org/samba/docs/man/Samba-HOWTO-Collection/passdb.html*

[7] *http://download.gna.org/smbldap-tools/docs/samba-ldap-howto/*

- Again, for more information on **smbldap-tools** see the man pages: **man smbldap-useradd, man smbldap-groupadd, man smbldap-populate**, etc.
- Also, there is a list of *Ubuntu wiki*[8] articles with more information

6.3. Kerberos

Kerberos is a network authentication system based on the principal of a trusted third party. The other two parties being the user and the service the user wishes to authenticate to. Not all services and applications can use Kerberos, but for those that can, it brings the network environment one step closer to being Single Sign On (SSO).

This section covers installation and configuration of a Kerberos server, and some example client configurations.

6.3.1. Overview

If you are new to Kerberos there are a few terms that are good to understand before setting up a Kerberos server. Most of the terms will relate to things you may be familiar with in other environments:

- *Principal:* any users, computers, and services provided by servers need to be defined as Kerberos Principals.
- *Instances:* are used for service principals and special administrative principals.
- *Realms:* the unique realm of control provided by the Kerberos installation. Usually the DNS domain converted to uppercase (EXAMPLE.COM).
- *Key Distribution Center:* (KDC) consist of three parts, a database of all principals, the authentication server, and the ticket granting server. For each realm there must be at least one KDC.
- *Ticket Granting Ticket:* issued by the Authentication Server (AS), the Ticket Granting Ticket (TGT) is encrypted in the user's password which is known only to the user and the KDC.
- *Ticket Granting Server:* (TGS) issues service tickets to clients upon request.
- *Tickets:* confirm the identity of the two principals. One principal being a user and the other a service requested by the user. Tickets establish an encryption key used for secure communication during the authenticated session.
- *Keytab Files:* are files extracted from the KDC principal database and contain the encryption key for a service or host.

---

[8] *https://help.ubuntu.com/community/Samba#samba-ldap*

To put the pieces together, a Realm has at least one KDC, preferably two for redundancy, which contains a database of Principals. When a user principal logs into a workstation, configured for Kerberos authentication, the KDC issues a Ticket Granting Ticket (TGT). If the user supplied credentials match, the user is authenticated and can then request tickets for Kerberized services from the Ticket Granting Server (TGS). The service tickets allow the user to authenticate to the service without entering another username and password.

6.3.2. Kerberos Server

6.3.2.1. Installation

Before installing the Kerberos server a properly configured DNS server is needed for your domain. Since the Kerberos Realm by convention matches the domain name, this section uses the *example.com* domain configured in the Section 7.2.3, *Primary Master*.

Also, Kerberos is a time sensitive protocol. So if the local system time between a client machine and the server differs by more than five minutes (by default), the workstation will not be able to authenticate. To correct the problem all hosts should have their time synchronized using the *Network Time Protocol (NTP)*. For details on setting up NTP see the Section 4.4, *Time Synchronisation with NTP*.

The first step in installing a Kerberos Realm is to install the **krb5-kdc** and **krb5-admin-server** packages. From a terminal enter:

```
sudo apt-get install krb5-kdc krb5-admin-server
```

You will be asked at the end of the install to supply a name for the Kerberos and Admin servers, which may or may not be the same server, for the realm.

Next, create the new realm with the **kdb5_newrealm** utility:

```
sudo krb5_newrealm
```

6.3.2.2. Configuration

The questions asked during installation are used to configure the /etc/krb5.conf file. If you need to adjust the Key Distribution Center (KDC) settings simply edit the file and restart the **krb5-kdc** daemon.

1. Now that the KDC running an admin user is needed. It is recommended to use a different username from your everyday username. Using the **kadmin.local** utility in a terminal prompt enter:

    ```
    sudo kadmin.local
    Authenticating as principal root/admin@EXAMPLE.COM with password.
    kadmin.local: addprinc steve/admin
    WARNING: no policy specified for steve/admin@EXAMPLE.COM;
                                            defaulting to no policy
    ```

```
Enter password for principal "steve/admin@EXAMPLE.COM":
Re-enter password for principal "steve/admin@EXAMPLE.COM":
Principal "steve/admin@EXAMPLE.COM" created.
kadmin.local: quit
```

In the above example steve is the *Principal*, /admin is an *Instance*, and @EXAMPLE.COM signifies the realm. The "every day" Principal would be *steve@EXAMPLE.COM*, and should have only normal user rights.

Note

Replace *EXAMPLE.COM* and *steve* with your Realm and admin username.

2. Next, the new admin user needs to have the appropriate Access Control List (ACL) permissions. The permissions are configured in the /etc/krb5kdc/kadm5.acl file:

```
steve/admin@EXAMPLE.COM                    *
```

This entry grants *steve/admin* the ability to perform any operation on all principals in the realm.

3. Now restart the **krb5-admin-server** for the new ACL to take affect:

```
sudo /etc/init.d/krb5-admin-server restart
```

4. The new user principal can be tested using the **kinit utility**:

```
kinit steve/admin
steve/admin@EXAMPLE.COM's Password:
```

After entering the password, use the **klist** utility to view information about the Ticket Granting Ticket (TGT):

```
klist
Credentials cache: FILE:/tmp/krb5cc_1000
        Principal: steve/admin@EXAMPLE.COM

  Issued             Expires           Principal
Jul 13 17:53:34   Jul 14 03:53:34   krbtgt/EXAMPLE.COM@EXAMPLE.COM
```

You may need to add an entry into the /etc/hosts for the KDC. For example:

```
192.168.0.1    kdc01.example.com        kdc01
```

Replacing *192.168.0.1* with the IP address of your KDC.

5. In order for clients to determine the KDC for the Realm some DNS SRV records are needed. Add the following to /etc/named/db.example.com:

```
_kerberos._udp.EXAMPLE.COM.       IN SRV 1   0 88  kdc01.example.com.
_kerberos._tcp.EXAMPLE.COM.       IN SRV 1   0 88  kdc01.example.com.
_kerberos._udp.EXAMPLE.COM.       IN SRV 10  0 88  kdc02.example.com.
_kerberos._tcp.EXAMPLE.COM.       IN SRV 10  0 88  kdc02.example.com.
_kerberos-adm._tcp.EXAMPLE.COM.   IN SRV 1   0 749 kdc01.example.com.
_kpasswd._udp.EXAMPLE.COM.        IN SRV 1   0 464 kdc01.example.com.
```

Note

Replace *EXAMPLE.COM*, *kdc01*, and *kdc02* with your domain name, primary KDC, and secondary KDC.

See Chapter 7, *Domain Name Service (DNS)* for detailed instructions on setting up DNS.

Your new Kerberos Realm is now ready to authenticate clients.

6.3.3. Secondary KDC

Once you have one Key Distribution Center (KDC) on your network, it is good practice to have a Secondary KDC in case the primary becomes unavailable.

1. First, install the packages, and when asked for the Kerberos and Admin server names enter the name of the Primary KDC:

   ```
   sudo apt-get install krb5-kdc krb5-admin-server
   ```

2. Once you have the packages installed, create the Secondary KDC's host principal. From a terminal prompt, enter:

   ```
   kadmin -q "addprinc -randkey host/kdc02.example.com"
   ```

Note

After, issuing any **kadmin** commands you will be prompted for your *username/admin@EXAMPLE.COM* principal password.

3. Extract the *keytab* file:

   ```
   kadmin -q "ktadd -k keytab.kdc02 host/kdc02.example.com"
   ```

4. There should now be a `keytab.kdc02` in the current directory, move the file to `/etc/krb5.keytab`:

   ```
   sudo mv keytab.kdc02 /etc/krb5.keytab
   ```

Note

If the path to the `keytab.kdc02` file is different adjust accordingly.

Also, you can list the principals in a Keytab file, which can be useful when troubleshooting, using the **klist** utility:

```
sudo klist -k /etc/krb5.keytab
```

5. Next, there needs to be a `kpropd.acl` file on each KDC that lists all KDCs for the Realm. For example, on both primary and secondary KDC, create `/etc/krb5kdc/kpropd.acl`:

   ```
   host/kdc01.example.com@EXAMPLE.COM
   host/kdc02.example.com@EXAMPLE.COM
   ```

6. Create an empty database on the *Secondary KDC*:

```
sudo kdb5_util -s create
```

7. Now start the **kpropd** daemon, which listens for connections from the **kprop** utility. **kprop** is used to transfer dump files:

```
sudo kpropd -S
```

8. From a terminal on the *Primary KDC*, create a dump file of the principal database:

```
sudo kdb5_util dump /var/lib/krb5kdc/dump
```

9. Extract the Primary KDC's *keytab* file and copy it to `/etc/krb5.keytab`:

```
kadmin -q "ktadd -k keytab.kdc01 host/kdc01.example.com"
sudo mv keytab.kdc01 /etc/krb5.keytab
```

Note

Make sure there is a *host* for *kdc01.example.com* before extracting the Keytab.

10. Using the **kprop** utility push the database to the Secondary KDC:

```
sudo kprop -r EXAMPLE.COM -f /var/lib/krb5kdc/dump kdc02.example.com
```

Note

There should be a *SUCCEEDED* message if the propagation worked. If there is an error message check `/var/log/syslog` on the secondary KDC for more information.

You may also want to create a **cron** job to periodically update the database on the Secondary KDC. For example, the following will push the database every hour:

```
# m h   dom mon dow    command
0 * * * * /usr/sbin/kdb5_util dump /var/lib/krb5kdc/dump && /usr/sbin
         /kprop -r EXAMPLE.COM -f /var/lib/krb5kdc/dump kdc02.example.com
```

11. Back on the *Secondary KDC*, create a *stash* file to hold the Kerberos master key:

```
sudo kdb5_util stash
```

12. Finally, start the **krb5-kdc** daemon on the Secondary KDC:

```
sudo /etc/init.d/krb5-kdc start
```

The *Secondary KDC* should now be able to issue tickets for the Realm. You can test this by stopping the **krb5-kdc** daemon on the Primary KDC, then use **kinit** to request a ticket. If all goes well you should receive a ticket from the Secondary KDC.

6.3.4. Kerberos Linux Client

This section covers configuring a Linux system as a **Kerberos** client. This will allow access to any kerberized services once a user has successfully logged into the system.

6.3.4.1. Installation

In order to authenticate to a Kerberos Realm, the **krb5-user** and **libpam-krb5** packages are needed, along with a few others that are not strictly necessary but make life easier. To install the packages enter the following in a terminal prompt:

```
sudo apt-get install krb5-user libpam-krb5 libpam-ccreds auth-client-config
```

The **auth-client-config** package allows simple configuration of PAM for authentication from multiple sources, and the **libpam-ccreds** will cache authentication credentials allowing you to login in case the Key Distribution Center (KDC) is unavailable. This package is also useful for laptops that may authenticate using Kerberos while on the corporate network, but will need to be accessed off the network as well.

6.3.4.2. Configuration

To configure the client in a terminal enter:

```
sudo dpkg-reconfigure krb5-config
```

You will then be prompted to enter the name of the Kerberos Realm. Also, if you don't have DNS configured with Kerberos *SRV* records, the menu will prompt you for the hostname of the Key Distribution Center (KDC) and Realm Administration server.

The **dpkg-reconfigure** adds entries to the /etc/krb5.conf file for your Realm. You should have entries similar to the following:

```
[libdefaults]
        default_realm = EXAMPLE.COM
...
[realms]
        EXAMPLE.COM = }
                kdc = 192.168.0.1
                admin_server = 192.168.0.1
        }
```

You can test the configuration by requesting a ticket using the **kinit** utility. For example:

```
kinit steve@EXAMPLE.COM
Password for steve@EXAMPLE.COM:
```

When a ticket has been granted, the details can be viewed using **klist**:

```
klist
Ticket cache: FILE:/tmp/krb5cc_1000
Default principal: steve@EXAMPLE.COM

Valid starting       Expires                  Service principal
07/24/08 05:18:56    07/24/08 15:18:56   krbtgt/EXAMPLE.COM@EXAMPLE.COM
        renew until 07/25/08 05:18:57

Kerberos 4 ticket cache: /tmp/tkt1000
klist: You have no tickets cached
```

Next, use the **auth-client-config** to configure the **libpam-krb5** module to request a ticket during login:

```
sudo auth-client-config -a -p kerberos_example
```

You will should now receive a ticket upon successful login authentication.

6.3.5. Resources

- For more information on Kerberos see the *MIT Kerberos*[9] site.
- The *Ubuntu Wiki Kerberos*[10] page has more details.
- O'Reilly's *Kerberos: The Definitive Guide*[11] is a great reference when setting up Kerberos.
- Also, feel free to stop by the *#ubuntu-server* IRC channel on *Freenode*[12] if you have Kerberos questions.

6.4. Kerberos and LDAP

Replicating a Kerberos principal database between two servers can be complicated, and adds an additional user database to your network. Fortunately, MIT Kerberos can be configured to use an **LDAP** directory as a principal database. This section covers configuring a primary and secondary kerberos server to use **OpenLDAP** for the principal database.

6.4.1. Configuring OpenLDAP

First, the necessary *schema* needs to be loaded on an **OpenLDAP** server that has network connectivity to the Primary and Secondary KDCs. The rest of this section assumes that you also have LDAP replication configured between at least two servers. For information on setting up OpenLDAP see the Section 6.1, *OpenLDAP Server*.

It is also required to configure OpenLDAP for TLS and SSL connections, so that traffic between the KDC and LDAP server is encrypted. See the Section 6.1.6, *TLS and SSL* for details.

- To load the schema into LDAP, on the LDAP server install the **krb5-kdc-ldap** package. From a terminal enter:
  ```
  sudo apt-get install krb5-kdc-ldap
  ```

---

[9] *http://web.mit.edu/Kerberos/*
[10] *https://help.ubuntu.com/community/Kerberos*
[11] *http://oreilly.com/catalog/9780596004033/*
[12] *http://freenode.net/*

- Next, extract the `kerberos.schema.gz` file:

```
sudo gzip -d /usr/share/doc/krb5-kdc-ldap/kerberos.schema.gz
sudo cp /usr/share/doc/krb5-kdc-ldap/kerberos.schema /etc/ldap/schema/
```

- The *kerberos* schema needs to be added to the *cn=config* tree. The procedure to add a new schema to **slapd** is also detailed in the Section 6.1.3, *Further Configuration*.

  1. First, create a configuration file named `schema_convert.conf`, or a similar descriptive name, containing the following lines:

```
include /etc/ldap/schema/core.schema
include /etc/ldap/schema/collective.schema
include /etc/ldap/schema/corba.schema
include /etc/ldap/schema/cosine.schema
include /etc/ldap/schema/duaconf.schema
include /etc/ldap/schema/dyngroup.schema
include /etc/ldap/schema/inetorgperson.schema
include /etc/ldap/schema/java.schema
include /etc/ldap/schema/misc.schema
include /etc/ldap/schema/nis.schema
include /etc/ldap/schema/openldap.schema
include /etc/ldap/schema/ppolicy.schema
include /etc/ldap/schema/kerberos.schema
```

  2. Create a temporary directory to hold the LDIF files:

```
mkdir /tmp/ldif_output
```

  3. Now use **slapcat** to convert the schema files:

```
slapcat -f schema_convert.conf -F /tmp/ldif_output -n0 -s "cn={12}
                 kerberos,cn=schema,cn=config" > /tmp/cn=kerberos.ldif
```

     Change the above file and path names to match your own if they are different.

  4. Edit the generated `/tmp/cn\=kerberos.ldif` file, changing the following attributes:

```
dn: cn=kerberos,cn=schema,cn=config
...
cn: kerberos
```

     And remove the following lines from the end of the file:

```
structuralObjectClass: olcSchemaConfig
entryUUID: 18ccd010-746b-102d-9fbe-3760cca765dc
creatorsName: cn=config
createTimestamp: 20090111203515Z
entryCSN: 20090111203515.326445Z#000000#000#000000
modifiersName: cn=config
modifyTimestamp: 20090111203515Z
```

Note

The attribute values will vary, just be sure the attributes are removed.

  5. Load the new schema with **ldapadd**:

```
ldapadd -x -D cn=admin,cn=config -W -f /tmp/cn\=kerberos.ldif
```

6. Add an index for the *krb5principalname* attribute:

```
ldapmodify -x -D cn=admin,cn=config -W
Enter LDAP Password:
dn: olcDatabase={1}hdb,cn=config
add: olcDbIndex
olcDbIndex: krbPrincipalName eq,pres,sub

modifying entry "olcDatabase={1}hdb,cn=config"
```

7. Finally, update the Access Control Lists (ACL):

```
ldapmodify -x -D cn=admin,cn=config -W
Enter LDAP Password:
dn: olcDatabase={1}hdb,cn=config
replace: olcAccess
olcAccess: to attrs=userPassword,shadowLastChange,krbPrincipalKey by
        dn="cn=admin,dc=example,dc=com" write by anonymous
        auth by self write by * none
-
add: olcAccess
olcAccess: to dn.base="" by * read
-
add: olcAccess
olcAccess: to * by dn="cn=admin,dc=example,dc=com" write by * read

modifying entry "olcDatabase={1}hdb,cn=config"
```

That's it, your LDAP directory is now ready to serve as a Kerberos principal database.

6.4.2. Primary KDC Configuration

With **OpenLDAP** configured it is time to configure the KDC.

- First, install the necessary packages, from a terminal enter:

```
sudo apt-get install krb5-kdc krb5-admin-server krb5-kdc-ldap
```

- Now edit /etc/krb5.conf adding the following options to under the appropriate sections:

```
[libdefaults]
        default_realm = EXAMPLE.COM

...

[realms]
        EXAMPLE.COM = {
                kdc = kdc01.example.com
                kdc = kdc02.example.com
                admin_server = kdc01.example.com
                admin_server = kdc02.example.com
                default_domain = example.com
                database_module = openldap_ldapconf
        }

...
```

```
[domain_realm]
        .example.com = EXAMPLE.COM

...

[dbdefaults]
        ldap_kerberos_container_dn = dc=example,dc=com

[dbmodules]
        openldap_ldapconf = {
                db_library = kldap
                ldap_kdc_dn = "cn=admin,dc=example,dc=com"

                # this object needs to have read rights on
                # the realm container, principal container and realm sub-trees
                ldap_kadmind_dn = "cn=admin,dc=example,dc=com"

                # this object needs to have read and write rights on
                # the realm container, principal container and realm sub-trees
                ldap_service_password_file = /etc/krb5kdc/service.keyfile
                ldap_servers = ldaps://ldap01.example.com ldaps://ldap02.example.com
                ldap_conns_per_server = 5
        }
```

Note

Change *example.com, dc=example,dc=com, cn=admin,dc=example,dc=com,* and
ldap01.example.com to the appropriate domain, LDAP object, and LDAP server for
your network.

- Next, use the **kdb5_ldap_util** utility to create the realm:

```
sudo kdb5_ldap_util -D  cn=admin,dc=example,dc=com create -subtrees
          dc=example,dc=com -r EXAMPLE.COM -s -H ldap://ldap01.example.com
```

- Create a stash of the password used to bind to the LDAP server. This password is
  used by the *ldap_kdc_dn* and *ldap_kadmin_dn* options in /etc/krb5.conf:

```
sudo kdb5_ldap_util -D  cn=admin,dc=example,dc=com stashsrvpw -f
                    /etc/krb5kdc/service.keyfile cn=admin,dc=example,dc=com
```

- Copy the CA certificate from the LDAP server:

```
scp ldap01:/etc/ssl/certs/cacert.pem .
sudo cp cacert.pem /etc/ssl/certs
```

And edit /etc/ldap/ldap.conf to use the certificate:

```
TLS_CACERT /etc/ssl/certs/cacert.pem
```

Note

The certificate will also need to be copied to the Secondary KDC, to allow the
connection to the LDAP servers using LDAPS.

You can now add Kerberos principals to the LDAP database, and they will be copied to any
other LDAP servers configured for replication. To add a principal using the **kadmin.local**
utility enter:

```
sudo kadmin.local
Authenticating as principal root/admin@EXAMPLE.COM with password.
kadmin.local:  addprinc -x dn="uid=steve,ou=people,dc=example,dc=com" steve
WARNING: no policy specified for steve@EXAMPLE.COM; defaulting to no policy
Enter password for principal "steve@EXAMPLE.COM":
Re-enter password for principal "steve@EXAMPLE.COM":
Principal "steve@EXAMPLE.COM" created.
```

There should now be krbPrincipalName, krbPrincipalKey, krbLastPwdChange, and krbExtraData attributes added to the *uid=steve,ou=people,dc=example,dc=com* user object. Use the **kinit** and **klist** utilities to test that the user is indeed issued a ticket.

Note

If the user object is already created the *-x dn="..."* option is needed to add the Kerberos attributes. Otherwise a new *principal* object will be created in the realm subtree.

6.4.3. Secondary KDC Configuration

Configuring a Secondary KDC using the LDAP backend is similar to configuring one using the normal Kerberos database.

- First, install the necessary packages. In a terminal enter:
  ```
  sudo apt-get install krb5-kdc krb5-admin-server krb5-kdc-ldap
  ```

- Next, edit /etc/krb5.conf to use the LDAP backend:
  ```
  [libdefaults]
          default_realm = EXAMPLE.COM

  ...

  [realms]
          EXAMPLE.COM = {
                  kdc = kdc01.example.com
                  kdc = kdc02.example.com
                  admin_server = kdc01.example.com
                  admin_server = kdc02.example.com
                  default_domain = example.com
                  database_module = openldap_ldapconf
          }

  ...

  [domain_realm]
          .example.com = EXAMPLE.COM

  ...

  [dbdefaults]
          ldap_kerberos_container_dn = dc=example,dc=com

  [dbmodules]
          openldap_ldapconf = {
                  db_library = kldap
                  ldap_kdc_dn = "cn=admin,dc=example,dc=com"
  ```

```
# this object needs to have read rights on
# the realm container, principal container and realm sub-trees
ldap_kadmind_dn = "cn=admin,dc=example,dc=com"

# this object needs to have read and write rights on
# the realm container, principal container and realm sub-trees
ldap_service_password_file = /etc/krb5kdc/service.keyfile
ldap_servers = ldaps://ldap01.example.com ldaps://ldap02.example.com
ldap_conns_per_server = 5
}
```

- Create the stash for the LDAP bind password:

```
sudo kdb5_ldap_util -D  cn=admin,dc=example,dc=com stashsrvpw -f /etc
                        /krb5kdc/service.keyfile cn=admin,dc=example,dc=com
```

- Now, on the *Primary KDC* copy the `/etc/krb5kdc/.k5.EXAMPLE.COM` *Master Key* stash to the Secondary KDC. Be sure to copy the file over an encrypted connection such as **scp**, or on physical media.

```
sudo scp /etc/krb5kdc/.k5.EXAMPLE.COM steve@kdc02.example.com:~
sudo mv .k5.EXAMPLE.COM /etc/krb5kdc/
```

 Note

Again, replace *EXAMPLE.COM* with your actual realm.

- Finally, start the **krb5-kdc** daemon:

```
sudo /etc/init.d/krb5-kdc start
```

You now have redundant KDCs on your network, and with redundant LDAP servers you should be able to continue to authenticate users if one LDAP server, one Kerberos server, or one LDAP and one Kerberos server become unavailable.

6.4.4. Resources

- The *Kerberos Admin Guide*[13] has some additional details.

- For more information on **kdb5_ldap_util** see *Section 5.6*[14] and the *kdb5_ldap_util man page*[15].

- Another useful link is the *krb5.conf man page*[16].

- Also, see the *Kerberos and LDAP*[17] Ubuntu wiki page.

---

[13] *http://web.mit.edu/Kerberos/krb5-1.6/krb5-1.6.3/doc/krb5-admin.html#Configuring-Kerberos-with-OpenLDAP-back_002dend*

[14] *http://web.mit.edu/Kerberos/krb5-1.6/krb5-1.6.3/doc/krb5-admin.html#Global-Operations-on-the-Kerberos-LDAP-Database*

[15] *http://manpages.ubuntu.com/manpages/natty/en/man8/kdb5_ldap_util.8.html*

[16] *http://manpages.ubuntu.com/manpages/natty/en/man5/krb5.conf.5.html*

[17] *https://help.ubuntu.com/community/Kerberos#kerberos-ldap*

Chapter 7.
Domain Name Service (DNS)

Domain Name Service (DNS) is an Internet service that maps IP addresses and fully qualified domain names (FQDN) to one another. In this way, DNS alleviates the need to remember IP addresses. Computers that run DNS are called *name servers*. Ubuntu ships with **BIND** (Berkley Internet Naming Daemon), the most common program used for maintaining a name server on Linux.

7.1. Installation

At a terminal prompt, enter the following command to install **dns**:

```
sudo apt-get install bind9
```

A very useful package for testing and troubleshooting DNS issues is the dnsutils package. To install **dnsutils** enter the following:

```
sudo apt-get install dnsutils
```

7.2. Configuration

There are many ways to configure **BIND9**. Some of the most common configurations are a caching nameserver, primary master, and as a secondary master.

- When configured as a caching nameserver BIND9 will find the answer to name queries and remember the answer when the domain is queried again.
- As a primary master server BIND9 reads the data for a zone from a file on it's host and is authoritative for that zone.
- In a secondary master configuration BIND9 gets the zone data from another nameserver authoritative for the zone.

7.2.1. Overview

The DNS configuration files are stored in the /etc/bind directory. The primary configuration file is /etc/bind/named.conf.

The *include* line specifies the filename which contains the DNS options. The *directory* line in the /etc/bind/named.conf.options file tells DNS where to look for files. All files BIND uses will be relative to this directory.

The file named `/etc/bind/db.root` describes the root nameservers in the world. The servers change over time, so the `/etc/bind/db.root` file must be maintained now and then. This is usually done as updates to the **bind9** package. The *zone* section defines a master server, and it is stored in a file mentioned in the *file* option.

It is possible to configure the same server to be a caching name server, primary master, and secondary master. A server can be the Start of Authority (SOA) for one zone, while providing secondary service for another zone. All the while providing caching services for hosts on the local LAN.

7.2.2. Caching Nameserver

The default configuration is setup to act as a caching server. All that is required is simply adding the IP Addresses of your ISP's DNS servers. Simply uncomment and edit the following in `/etc/bind/named.conf.options`:

```
forwarders {
        1.2.3.4;
        5.6.7.8;
    };
```

 Note

Replace *1.2.3.4* and *5.6.7.8* with the IP Adresses of actual nameservers.

Now restart the DNS server, to enable the new configuration. From a terminal prompt:

```
sudo /etc/init.d/bind9 restart
```

See the Section 7.3.1.2, *dig* for information on testing a caching DNS server.

7.2.3. Primary Master

In this section **BIND9** will be configured as the Primary Master for the domain *example.com*. Simply replace example.com with your FQDN (Fully Qualified Domain Name).

7.2.3.1. Forward Zone File

To add a DNS zone to BIND9, turning BIND9 into a Primary Master server, the first step is to edit `/etc/bind/named.conf.local`:

```
zone "example.com" {
  type master;
        file "/etc/bind/db.example.com";
};
```

Now use an existing zone file as a template to create the `/etc/bind/db.example.com` file:

```
sudo cp /etc/bind/db.local /etc/bind/db.example.com
```

Edit the new zone file /etc/bind/db.example.com change *localhost.* to the FQDN of your server, leaving the additional "." at the end. Change *127.0.0.1* to the nameserver's IP Address and *root.localhost* to a valid email address, but with a "." instead of the usual "@" symbol, again leaving the "." at the end.

Also, create an *A record* for ns.example.com. The name server in this example:

```
;
; BIND data file for local loopback interface
;
$TTL      604800
@         IN        SOA       ns.example.com. root.example.com. (
                                    2            ; Serial
                              604800            ; Refresh
                               86400            ; Retry
                             2419200            ; Expire
                              604800 )          ; Negative Cache TTL
;
@         IN        NS        ns.example.com.
@         IN        A         127.0.0.1
@         IN        AAAA      ::1
ns        IN        A         192.168.1.10
```

You must increment the *Serial Number* every time you make changes to the zone file. If you make multiple changes before restarting BIND9, simply increment the Serial once.

Now, you can add DNS records to the bottom of the zone file. See the Section 7.4.1, *Common Record Types* for details.

Note

Many admins like to use the last date edited as the serial of a zone, such as *2007010100* which is yyyymmddss (where *ss* is the Serial Number)

Once you have made a change to the zone file **BIND9** will need to be restarted for the changes to take effect:

```
sudo /etc/init.d/bind9 restart
```

7.2.3.2. Reverse Zone File

Now that the zone is setup and resolving names to IP Adresses a *Reverse zone* is also required. A Reverse zone allows DNS to resolve an address to a name.

Edit /etc/bind/named.conf.local and add the following:

```
zone "1.168.192.in-addr.arpa" {
        type master;
        notify no;
        file "/etc/bind/db.192";
};
```

Note

Replace *1.168.192* with the first three octets of whatever network you are using. Also, name the zone file `/etc/bind/db.192` appropriately. It should match the first octet of your network.

Now create the `/etc/bind/db.192` file:

```
sudo cp /etc/bind/db.127 /etc/bind/db.192
```

Next edit `/etc/bind/db.192` changing the basically the same options as `/etc/bind/db.example.com`:

```
;
; BIND reverse data file for local loopback interface
;
$TTL    604800
@       IN      SOA     ns.example.com. root.example.com. (
                               2          ; Serial
                          604800          ; Refresh
                           86400          ; Retry
                         2419200          ; Expire
                          604800 )        ; Negative Cache TTL
;
@       IN      NS      ns.
10      IN      PTR     ns.example.com.
```

The *Serial Number* in the Reverse zone needs to be incremented on each change as well. For each *A record* you configure in `/etc/bind/db.example.com` you need to create a *PTR record* in `/etc/bind/db.192`.

After creating the reverse zone file restart **BIND9**:

```
sudo /etc/init.d/bind9 restart
```

7.2.4. Secondary Master

Once a *Primary Master* has been configured a *Secondary Master* is needed in order to maintain the availability of the domain should the Primary become unavailable.

First, on the Primary Master server, the zone transfer needs to be allowed. Add the *allow-transfer* option to the example Forward and Reverse zone definitions in `/etc/bind/named.conf.local`:

```
zone "example.com" {
        type master;
   file "/etc/bind/db.example.com";
        allow-transfer { 192.168.1.11; };
};

zone "1.168.192.in-addr.arpa" {
        type master;
        notify no;
```

```
      file "/etc/bind/db.192";
  allow-transfer { 192.168.1.11; };
};
```

Note

Replace *192.168.1.11* with the IP Address of your Secondary nameserver.

Next, on the Secondary Master, install the **bind9** package the same way as on the Primary. Then edit the `/etc/bind/named.conf.local` and add the following declarations for the Forward and Reverse zones:

```
zone "example.com" {
  type slave;
        file "db.example.com";
        masters { 192.168.1.10; };
};

zone "1.168.192.in-addr.arpa" {
  type slave;
        file "db.192";
        masters { 192.168.1.10; };
};
```

Note

Replace *192.168.1.10* with the IP Address of your Primary nameserver.

Restart **BIND9** on the Secondary Master:

```
sudo /etc/init.d/bind9 restart
```

In `/var/log/syslog` you should see something similar to:

```
slave zone "example.com" (IN) loaded (serial 6)
slave zone "100.18.172.in-addr.arpa" (IN) loaded (serial 3)
```

Note

A zone is only transferred if the *Serial Number* on the Primary is larger than the one on the Secondary.

Note

The default directory for non-authoritative zone files is `/var/cache/bind/`. This directory is also configured in **AppArmor** to allow the **named** daemon to write to it. For more information on AppArmor see the Section 8.4, *AppArmor*.

7.3. Troubleshooting

This section covers ways to help determine the cause when problems happen with DNS and BIND9.

7.3.1. Testing

7.3.1.1. resolv.conf

The first step in testing **BIND9** is to add the nameserver's IP Address to a hosts resolver. The Primary nameserver should be configured as well as another host to double check things. Simply edit /etc/resolv.conf and add the following:

```
nameserver    192.168.1.10
nameserver    192.168.1.11
```

 Note

> You should also add the IP Address of the Secondary nameserver in case the Primary becomes unavailable.

7.3.1.2. dig

If you installed the **dnsutils** package you can test your setup using the DNS lookup utility **dig**:

- After installing **BIND9** use **dig** against the loopback interface to make sure it is listening on port 53. From a terminal prompt:

  ```
  dig -x 127.0.0.1
  ```

  You should see lines similar to the following in the command output:

  ```
  ;; Query time: 1 msec
  ;; SERVER: 192.168.1.10#53(192.168.1.10)
  ```

- If you have configured **BIND9** as a *Caching* nameserver "dig" an outside domain to check the query time:

  ```
  dig ubuntu.com
  ```

  Note the query time toward the end of the command output:

  ```
  ;; Query time: 49 msec
  ```

  After a second dig there should be improvement:

  ```
  ;; Query time: 1 msec
  ```

7.3.1.3. ping

Now to demonstrate how applications make use of DNS to resolve a host name use the **ping** utility to send an ICMP echo request. From a terminal prompt enter:

```
ping example.com
```

This tests if the nameserver can resolve the name *ns.example.com* to an IP Address. The command output should resemble:

```
PING ns.example.com (192.168.1.10) 56(84) bytes of data.
64 bytes from 192.168.1.10: icmp_seq=1 ttl=64 time=0.800 ms
64 bytes from 192.168.1.10: icmp_seq=2 ttl=64 time=0.813 ms
```

7.3.1.4. named-checkzone

A great way to test your zone files is by using the **named-checkzone** utility installed with the **bind9** package. This utility allows you to make sure the configuration is correct before restarting **BIND9** and making the changes live.

- To test our example Forward zone file enter the following from a command prompt:

```
named-checkzone example.com /etc/bind/db.example.com
```

  If everything is configured correctly you should see output similar to:

```
zone example.com/IN: loaded serial 6
OK
```

- Similarly, to test the Reverse zone file enter the following:

```
named-checkzone example.com /etc/bind/db.192
```

  The output should be similar to:

```
zone example.com/IN: loaded serial 3
OK
```

 Note

The *Serial Number* of your zone file will probably be different.

7.3.2. Logging

BIND9 has a wide variety of logging configuration options available. There are two main options. The *channel* option configures where logs go, and the *category* option determines what information to log.

If no logging option is configured the default option is:

```
logging {
     category default { default_syslog; default_debug; };
     category unmatched { null; };
};
```

This section covers configuring **BIND9** to send *debug* messages related to DNS queries to a separate file.

- First, we need to configure a channel to specify which file to send the messages to. Edit /etc/bind/named.conf.local and add the following:

```
logging {
    channel query.log {
        file "/var/log/query.log";
        severity debug 3;
    };
};
```

- Next, configure a category to send all DNS queries to the query file:

```
logging {
    channel query.log {
        file "/var/log/query.log";
        severity debug 3;
    };


category queries { query.log; };
};
```

 Note

The *debug* option can be set from 1 to 3. If a level isn't specified level 1 is the default.

- Since the *named daemon* runs as the *bind* user the /var/log/query.log file must be created and the ownership changed:

```
sudo touch /var/log/query.log
sudo chown bind /var/log/query.log
```

- Before **named** daemon can write to the new log file the **AppArmor** profile must be updated. First, edit /etc/apparmor.d/usr.sbin.named and add:

```
/var/log/query.log w,
```

Next, reload the profile:

```
cat /etc/apparmor.d/usr.sbin.named | sudo apparmor_parser -r
```

For more information on **AppArmor** see the Section 8.4, *AppArmor*

- Now restart **BIND9** for the changes to take effect:

```
sudo /etc/init.d/bind9 restart
```

You should see the file /var/log/query.log fill with query information. This is a simple example of the **BIND9** logging options. For coverage of advanced options see the Section 7.4.2, *More Information*.

7.4. References

7.4.1. Common Record Types

This section covers some of the most common DNS record types.

- *A record*: This record maps an IP Address to a hostname.
```
www      IN    A      192.168.1.12
```
- *CNAME record*: Used to create an alias to an existing A record. You cannot create a CNAME record pointing to another CNAME record.
```
web      IN    CNAME  www
```
- *MX record*: Used to define where email should be sent to. Must point to an A record, not a CNAME.

```
         IN    MX        mail.example.com.
mail     IN    A         192.168.1.13
```

- *NS* record: Used to define which servers serve copies of a zone. It must point to an A record, not a CNAME. This is where Primary and Secondary servers are defined.

```
         IN    NS        ns.example.com.
         IN    NS        ns2.example.com.
ns       IN    A         192.168.1.10
ns2      IN    A         192.168.1.11
```

7.4.2. More Information

- The *DNS HOWTO*[1] explains more advanced options for configuring BIND9.
- For in depth coverage of *DNS* and **BIND9** see *Bind9.net*[2].
- *DNS and BIND*[3] is a popular book now in it's fifth edition.
- A great place to ask for **BIND9** assistance, and get involved with the Ubuntu Server community, is the *#ubuntu-server* IRC channel on *freenode*[4].
- Also, see the *BIND9 Server HOWTO*[5] in the Ubuntu Wiki

---

[1] *http://www.tldp.org/HOWTO/DNS-HOWTO.html*

[2] *http://www.bind9.net/*

[3] *http://www.oreilly.com/catalog/dns5/index.html*

[4] *http://freenode.net/*

[5] *https://help.ubuntu.com/community/BIND9ServerHowto*

Chapter 8.
Security

Security should always be considered when installing, deploying, and using any type of computer system. Although a fresh installation of Ubuntu is relatively safe for immediate use on the Internet, it is important to have a balanced understanding of your systems security posture based on how it will be used after deployment.

This chapter provides an overview of security related topics as they pertain to Ubuntu 11.04 Server Edition, and outlines simple measures you may use to protect your server and network from any number of potential security threats.

8.1. User Management

User management is a critical part of maintaining a secure system. Ineffective user and privilege management often lead many systems into being compromised. Therefore, it is important that you understand how you can protect your server through simple and effective user account management techniques.

8.1.1. Where is root?

Ubuntu developers made a conscientious decision to disable the administrative root account by default in all Ubuntu installations. This does not mean that the root account has been deleted or that it may not be accessed. It merely has been given a password which matches no possible encrypted value, therefore may not log in directly by itself.

Instead, users are encouraged to make use of a tool by the name of **sudo** to carry out system administrative duties. **Sudo** allows an authorized user to temporarily elevate their privileges using their own password instead of having to know the password belonging to the root account. This simple yet effective methodology provides accountability for all user actions, and gives the administrator granular control over which actions a user can perform with said privileges.

- If for some reason you wish to enable the root account, simply give it a password:

  ```
  sudo passwd
  ```

  Sudo will prompt you for your password, and then ask you to supply a new password for root as shown below:

```
[sudo] password for username: (enter your own password)
Enter new UNIX password: (enter a new password for root)
Retype new UNIX password: (repeat new password for root)
passwd: password updated successfully
```

- To disable the root account, use the following passwd syntax:

```
sudo passwd -l root
```

- You should read more on **Sudo** by checking out it's man page:

```
man sudo
```

By default, the initial user created by the Ubuntu installer is a member of the group "admin" which is added to the file /etc/sudoers as an authorized sudo user. If you wish to give any other account full root access through **sudo**, simply add them to the admin group.

8.1.2. Adding and Deleting Users

The process for managing local users and groups is straight forward and differs very little from most other GNU/Linux operating systems. Ubuntu and other Debian based distributions, encourage the use of the "adduser" package for account management.

- To add a user account, use the following syntax, and follow the prompts to give the account a password and identifiable characteristics such as a full name, phone number, etc.

```
sudo adduser username
```

- To delete a user account and its primary group, use the following syntax:

```
sudo deluser username
```

Deleting an account does not remove their respective home folder. It is up to you whether or not you wish to delete the folder manually or keep it according to your desired retention policies.

Remember, any user added later on with the same UID/GID as the previous owner will now have access to this folder if you have not taken the necessary precautions.

You may want to change these UID/GID values to something more appropriate, such as the root account, and perhaps even relocate the folder to avoid future conflicts:

```
sudo chown -R root:root /home/username/
sudo mkdir /home/archived_users/
sudo mv /home/username /home/archived_users/
```

- To temporarily lock or unlock a user account, use the following syntax, respectively:

```
sudo passwd -l username
sudo passwd -u username
```

- To add or delete a personalized group, use the following syntax, respectively:

```
sudo addgroup groupname
sudo delgroup groupname
```

- To add a user to a group, use the following syntax:

```
sudo adduser username groupname
```

8.1.3. User Profile Security

When a new user is created, the adduser utility creates a brand new home directory named /home/username, respectively. The default profile is modeled after the contents found in the directory of /etc/skel, which includes all profile basics.

If your server will be home to multiple users, you should pay close attention to the user home directory permissions to ensure confidentiality. By default, user home directories in Ubuntu are created with world read/execute permissions. This means that all users can browse and access the contents of other users home directories. This may not be suitable for your environment.

- To verify your current users home directory permissions, use the following syntax:

```
ls -ld /home/username
```

The following output shows that the directory /home/username has world readable permissions:

```
drwxr-xr-x  2 username username    4096 2007-10-02 20:03 username
```

- You can remove the world readable permissions using the following syntax:

```
sudo chmod 0750 /home/username
```

 Note

Some people tend to use the recursive option (-R) indiscriminately which modifies all child folders and files, but this is not necessary, and may yield other undesirable results. The parent directory alone is sufficient for preventing unauthorized access to anything below the parent.

- A much more efficient approach to the matter would be to modify the **adduser** global default permissions when creating user home folders. Simply edit the file /etc/adduser.conf and modify the DIR_MODE variable to something appropriate, so that all new home directories will receive the correct permissions.

```
DIR_MODE=0750
```

- After correcting the directory permissions using any of the previously mentioned techniques, verify the results using the following syntax:

```
ls -ld /home/username
```

The results below show that world readable permissions have been removed:

```
drwxr-x---  2 username username    4096 2007-10-02 20:03 username
```

8.1.4. Password Policy

A strong password policy is one of the most important aspects of your security posture. Many successful security breaches involve simple brute force and dictionary attacks against weak passwords. If you intend to offer any form of remote access involving your local password system, make sure you adequately address minimum password complexity requirements, maximum password lifetimes, and frequent audits of your authentication systems.

8.1.4.1. Minimum Password Length

By default, Ubuntu requires a minimum password length of 6 characters, as well as some basic entropy checks. These values are controlled in the file /etc/pam.d/common-password, which is outlined below.

```
password        [success=2 default=ignore]        pam_unix.so obscure sha512
```

If you would like to adjust the minimum length to 6 characters, change the appropriate variable to min=6. The modification is outlined below.

```
password        [success=2 default=ignore]        pam_unix.so obscure sha512 min=8
```

8.1.4.2. Password Expiration

When creating user accounts, you should make it a policy to have a minimum and maximum password age forcing users to change their passwords when they expire.

- To easily view the current status of a user account, use the following syntax:
  ```
  sudo chage -l username
  ```
  The output below shows interesting facts about the user account, namely that there are no policies applied:

  ```
  Last password change                                 : Jan 20, 2008
  Password expires                                     : never
  Password inactive                                    : never
  Account expires                                      : never
  Minimum number of days between password change       : 0
  Maximum number of days between password change       : 99999
  Number of days of warning before password expires    : 7
  ```

- To set any of these values, simply use the following syntax, and follow the interactive prompts:
  ```
  sudo chage username
  ```
  The following is also an example of how you can manually change the explicit expiration date (-E) to 01/31/2008, minimum password age (-m) of 5 days, maximum password age (-M) of 90 days, inactivity period (-I) of 5 days after

password expiration, and a warning time period (-W) of 14 days before password expiration.

```
sudo chage -E 01/31/2011 -m 5 -M 90 -I 30 -W 14 username
```

- To verify changes, use the same syntax as mentioned previously:

```
sudo chage -l username
```

The output below shows the new policies that have been established for the account:

```
Last password change                              : Jan 20, 2008
Password expires                                  : Apr 19, 2008
Password inactive                                 : May 19, 2008
Account expires                                   : Jan 31, 2008
Minimum number of days between password change    : 5
Maximum number of days between password change    : 90
Number of days of warning before password expires : 14
```

8.1.5. Other Security Considerations

Many applications use alternate authentication mechanisms that can be easily overlooked by even experienced system administrators. Therefore, it is important to understand and control how users authenticate and gain access to services and applications on your server.

8.1.5.1. SSH Access by Disabled Users

Simply disabling/locking a user account will not prevent a user from logging into your server remotely if they have previously set up RSA public key authentication. They will still be able to gain shell access to the server, without the need for any password. Remember to check the users home directory for files that will allow for this type of authenticated SSH access. e.g. /home/username/.ssh/authorized_keys.

Remove or rename the directory .ssh/ in the user's home folder to prevent further SSH authentication capabilities.

Be sure to check for any established SSH connections by the disabled user, as it is possible they may have existing inbound or outbound connections. Kill any that are found.

Restrict SSH access to only user accounts that should have it. For example, you may create a group called "sshlogin" and add the group name as the value associated with the AllowGroups variable located in the file /etc/ssh/sshd_config.

```
AllowGroups sshlogin
```

Then add your permitted SSH users to the group "sshlogin", and restart the SSH service.

```
sudo adduser username sshlogin
sudo /etc/init.d/ssh restart
```

8.1.5.2. External User Database Authentication

Most enterprise networks require centralized authentication and access controls for all system resources. If you have configured your server to authenticate users against external databases, be sure to disable the user accounts both externally and locally, this way you ensure that local fallback authentication is not possible.

8.2. Console Security

As with any other security barrier you put in place to protect your server, it is pretty tough to defend against untold damage caused by someone with physical access to your environment, for example, theft of hard drives, power or service disruption and so on. Therefore, console security should be addressed merely as one component of your overall physical security strategy. A locked "screen door" may deter a casual criminal, or at the very least slow down a determined one, so it is still advisable to perform basic precautions with regard to console security.

The following instructions will help defend your server against issues that could otherwise yield very serious consequences.

8.2.1. Disable Ctrl+Alt+Delete

First and foremost, anyone that has physical access to the keyboard can simply use the **Ctrl+ Alt+ Delete** key combination to reboot the server without having to log on. Sure, someone could simply unplug the power source, but you should still prevent the use of this key combination on a production server. This forces an attacker to take more drastic measures to reboot the server, and will prevent accidental reboots at the same time.

- To disable the reboot action taken by pressing the **Ctrl+Alt+Delete** key combination, comment out the following line in the file `/etc/init/control-alt-delete.conf`

```
#exec shutdown -r now "Control-Alt-Delete pressed"
```

8.3. Firewall

8.3.1. Introduction

The Linux kernel includes the *Netfilter* subsystem, which is used to manipulate or decide the fate of network traffic headed into or through your server. All modern Linux firewall solutions use this system for packet filtering.

The kernel's packet filtering system would be of little use to administrators without a userspace interface to manage it. This is the purpose of iptables. When a packet reaches your server, it will be handed off to the Netfilter subsystem for acceptance, manipulation, or rejection based on the rules supplied to it from userspace via iptables. Thus, iptables is all you need to manage your firewall if you're familiar with it, but many frontends are available to simplify the task.

8.3.2. ufw - Uncomplicated Firewall

The default firewall configuration tool for Ubuntu is **ufw**. Developed to ease iptables firewall configuration, **ufw** provides a user friendly way to create an IPv4 or IPv6 host-based firewall.

ufw by default is initially disabled. From the **ufw** man page:

"ufw is not intended to provide complete firewall functionality via its command interface, but instead provides an easy way to add or remove simple rules. It is currently mainly used for host-based firewalls. "

The following are some examples of how to use **ufw**:

- First, **ufw** needs to be enabled. From a terminal prompt enter:
  ```
  sudo ufw enable
  ```
- To open a port (ssh in this example):
  ```
  sudo ufw allow 22
  ```
- Rules can also be added using a *numbered* format:
  ```
  sudo ufw insert 1 allow 80
  ```
- Similarly, to close an opened port:
  ```
  sudo ufw deny 22
  ```
- To remove a rule, use delete followed by the rule:
  ```
  sudo ufw delete deny 22
  ```
- It is also possible to allow access from specific hosts or networks to a port. The following example allows ssh access from host 192.168.0.2 to any ip address on this host:
  ```
  sudo ufw allow proto tcp from 192.168.0.2 to any port 22
  ```
  Replace 192.168.0.2 with 192.168.0.0/24 to allow ssh access from the entire subnet.
- Adding the *--dry-run* option to a *ufw* command will output the resulting rules, but not apply them. For example, the following is what would be applied if opening the HTTP port:
  ```
  sudo ufw --dry-run allow http
  ```
  ```
  *filter
  :ufw-user-input - [0:0]
  :ufw-user-output - [0:0]
  :ufw-user-forward - [0:0]
  :ufw-user-limit - [0:0]
  ```

```
:ufw-user-limit-accept - [0:0]
### RULES ###

### tuple ### allow tcp 80 0.0.0.0/0 any 0.0.0.0/0
-A ufw-user-input -p tcp --dport 80 -j ACCEPT

### END RULES ###
-A ufw-user-input -j RETURN
-A ufw-user-output -j RETURN
-A ufw-user-forward -j RETURN
-A ufw-user-limit -m limit --limit 3/minute -j LOG --log-prefix "[UFW LIMIT]:"
-A ufw-user-limit -j REJECT
-A ufw-user-limit-accept -j ACCEPT
COMMIT
Rules updated
```

- **ufw** can be disabled by:

  ```
  sudo ufw disable
  ```

- To see the firewall status, enter:

  ```
  sudo ufw status
  ```

- And for more verbose status information use:

  ```
  sudo ufw status verbose
  ```

- To view the *numbered* format:

  ```
  sudo ufw status numbered
  ```

 Note

If the port you want to open or close is defined in /etc/services, you can use the port name instead of the number. In the above examples, replace 22 with *ssh*.

This is a quick introduction to using **ufw**. Please refer to the **ufw** man page for more information.

8.3.2.1. ufw Application Integration

Applications that open ports can include an **ufw** profile, which details the ports needed for the application to function properly. The profiles are kept in /etc/ufw/applications.d, and can be edited if the default ports have been changed.

- To view which applications have installed a profile, enter the following in a terminal:

  ```
  sudo ufw app list
  ```

- Similar to allowing traffic to a port, using an application profile is accomplished by entering:

  ```
  sudo ufw allow Samba
  ```

- An extended syntax is available as well:

  ```
  ufw allow from 192.168.0.0/24 to any app Samba
  ```

Replace *Samba* and *192.168.0.0/24* with the application profile you are using and the IP range for your network.

Note

There is no need to specify the *protocol* for the application, because that information is detailed in the profile. Also, note that the *app* name replaces the *port* number.

- To view details about which ports, protocols, etc are defined for an application, enter:

```
sudo ufw app info Samba
```

Not all applications that require opening a network port come with **ufw** profiles, but if you have profiled an application and want the file to be included with the package, please file a bug against the package in *Launchpad*[1].

8.3.3. IP Masquerading

The purpose of IP Masquerading is to allow machines with private, non-routable IP addresses on your network to access the Internet through the machine doing the masquerading. Traffic from your private network destined for the Internet must be manipulated for replies to be routable back to the machine that made the request. To do this, the kernel must modify the *source* IP address of each packet so that replies will be routed back to it, rather than to the private IP address that made the request, which is impossible over the Internet. Linux uses *Connection Tracking* (conntrack) to keep track of which connections belong to which machines and reroute each return packet accordingly. Traffic leaving your private network is thus "masqueraded" as having originated from your Ubuntu gateway machine. This process is referred to in Microsoft documentation as Internet Connection Sharing.

8.3.3.1. ufw Masquerading

IP Masquerading can be achieved using custom **ufw** rules. This is possible because the current back-end for **ufw** is **iptables-restore** with the rules files located in `/etc/ufw/*.rules`. These files are a great place to add legacy iptables rules used without **ufw**, and rules that are more network gateway or bridge related.

The rules are split into two different files, rules that should be executed before **ufw** command line rules, and rules that are executed after **ufw** command line rules.

- First, packet forwarding needs to be enabled in **ufw**. Two configuration files will need to be adjusted, in `/etc/default/ufw` change the *DEFAULT_FORWARD_POLICY* to "ACCEPT":

```
DEFAULT_FORWARD_POLICY="ACCEPT"
```

---

[1] *https://launchpad.net/*

Then edit `/etc/ufw/sysctl.conf` and uncomment:

```
net/ipv4/ip_forward=1
```

Similarly, for IPv6 forwarding uncomment:

```
net/ipv6/conf/default/forwarding=1
```

- Now we will add rules to the `/etc/ufw/before.rules` file. The default rules only configure the *filter* table, and to enable masquerading the *nat* table will need to be configured. Add the following to the top of the file just after the header comments:

```
# nat Table rules
*nat
:POSTROUTING ACCEPT [0:0]

# Forward traffic from eth1 through eth0.
-A POSTROUTING -s 192.168.0.0/24 -o eth0 -j MASQUERADE

# don't delete the 'COMMIT' line or these nat table rules won't be processed
COMMIT
```

The comments are not strictly necessary, but it is considered good practice to document your configuration. Also, when modifying any of the *rules* files in `/etc/ufw`, make sure these lines are the last line for each table modified:

```
# don't delete the 'COMMIT' line or these rules won't be processed
COMMIT
```

For each *Table* a corresponding *COMMIT* statement is required. In these examples only the *nat* and *filter* tables are shown, but you can also add rules for the *raw* and *mangle* tables.

 Note

In the above example replace *eth0*, *eth1*, and *192.168.0.0/24* with the appropriate interfaces and IP range for your network.

- Finally, disable and re-enable **ufw** to apply the changes:

```
sudo ufw disable && sudo ufw enable
```

IP Masquerading should now be enabled. You can also add any additional FORWARD rules to the `/etc/ufw/before.rules`. It is recommended that these additional rules be added to the *ufw-before-forward* chain.

8.3.3.2. iptables Masquerading

iptables can also be used to enable masquerading.

- Similar to **ufw**, the first step is to enable IPv4 packet forwarding by editing `/etc/sysctl.conf` and uncomment the following line

```
net.ipv4.ip_forward=1
```

If you wish to enable IPv6 forwarding also uncomment:

```
net.ipv6.conf.default.forwarding=1
```

- Next, execute the **sysctl** command to enable the new settings in the configuration file:

```
sudo sysctl -p
```

- IP Masquerading can now be accomplished with a single iptables rule, which may differ slightly based on your network configuration:

```
sudo iptables -t nat -A POSTROUTING -s 192.168.0.0/16 -o ppp0 -j MASQUERADE
```

The above command assumes that your private address space is 192.168.0.0/16 and that your Internet-facing device is ppp0. The syntax is broken down as follows:

- -t nat -- the rule is to go into the nat table
- -A POSTROUTING -- the rule is to be appended (-A) to the POSTROUTING chain
- -s 192.168.0.0/16 -- the rule applies to traffic originating from the specified address space
- -o ppp0 -- the rule applies to traffic scheduled to be routed through the specified network device
- -j MASQUERADE -- traffic matching this rule is to "jump" (-j) to the MASQUERADE target to be manipulated as described above

- Also, each chain in the filter table (the default table, and where most or all packet filtering occurs) has a default *policy* of ACCEPT, but if you are creating a firewall in addition to a gateway device, you may have set the policies to DROP or REJECT, in which case your masqueraded traffic needs to be allowed through the FORWARD chain for the above rule to work:

```
sudo iptables -A FORWARD -s 192.168.0.0/16 -o ppp0 -j ACCEPT
sudo iptables -A FORWARD -d 192.168.0.0/16 -m state --state ESTABLISHED,
                                      RELATED -i ppp0 -j ACCEPT
```

The above commands will allow all connections from your local network to the Internet and all traffic related to those connections to return to the machine that initiated them.

- If you want masquerading to be enabled on reboot, which you probably do, edit /etc/rc.local and add any commands used above. For example add the first command with no filtering:

```
iptables -t nat -A POSTROUTING -s 192.168.0.0/16 -o ppp0 -j MASQUERADE
```

8.3.4. Logs

Firewall logs are essential for recognizing attacks, troubleshooting your firewall rules, and noticing unusual activity on your network. You must include logging rules in your firewall for them to be generated, though, and logging rules must come before any applicable terminating rule (a rule with a target that decides the fate of the packet, such as ACCEPT, DROP, or REJECT).

If you are using **ufw**, you can turn on logging by entering the following in a terminal:

```
sudo ufw logging on
```

To turn logging off in **ufw**, simply replace on with off in the above command.

If using **iptables** instead of **ufw**, enter:

```
sudo iptables -A INPUT -m state --state NEW -p tcp --dport 80 -j LOG
                                  --log-prefix "NEW_HTTP_CONN: "
```

A request on port 80 from the local machine, then, would generate a log in dmesg that looks like this:

```
[4304885.870000] NEW_HTTP_CONN: IN=lo OUT= MAC=00:00:00:00:00:00:00:00:00:00:00:
00:08:00 SRC=127.0.0.1 DST=127.0.0.1 LEN=60 TOS=0x00 PREC=0x00 TTL=64 ID=58288 DF
PROTO=TCP SPT=53981 DPT=80 WINDOW=32767 RES=0x00 SYN URGP=0
```

The above log will also appear in `/var/log/messages`, `/var/log/syslog`, and `/var/log/kern.log`. This behavior can be modified by editing `/etc/syslog.conf` appropriately or by installing and configuring **ulogd** and using the ULOG target instead of LOG. The **ulogd** daemon is a userspace server that listens for logging instructions from the kernel specifically for firewalls, and can log to any file you like, or even to a **PostgreSQL** or **MySQL** database. Making sense of your firewall logs can be simplified by using a log analyzing tool such as **fwanalog**, **fwlogwatch**, or **lire**.

8.3.5. Other Tools

There are many tools available to help you construct a complete firewall without intimate knowledge of iptables. For the GUI-inclined:

- *Firestarter*[2] is quite popular and easy to use.
- *fwbuilder*[3] is very powerful and will look familiar to an administrator who has used a commercial firewall utility such as **Checkpoint FireWall-1**.

If you prefer a command-line tool with plain-text configuration files:

---

[2] *http://www.fs-security.com/*
[3] *http://www.fwbuilder.org/*

- *Shorewall*[4] is a very powerful solution to help you configure an advanced firewall for any network.

- *ipkungfu*[5] should give you a working firewall "out of the box" with zero configuration, and will allow you to easily set up a more advanced firewall by editing simple, well-documented configuration files.

- *fireflier*[6] is designed to be a desktop firewall application. It is made up of a server (fireflier-server) and your choice of GUI clients (GTK or QT), and behaves like many popular interactive firewall applications for Windows.

8.3.6. References

- The *Ubuntu Firewall*[7] wiki page contains information on the development of **ufw**.

- Also, the **ufw** manual page contains some very useful information: **man ufw**.

- See the *packet-filtering-HOWTO*[8] for more information on using **iptables**.

- The *nat-HOWTO*[9] contains further details on masquerading.

- The *IPTables HowTo*[10] in the Ubuntu wiki is a great resource.

8.4. AppArmor

AppArmor is a Linux Security Module implementation of name-based mandatory access controls. AppArmor confines individual programs to a set of listed files and posix 1003.1e draft capabilities.

AppArmor is installed and loaded by default. It uses *profiles* of an application to determine what files and permissions the application requires. Some packages will install their own profiles, and additional profiles can be found in the **apparmor-profiles** package.

To install the **apparmor-profiles** package from a terminal prompt:

```
sudo apt-get install apparmor-profiles
```

AppArmor profiles have two modes of execution:

- Complaining/Learning: profile violations are permitted and logged. Useful for testing and developing new profiles.

- Enforced/Confined: enforces profile policy as well as logging the violation.

---

[4] *http://www.shorewall.net/*

[5] *http://www.linuxkungfu.org/*

[6] *http://fireflier.sourceforge.net/*

[7] *https://wiki.ubuntu.com/UbuntuFirewall*

[8] *http://www.netfilter.org/documentation/HOWTO/packet-filtering-HOWTO.html*

[9] *http://www.netfilter.org/documentation/HOWTO/NAT-HOWTO.html*

[10] *https://help.ubuntu.com/community/IptablesHowTo*

8.4.1. Using AppArmor

The **apparmor-utils** package contains command line utilities that you can use to change the **AppArmor** execution mode, find the status of a profile, create new profiles, etc.

- **apparmor_status** is used to view the current status of AppArmor profiles.

```
sudo apparmor_status
```

- **aa-complain** places a profile into *complain* mode.

```
sudo aa-complain /path/to/bin
```

- **aa-enforce** places a profile into *enforce* mode.

```
sudo aa-enforce /path/to/bin
```

- The `/etc/apparmor.d` directory is where the AppArmor profiles are located. It can be used to manipulate the *mode* of all profiles.

    Enter the following to place all profiles into complain mode:

```
sudo aa-complain /etc/apparmor.d/*
```

    To place all profiles in enforce mode:

```
sudo aa-enforce /etc/apparmor.d/*
```

- **apparmor_parser** is used to load a profile into the kernel. It can also be used to reload a currently loaded profile using the *-r* option. To load a profile:

```
cat /etc/apparmor.d/profile.name | sudo apparmor_parser -a
```

    To reload a profile:

```
cat /etc/apparmor.d/profile.name | sudo apparmor_parser -r
```

- `/etc/init.d/apparmor` can be used to *reload* all profiles:

```
sudo /etc/init.d/apparmor reload
```

- The `/etc/apparmor.d/disable` directory can be used along with the **apparmor_parser -R** option to *disable* a profile.

```
sudo ln -s /etc/apparmor.d/profile.name /etc/apparmor.d/disable/
sudo apparmor_parser -R /etc/apparmor.d/profile.name
```

    To *re-enable* a disabled profile remove the symbolic link to the profile in `/etc/apparmor.d/disable/`. Then load the profile using the *-a* option.

```
sudo rm /etc/apparmor.d/disable/profile.name
cat /etc/apparmor.d/profile.name | sudo apparmor_parser -a
```

- **AppArmor** can be disabled, and the kernel module unloaded by entering the following:

```
sudo /etc/init.d/apparmor stop
sudo update-rc.d -f apparmor remove
```

- To re-enable **AppArmor** enter:

```
sudo /etc/init.d/apparmor start
sudo update-rc.d apparmor defaults
```

 Note

Replace *profile.name* with the name of the profile you want to manipulate. Also, replace /path/to/bin/ with the actual executable file path. For example for the **ping** command use /bin/ping

8.4.2. Profiles

AppArmor profiles are simple text files located in /etc/apparmor.d/. The files are named after the full path to the executable they profile replacing the "/" with ".". For example /etc/apparmor.d/bin.ping is the AppArmor profile for the /bin/ping command.

There are two main type of rules used in profiles:

- *Path entries:* which detail which files an application can access in the file system.
- *Capability entries:* determine what privileges a confined process is allowed to use.

As an example take a look at /etc/apparmor.d/bin.ping:

```
#include <tunables/global>
/bin/ping flags=(complain) {
  #include <abstractions/base>
  #include <abstractions/consoles>
  #include <abstractions/nameservice>

  capability net_raw,
  capability setuid,
  network inet raw,

  /bin/ping mixr,
  /etc/modules.conf r,
}
```

- *#include <tunables/global>:* include statements from other files. This allows statements pertaining to multiple applications to be placed in a common file.
- */bin/ping flags=(complain):* path to the profiled program, also setting the mode to *complain*.
- *capability net_raw,:* allows the application access to the CAP_NET_RAW Posix.1e capability.
- */bin/ping mixr,:* allows the application read and execute access to the file.

 Note

After editing a profile file the profile must be reloaded. See the Section 8.4.1, *Using AppArmor* for details.

8.4.2.1. Creating a Profile

- *Design a test plan:* Try to think about how the application should be exercised. The test plan should be divided into small test cases. Each test case should have a small description and list the steps to follow.

  Some standard test cases are:

  - Starting the program.
  - Stopping the program.
  - Reloading the program.
  - Testing all the commands supported by the init script.

- *Generate the new profile:* Use **aa-genprof** to generate a new profile. From a terminal:

  ```
  sudo aa-genprof executable
  ```

  For example:

  ```
  sudo aa-genprof slapd
  ```

- To get your new profile included in the **apparmor-profiles** package, file a bug in *Launchpad* against the *AppArmor*[11] package:

  - Include your test plan and test cases.
  - Attach your new profile to the bug.

8.4.2.2. Updating Profiles

When the program is misbehaving, audit messages are sent to the log files. The program **aa-logprof** can be used to scan log files for **AppArmor** audit messages, review them and update the profiles. From a terminal:

```
sudo aa-logprof
```

8.4.3. References

- See the *AppArmor Administration Guide*[12] for advanced configuration options.
- For details using AppArmor with other Ubuntu releases see the *AppArmor Community Wiki*[13] page.
- The *OpenSUSE AppArmor*[14] page is another introduction to AppArmor.

---

[11] *https://bugs.launchpad.net/ubuntu/+source/apparmor/+filebug*

[12] *http://www.novell.com/documentation/apparmor/apparmor201_sp10_admin/index.html?page=/documentation/apparmor/apparmor201_sp10_admin/data/book_apparmor_admin.html*

[13] *https://help.ubuntu.com/community/AppArmor*

[14] *http://en.opensuse.org/AppArmor*

- A great place to ask for **AppArmor** assistance, and get involved with the Ubuntu Server community, is the *#ubuntu-server* IRC channel on *freenode*[15].

8.5. Certificates

One of the most common forms of cryptography today is *public-key* cryptography. Public-key cryptography utilizes a *public key* and a *private key*. The system works by *encrypting* information using the public key. The information can then only be *decrypted* using the private key.

A common use for public-key cryptography is encrypting application traffic using a Secure Socket Layer (SSL) or Transport Layer Security (TLS) connection. For example, configuring Apache to provide *HTTPS*, the HTTP protocol over SSL. This allows a way to encrypt traffic using a protocol that does not itself provide encryption.

A *Certificate* is a method used to distribute a *public key* and other information about a server and the organization who is responsible for it. Certificates can be digitally signed by a *Certification Authority* or CA. A CA is a trusted third party that has confirmed that the information contained in the certificate is accurate.

8.5.1. Types of Certificates

To set up a secure server using public-key cryptography, in most cases, you send your certificate request (including your public key), proof of your company's identity, and payment to a CA. The CA verifies the certificate request and your identity, and then sends back a certificate for your secure server. Alternatively, you can create your own *self-signed* certificate.

 Note

Note, that self-signed certificates should not be used in most production environments.

Continuing the HTTPS example, a CA-signed certificate provides two important capabilities that a self-signed certificate does not:

- Browsers (usually) automatically recognize the certificate and allow a secure connection to be made without prompting the user.
- When a CA issues a signed certificate, it is guaranteeing the identity of the organization that is providing the web pages to the browser.

Most Web browsers, and computers, that support SSL have a list of CAs whose certificates they automatically accept. If a browser encounters a certificate whose authorizing CA is not

---

[15] *http://freenode.net/*

in the list, the browser asks the user to either accept or decline the connection. Also, other applications may generate an error message when using a self-singed certificate.

The process of getting a certificate from a CA is fairly easy. A quick overview is as follows:

1. Create a private and public encryption key pair.
2. Create a certificate request based on the public key. The certificate request contains information about your server and the company hosting it.
3. Send the certificate request, along with documents proving your identity, to a CA. We cannot tell you which certificate authority to choose. Your decision may be based on your past experiences, or on the experiences of your friends or colleagues, or purely on monetary factors.
4. Once you have decided upon a CA, you need to follow the instructions they provide on how to obtain a certificate from them.
5. When the CA is satisfied that you are indeed who you claim to be, they send you a digital certificate.
6. Install this certificate on your secure server, and configure the appropriate applications to use the certificate.

8.5.2. Generating a Certificate Signing Request (CSR)

Whether you are getting a certificate from a CA or generating your own self-signed certificate, the first step is to generate a key.

If the certificate will be used by service daemons, such as Apache, Postfix, Dovecot, etc, a key without a passphrase is often appropriate. Not having a passphrase allows the services to start without manual intervention, usually the preferred way to start a daemon.

This section will cover generating a key with a passphrase, and one without. The non-passphrase key will then be used to generate a certificate that can be used with various service daemons.

 Warning

Running your secure service without a passphrase is convenient because you will not need to enter the passphrase every time you start your secure service. But it is insecure and a compromise of the key means a compromise of the server as well.

To generate the *keys* for the Certificate Signing Request (CSR) run the following command from a terminal prompt:

```
openssl genrsa -des3 -out server.key 1024

Generating RSA private key, 1024 bit long modulus
.......................++++++
..................++++++
```

```
unable to write 'random state'
e is 65537 (0x10001)
Enter pass phrase for server.key:
```

You can now enter your passphrase. For best security, it should at least contain eight characters. The minimum length when specifying -des3 is four characters. It should include numbers and/or punctuation and not be a word in a dictionary. Also remember that your passphrase is case-sensitive.

Re-type the passphrase to verify. Once you have re-typed it correctly, the server key is generated and stored in the `server.key` file.

Now create the insecure key, the one without a passphrase, and shuffle the key names:

```
openssl rsa -in server.key -out server.key.insecure
mv server.key server.key.secure
mv server.key.insecure server.key
```

The insecure key is now named `server.key`, and you can use this file to generate the CSR without passphrase.

To create the CSR, run the following command at a terminal prompt:

```
openssl req -new -key server.key -out server.csr
```

It will prompt you enter the passphrase. If you enter the correct passphrase, it will prompt you to enter Company Name, Site Name, Email Id, etc. Once you enter all these details, your CSR will be created and it will be stored in the `server.csr` file

You can now submit this CSR file to a CA for processing. The CA will use this CSR file and issue the certificate. On the other hand, you can create self-signed certificate using this CSR.

8.5.3. Creating a Self-Signed Certificate

To create the self-signed certificate, run the following command at a terminal prompt:

```
openssl x509 -req -days 365 -in server.csr -signkey server.key -out server.crt
```

The above command will prompt you to enter the passphrase. Once you enter the correct passphrase, your certificate will be created and it will be stored in the `server.crt` file.

 Warning

> If your secure server is to be used in a production environment, you probably need a CA-signed certificate. It is not recommended to use self-signed certificate.

8.5.4. Installing the Certificate

You can install the key file `server.key` and certificate file `server.crt`, or the certificate file issued by your CA, by running following commands at a terminal prompt:

```
sudo cp server.crt /etc/ssl/certs
sudo cp server.key /etc/ssl/private
```

Now simply configure any applications, with the ability to use public-key cryptography, to use the *certificate* and *key* files. For example, **Apache** can provide HTTPS, **Dovecot** can provide IMAPS and POP3S, etc.

8.5.5. Certification Authority

If the services on your network require more than a few self-signed certificates it may be worth the additional effort to setup your own internal *Certification Authority (CA)*. Using certificates signed by your own CA, allows the various services using the certificates to easily trust other services using certificates issued from the same CA.

1. First, create the directories to hold the CA certificate and related files:

   ```
   sudo mkdir /etc/ssl/CA
   sudo mkdir /etc/ssl/newcerts
   ```

2. The CA needs a few additional files to operate, one to keep track of the last serial number used by the CA, each certificate must have a unique serial number, and another file to record which certificates have been issued:

   ```
   sudo sh -c "echo '01' > /etc/ssl/CA/serial"
   sudo touch /etc/ssl/CA/index.txt
   ```

3. The third file is a CA configuration file. Though not strictly necessary, it is very convenient when issuing multiple certificates. Edit /etc/ssl/openssl.cnf, and in the *[CA_default]* change:

   ```
   dir             = /etc/ssl/          # Where everything is kept
   database        = $dir/CA/index.txt  # database index file.
   certificate     = $dir/certs/cacert.pem # The CA certificate
   serial          = $dir/CA/serial     # The current serial number
   private_key     = $dir/private/cakey.pem # The private key
   ```

4. Next, create the self-singed root certificate:

   ```
   openssl req -new -x509 -extensions v3_ca -keyout cakey.pem -out cacert.pem
                                                               -days 3650
   ```

   You will then be asked to enter the details about the certificate.

5. Now install the root certificate and key:

   ```
   sudo mv cakey.pem /etc/ssl/private/
   sudo mv cacert.pem /etc/ssl/certs/
   ```

6. You are now ready to start signing certificates. The first item needed is a Certificate Signing Request (CSR), see the Section 8.5.2, *Generating a Certificate Signing Request (CSR)* for details. Once you have a CSR, enter the following to generate a certificate signed by the CA:

   ```
   sudo openssl ca -in server.csr -config /etc/ssl/openssl.cnf
   ```

After entering the password for the CA key, you will be prompted to sign the certificate, and again to commit the new certificate. You should then see a somewhat large amount of output related to the certificate creation.

7. There should now be a new file, `/etc/ssl/newcerts/01.pem`, containing the same output. Copy and paste everything beginning with the line: -----*BEGIN CERTIFICATE*----- and continuing through the line: ----*END CERTIFICATE*----- lines to a file named after the hostname of the server where the certificate will be installed. For example `mail.example.com.crt`, is a nice descriptive name.

   Subsequent certificates will be named `02.pem`, `03.pem`, etc.

 Note

Replace *mail.example.com.crt* with your own descriptive name.

8. Finally, copy the new certificate to the host that needs it, and configure the appropriate applications to use it. The default location to install certificates is `/etc/ssl/certs`. This enables multiple services to use the same certificate without overly complicated file permissions.

   For applications that can be configured to use a CA certificate, you should also copy the `/etc/ssl/certs/cacert.pem` file to the `/etc/ssl/certs/` directory on each server.

8.5.6. References

- For more detailed instructions on using cryptography see the *SSL Certificates HOWTO*[16] by tlpd.org
- The Wikipedia *HTTPS*[17] page has more information regarding HTTPS.
- For more information on *OpenSSL* see the *OpenSSL Home Page*[18].
- Also, O'Reilly's *Network Security with OpenSSL*[19] is a good in depth reference.

8.6. eCryptfs

eCryptfs is a POSIX-compliant enterprise-class stacked cryptographic filesystem for Linux. Layering on top of the filesystem layer *eCryptfs* protects files no matter the underlying filesystem, partition type, etc.

---

[16] *http://tldp.org/HOWTO/SSL-Certificates-HOWTO/index.html*
[17] *http://en.wikipedia.org/wiki/Https*
[18] *http://www.openssl.org/*
[19] *http://oreilly.com/catalog/9780596002701/*

During installation there is an option to encrypt the /home partition. This will automatically configure everything needed to encrypt and mount the partition.

As an example, this section will cover configuring /srv to be encrypted using *eCryptfs*.

8.6.1. Using eCryptfs

First, install the necessary packages. From a terminal prompt enter:

```
sudo apt-get install ecryptfs-utils
```

Now mount the partition to be encrypted:

```
sudo mount -t ecryptfs /srv /srv
```

You will then be prompted for some details on how **ecryptfs** should encrypt the data.

To test that files placed in /srv are indeed encrypted copy the /etc/default folder to /srv:

```
sudo cp -r /etc/default /srv
```

Now unmount /srv, and try to view a file:

```
sudo umount /srv
cat /srv/default/cron
```

Remounting /srv using **ecryptfs** will make the data viewable once again.

8.6.2. Automatically Mounting Encrypted Partitions

There are a couple of ways to automatically mount an **ecryptfs** encrypted filesystem at boot. This example will use a /root/.ecryptfsrc file containing mount options, along with a passphrase file residing on a USB key.

First, create /root/.ecryptfsrc containing:

```
key=passphrase:passphrase_passwd_file=/mnt/usb/passwd_file.txt
ecryptfs_sig=5826dd62cf81c615
ecryptfs_cipher=aes
ecryptfs_key_bytes=16
ecryptfs_passthrough=n
ecryptfs_enable_filename_crypto=n
```

 Note

Adjust the *ecryptfs_sig* to the signature in /root/.ecryptfs/sig-cache.txt.

Next, create the /mnt/usb/passwd_file.txt passphrase file:

```
passphrase_passwd=[secrets]
```

Now add the necessary lines to /etc/fstab:

```
/dev/sdb1         /mnt/usb          ext3      ro        0 0
/srv /srv ecryptfs defaults 0 0
```

Make sure the USB drive is mounted before the encrypted partition.

Finally, reboot and the /srv should be mounted using *eCryptfs*.

8.6.3. Other Utilities

The **ecryptfs-utils** package includes several other useful utilities:

- *ecryptfs-setup-private:* creates a ~/Private directory to contain encrypted information. This utility can be run by unprivileged users to keep data private from other users on the system.
- *ecryptfs-mount-private and ecryptfs-umount-private:* will mount and unmount respectively, a users ~/Private directory.
- *ecryptfs-add-passphrase:* adds a new passphrase to the kernel keyring.
- *ecryptfs-manager:* manages **eCryptfs** objects such as keys.
- *ecryptfs-stat:* allows you to view the **ecryptfs** meta information for a file.

8.6.4. References

- For more information on *eCryptfs* see the *Launch Pad project page*[20]
- There is also a *Linux Journal*[21] article covering *eCryptfs*.
- Also, for more **ecryptfs** options see the *ecryptfs man page*[22].
- The *eCryptfs Ubuntu Wiki*[23] page also has more details.

---

[20] *https://launchpad.net/ecryptfs*
[21] *http://www.linuxjournal.com/article/9400*
[22] *http://manpages.ubuntu.com/manpages/natty/en/man7/ecryptfs.7.html*
[23] *https://help.ubuntu.com/community/eCryptfs*

Chapter 9.
Monitoring

9.1. Overview

The monitoring of essential servers and services is an important part of system administration. Most network services are monitored for performance, availability, or both. This section will cover installation and configuration of **Nagios** for availability monitoring, and **Munin** for performance monitoring.

The examples in this section will use two servers with hostnames *server01* and *server02*. *Server01* will be configured with **Nagios** to monitor services on itself and *server02*. Server01 will also be setup with the **munin** package to gather information from the network. Using the **munin-node** package, *server02* will be configured to send information to *server01*.

Hopefully these simple examples will allow you to monitor additional servers and services on your network.

9.2. Nagios

9.2.1. Installation

First, on *server01* install the **nagios** package. In a terminal enter:

```
sudo apt-get install nagios3 nagios-nrpe-plugin
```

You will be asked to enter a password for the *nagiosadmin* user. The user's credentials are stored in /etc/nagios3/htpasswd.users. To change the *nagiosadmin* password, or add additional users to the Nagios CGI scripts, use the **htpasswd** that is part of the **apache2-utils** package.

For example, to change the password for the *nagiosadmin* user enter:

```
sudo htpasswd /etc/nagios3/htpasswd.users nagiosadmin
```

To add a user:

```
sudo htpasswd /etc/nagios3/htpasswd.users steve
```

Next, on *server02* install the **nagios-nrpe-server** package. From a terminal on server02 enter:

```
sudo apt-get install nagios-nrpe-server
```

Note

NRPE allows you to execute local checks on remote hosts. There are other ways of accomplishing this through other Nagios plugins as well as other checks.

9.2.2. Configuration Overview

There are a couple of directories containing **Nagios** configuration and check files.

- `/etc/nagios3`: contains configuration files for the operation of the **nagios** daemon, CGI files, hosts, etc.

- `/etc/nagios-plugins`: houses configuration files for the service checks.

- `/etc/nagios`: on the remote host contains the **nagios-nrpe-server** configuration files.

- `/usr/lib/nagios/plugins/`: where the check binaries are stored. To see the options of a check use the *-h* option.

  For example: **/usr/lib/nagios/plugins/check_dhcp -h**

There are a plethora of checks **Nagios** can be configured to execute for any given host. For this example Nagios will be configured to check disk space, DNS, and a MySQL hostgroup. The DNS check will be on *server02*, and the MySQL hostgroup will include both *server01* and *server02*.

Note

See the Section 10.1, *HTTPD - Apache2 Web Server* for details on setting up Apache, Chapter 7, *Domain Name Service (DNS)* for DNS, and the Section 11.1, *MySQL* for MySQL.

Additionally, there are some terms that once explained will hopefully make understanding Nagios configuration easier:

- *Host*: a server, workstation, network device, etc that is being monitored.

- *Host Group*: a group of similar hosts. For example, you could group all web servers, file server, etc.

- *Service*: the service being monitored on the host. Such as HTTP, DNS, NFS, etc.

- *Service Group*: allows you to group multiple services together. This is useful for grouping multiple HTTP for example.

- *Contact*: person to be notified when an event takes place. Nagios can be configured to send emails, SMS messages, etc.

By default Nagios is configured to check HTTP, disk space, SSH, current users, processes, and load on the *localhost*. Nagios will also **ping** check the *gateway*.

Large Nagios installations can be quite complex to configure. It is usually best to start small, one or two hosts, get things configured the way you like then expand.

9.2.3. Configuration

1. First, create a *host* configuration file for *server02*. Unless otherwise specified, run all these commands on *server01*. In a terminal enter:

```
sudo cp /etc/nagios3/conf.d/localhost_nagios2.cfg /etc/nagios3/conf.d/server02.cfg
```

 Note

In the above and following command examples, replace *"server01"*, *"server02"* *172.18.100.100*, and *172.18.100.101* with the host names and IP addresses of your servers.

2. Next, edit /etc/nagios3/conf.d/server02.cfg:

```
define host{
        use                     generic-host  ; Name of host template to use
        host_name               server02
        alias                   Server 02
        address                 172.18.100.101
}

# check DNS service.
define service {
        use                             generic-service
        host_name                       server02
        service_description             DNS
        check_command                   check_dns!172.18.100.101
}
```

3. Restart the **nagios** daemon to enable the new configuration:

```
sudo /etc/init.d/nagios3 restart
```

1. Now add a service definition for the MySQL check by adding the following to /etc/nagios3/conf.d/services_nagios2.cfg:

```
# check MySQL servers.
define service {
        hostgroup_name          mysql-servers
        service_description     MySQL
        check_command
check_mysql_cmdlinecred!nagios!secret!$HOSTADDRESS
        use                     generic-service
        notification_interval   0 ; set > 0 if you want to be renotified
}
```

2. A *mysql-servers* hostgroup now needs to be defined. Edit /etc/nagios3/conf.d/hostgroups_nagios2.cfg adding:

```
# MySQL hostgroup.
define hostgroup {
        hostgroup_name  mysql-servers
                alias           MySQL servers
                members         localhost, server02
        }
```

3. The Nagios check needs to authenticate to MySQL. To add a *nagios* user to MySQL enter:

```
mysql -u root -p -e "create user nagios identified by 'secret';"
```

Note

The *nagios* user will need to be added all hosts in the *mysql-servers* hostgroup.

4. Restart **nagios** to start checking the MySQL servers.

```
sudo /etc/init.d/nagios3 restart
```

1. Lastly configure NRPE to check the disk space on *server02*.

    On *server01* add the service check to /etc/nagios3/conf.d/server02.cfg:

```
# NRPE disk check.
define service {
        use                     generic-service
        host_name               server02
        service_description     nrpe-disk
        check_command
check_nrpe_1arg!check_all_disks!172.18.100.101
}
```

2. Now on *server02* edit /etc/nagios/nrpe.cfg changing:

```
allowed_hosts=172.18.100.100
```

And below in the command definition area add:

```
command[check_all_disks]=/usr/lib/nagios/plugins/check_disk -w 20% -c 10% -e
```

3. Finally, restart **nagios-nrpe-server**:

```
sudo /etc/init.d/nagios-nrpe-server restart
```

4. Also, on *server01* restart **nagios**:

```
sudo /etc/init.d/nagios3 restart
```

You should now be able to see the host and service checks in the Nagios CGI files. To access them point a browser to http://server01/nagios3. You will then be prompted for the *nagiosadmin* username and password.

9.2.4. References

This section has just scratched the surface of Nagios' features. The **nagios-plugins-extra** and **nagios-snmp-plugins** contain many more service checks.

- For more information see *Nagios*[1] website.
- Specifically the *Online Documentation*[2] site.
- There is also a list of *books*[3] related to Nagios and network monitoring.
- The *Nagios Ubuntu Wiki*[4] page also has more details.

9.3. Munin

9.3.1. Installation

Before installing **Munin** on *server01* **apache2** will need to be installed. The default configuration is fine for running a **munin** server. For more information see Section 10.1, *HTTPD - Apache2 Web Server*.

First, on *server01* install **munin**. In a terminal enter:

```
sudo apt-get install munin
```

Now on *server02* install the **munin-node** package:

```
sudo apt-get install munin-node
```

9.3.2. Configuration

On *server01* edit the /etc/munin/munin.conf adding the IP address for *server02*:

```
## First our "normal" host.
[server02]
        address 172.18.100.101
```

 Note

Replace *server02* and *172.18.100.101* with the actual hostname and IP address for your server.

Next, configure **munin-node** on *server02*. Edit /etc/munin/munin-node.conf to allow access by *server01*:

```
allow ^172\.18\.100\.100$
```

---

[1] *http://www.nagios.org/*
[2] *http://nagios.sourceforge.net/docs/3_0/*
[3] *http://www.nagios.org/propaganda/books/*
[4] *https://help.ubuntu.com/community/Nagios*

Note

Replace ^172\.18\.100\.100$ with IP address for your **munin** server.

Now restart **munin-node** on *server02* for the changes to take effect:

```
sudo /etc/init.d/munin-node restart
```

Finally, in a browser go to *http://server01/munin*, and you should see links to nice graphs displaying information from the standard *munin-plugins* for disk, network, processes, and system.

Note

Since this is a new install it may take some time for the graphs to display anything useful.

9.3.3. Additional Plugins

The **munin-plugins-extra** package contains performance checks additional services such as DNS, DHCP, Samba, etc. To install the package, from a terminal enter:

```
sudo apt-get install munin-plugins-extra
```

Be sure to install the package on both the server and node machines.

9.3.4. References

- See the *Munin*[5] website for more details.
- Specifically the *Munin Documentation*[6] page includes information on additional plugins, writing plugins, etc.
- Also, there is a book in German by Open Source Press: *Munin Graphisches Netzwerk- und System-Monitoring*[7].
- Another resource is the *Munin Ubuntu Wiki*[8] page.

---

[5] *http://munin.projects.linpro.no/*

[6] *http://munin.projects.linpro.no/wiki/Documentation*

[7] *https://www.opensourcepress.de/index.php?26&backPID=178&tt_products=152*

[8] *https://help.ubuntu.com/community/Munin*

Chapter 10.
Web Servers

A Web server is a software responsible for accepting HTTP requests from clients, which are known as Web browsers, and serving them HTTP responses along with optional data contents, which usually are Web pages such as HTML documents and linked objects (images, etc.).

10.1. HTTPD - Apache2 Web Server

Apache is the most commonly used Web Server on Linux systems. Web Servers are used to serve Web Pages requested by client computers. Clients typically request and view Web Pages using Web Browser applications such as **Firefox, Opera**, or **Mozilla**.

Users enter a Uniform Resource Locator (URL) to point to a Web server by means of its Fully Qualified Domain Name (FQDN) and a path to the required resource. For example, to view the home page of the *Ubuntu Web site*[1] a user will enter only the FQDN. To request specific information about *paid support* [2], a user will enter the FQDN followed by a path.

The most common protocol used to transfer Web pages is the Hyper Text Transfer Protocol (HTTP). Protocols such as Hyper Text Transfer Protocol over Secure Sockets Layer (HTTPS), and File Transfer Protocol (FTP), a protocol for uploading and downloading files, are also supported.

Apache Web Servers are often used in combination with the **MySQL** database engine, the HyperText Preprocessor (**PHP**) scripting language, and other popular scripting languages such as **Python** and **Perl**. This configuration is termed LAMP (Linux, Apache, MySQL and Perl/Python/PHP) and forms a powerful and robust platform for the development and deployment of Web-based applications.

10.1.1. Installation

The Apache2 web server is available in Ubuntu Linux. To install Apache2:

- At a terminal prompt enter the following command:

```
sudo apt-get install apache2
```

---

[1] *http://www.ubuntu.com/*
[2] *http://www.ubuntu.com/support/services*

10.1.2. Configuration

Apache2 is configured by placing *directives* in plain text configuration files. These *directives* are separated between the following files and directories:

- *apache2.conf:* the main Apache2 configuration file. Contains settings that are *global* to Apache2.
- *conf.d:* contains configuration files which apply *globally* to Apache2. Other packages that use Apache2 to serve content may add files, or symlinks, to this directory.
- *envvars:* file where Apache2 *environment* variables are set.
- *httpd.conf:* historically the main Apache2 configuration file, named after the **httpd** daemon. The file can be used for *user specific* configuration options that globally effect Apache2.
- *mods-available:* this directory contains configuration files to both load *modules* and configure them. Not all modules will have specific configuration files, however.
- *mods-enabled:* holds *symlinks* to the files in /etc/apache2/mods-available. When a module configuration file is symlinked it will be enabled the next time **apache2** is restarted.
- *ports.conf:* houses the directives that determine which TCP ports Apache2 is listening on.
- *sites-available:* this directory has configuration files for Apache2 *Virtual Hosts*. Virtual Hosts allow Apache2 to be configured for multiple sites that have separate configurations.
- *sites-enabled:* like mods-enabled, sites-enabled contains symlinks to the /etc/apache2/sites-available directory. Similarly when a configuration file in sites-available is symlinked, the site configured by it will be active once Apache2 is restarted.

In addition, other configuration files may be added using the *Include* directive, and wildcards can be used to include many configuration files. Any directive may be placed in any of these configuration files. Changes to the main configuration files are only recognized by Apache2 when it is started or restarted.

The server also reads a file containing mime document types; the filename is set by the *TypesConfig* directive, and is /etc/mime.types by default.

10.1.2.1. Basic Settings

This section explains Apache2 server essential configuration parameters. Refer to the *Apache2 Documentation*[3] for more details.

---

[3] *http://httpd.apache.org/docs/2.2/*

- Apache2 ships with a virtual-host-friendly default configuration. That is, it is configured with a single default virtual host (using the *VirtualHost* directive) which can modified or used as-is if you have a single site, or used as a template for additional virtual hosts if you have multiple sites. If left alone, the default virtual host will serve as your default site, or the site users will see if the URL they enter does not match the *ServerName* directive of any of your custom sites. To modify the default virtual host, edit the file `/etc/apache2/sites-available/default`.

 Note

The directives set for a virtual host only apply to that particular virtual host. If a directive is set server-wide and not defined within the virtual host settings, the default setting is used. For example, you can define a Webmaster email address and not define individual email addresses for each virtual host.

If you wish to configure a new virtual host or site, copy that file into the same directory with a name you choose. For example:

```
sudo cp /etc/apache2/sites-available/default /etc/apache2/sites-
                                              available/mynewsite
```

Edit the new file to configure the new site using some of the directives described below.

- The *ServerAdmin* directive specifies the email address to be advertised for the server's administrator. The default value is webmaster@localhost. This should be changed to an email address that is delivered to you (if you are the server's administrator). If your website has a problem, Apache2 will display an error message containing this email address to report the problem to. Find this directive in your site's configuration file in /etc/apache2/sites-available.

- The *Listen* directive specifies the port, and optionally the IP address, Apache2 should listen on. If the IP address is not specified, Apache2 will listen on all IP addresses assigned to the machine it runs on. The default value for the Listen directive is 80. Change this to 127.0.0.1:80 to cause Apache2 to listen only on your loopback interface so that it will not be available to the Internet, to (for example) 81 to change the port that it listens on, or leave it as is for normal operation. This directive can be found and changed in its own file, `/etc/apache2/ports.conf`

- The *ServerName* directive is optional and specifies what FQDN your site should answer to. The default virtual host has no ServerName directive specified, so it will respond to all requests that do not match a ServerName directive in another virtual host. If you have just acquired the domain name ubunturocks.com and wish to host it on your Ubuntu server, the value of the ServerName directive in your virtual host configuration file should be ubunturocks.com. Add this directive to the new virtual host file you created earlier (`/etc/apache2/sites-available/mynewsite`).

You may also want your site to respond to www.ubunturocks.com, since many users will assume the www prefix is appropriate. Use the *ServerAlias* directive for this. You may also use wildcards in the ServerAlias directive.

For example, the following configuration will cause your site to respond to any domain request ending in *.ubunturocks.com*.

```
ServerAlias *.ubunturocks.com
```

- The *DocumentRoot* directive specifies where Apache2 should look for the files that make up the site. The default value is /var/www. No site is configured there, but if you uncomment the *RedirectMatch* directive in /etc/apache2/apache2.conf requests will be redirected to /var/www/apache2-default where the default Apache2 site awaits. Change this value in your site's virtual host file, and remember to create that directory if necessary!

Enable the new *VirtualHost* using the **a2ensite** utility and restart Apache2:

```
sudo a2ensite mynewsite
sudo /etc/init.d/apache2 restart
```

 Note

Be sure to replace *mynewsite* with a more descriptive name for the VirtualHost. One method is to name the file after the *ServerName* directive of the VirtualHost.

Similarly, use the **a2dissite** utility to disable sites. This is can be useful when troubleshooting configuration problems with multiple VirtualHosts:

```
sudo a2dissite mynewsite
sudo /etc/init.d/apache2 restart
```

10.1.2.2. Default Settings

This section explains configuration of the Apache2 server default settings. For example, if you add a virtual host, the settings you configure for the virtual host take precedence for that virtual host. For a directive not defined within the virtual host settings, the default value is used.

- The *DirectoryIndex* is the default page served by the server when a user requests an index of a directory by specifying a forward slash (/) at the end of the directory name.

  For example, when a user requests the page *http://www.example.com/this_directory/*, he or she will get either the DirectoryIndex page if it exists, a server-generated directory list if it does not and the Indexes option is specified, or a Permission Denied page if neither is true. The server will try to find one of the files listed in the DirectoryIndex directive and will return the first one it finds. If it does not find any of these files and if *Options Indexes* is set for that directory, the server will generate and return a list, in HTML format, of the subdirectories and files in the directory. The default value, found in `/etc/apache2/mods-available/dir.conf` is "index.html index.cgi index.pl index.php index.xhtml index.htm". Thus, if Apache2 finds a file in a requested directory matching any of these names, the first will be displayed.

- The *ErrorDocument* directive allows you to specify a file for Apache2 to use for specific error events. For example, if a user requests a resource that does not exist, a 404 error will occur, and per Apache2's default configuration, the file `/usr/share/apache2/error/HTTP_NOT_FOUND.html.var` will be displayed. That file is not in the server's DocumentRoot, but there is an Alias directive in `/etc/apache2/apache2.conf` that redirects requests to the /error directory to `/usr/share/apache2/error/`.

  To see a list of the default ErrorDocument directives, use this command:

  ```
  grep ErrorDocument /etc/apache2/apache2.conf
  ```

- By default, the server writes the transfer log to the file `/var/log/apache2/access.log`. You can change this on a per-site basis in your virtual host configuration files with the *CustomLog* directive, or omit it to accept the default, specified in `/etc/apache2/apache2.conf`. You may also specify the file to which errors are logged, via the *ErrorLog* directive, whose default is `/var/log/apache2/error.log`. These are kept separate from the transfer logs to aid in troubleshooting problems with your Apache2 server. You may also specify the *LogLevel* (the default value is "warn") and the *LogFormat* (see `/etc/apache2/apache2.conf` for the default value).

- Some options are specified on a per-directory basis rather than per-server. *Options* is one of these directives. A Directory stanza is enclosed in XML-like tags, like so:

  ```
  <Directory /var/www/mynewsite>
  ...
  </Directory>
  ```

  The *Options* directive within a Directory stanza accepts one or more of the following values (among others), separated by spaces:

  - **ExecCGI** - Allow execution of CGI scripts. CGI scripts are not executed if this option is not chosen.

 Tip

Most files should not be executed as CGI scripts. This would be very dangerous. CGI scripts should kept in a directory separate from and outside your DocumentRoot, and only this directory should have the ExecCGI option set. This is the default, and the default location for CGI scripts is `/usr/lib/cgi-bin`.

- **Includes** - Allow server-side includes. Server-side includes allow an HTML file to *include* other files. This is not a common option. See *the Apache2 SSI HOWTO*[4] for more information.

- **IncludesNOEXEC** - Allow server-side includes, but disable the *#exec* and *#include* commands in CGI scripts.

- **Indexes** - Display a formatted list of the directory's contents, if no *DirectoryIndex* (such as index.html) exists in the requested directory.

 Caution

For security reasons, this should usually not be set, and certainly should not be set on your DocumentRoot directory. Enable this option carefully on a per-directory basis only if you are certain you want users to see the entire contents of the directory.

- **Multiview** - Support content-negotiated multiviews; this option is disabled by default for security reasons. See the *Apache2 documentation on this option*[5].

- **SymLinksIfOwnerMatch** - Only follow symbolic links if the target file or directory has the same owner as the link.

10.1.2.3. httpd Settings

This section explains some basic **httpd** daemon configuration settings.

LockFile - The LockFile directive sets the path to the lockfile used when the server is compiled with either USE_FCNTL_SERIALIZED_ACCEPT or USE_FLOCK_SERIALIZED_ACCEPT. It must be stored on the local disk. It should be left to the default value unless the logs directory is located on an NFS share. If this is the case, the default value should be changed to a location on the local disk and to a directory that is readable only by root.

PidFile - The PidFile directive sets the file in which the server records its process ID (pid). This file should only be readable by root. In most cases, it should be left to the default value.

User - The User directive sets the userid used by the server to answer requests. This setting determines the server's access. Any files inaccessible to this user will also be inaccessible to your website's visitors. The default value for User is www-data.

 Warning

Unless you know exactly what you are doing, do not set the User directive to root. Using root as the User will create large security holes for your Web server.

---

[4] *http://httpd.apache.org/docs/2.2/howto/ssi.html*
[5] *http://httpd.apache.org/docs/2.2/mod/mod_negotiation.html#multiviews*

The Group directive is similar to the User directive. Group sets the group under which the server will answer requests. The default group is also www-data.

10.1.2.4. Apache2 Modules

Apache2 is a modular server. This implies that only the most basic functionality is included in the core server. Extended features are available through modules which can be loaded into Apache2. By default, a base set of modules is included in the server at compile-time. If the server is compiled to use dynamically loaded modules, then modules can be compiled separately, and added at any time using the LoadModule directive. Otherwise, Apache2 must be recompiled to add or remove modules.

Ubuntu compiles Apache2 to allow the dynamic loading of modules. Configuration directives may be conditionally included on the presence of a particular module by enclosing them in an *<IfModule>* block.

You can install additional Apache2 modules and use them with your Web server. For example, run the following command from a terminal prompt to install the *MySQL Authentication* module:

```
sudo apt-get install libapache2-mod-auth-mysql
```

See the /etc/apache2/mods-available directory, for additional modules.

Use the **a2enmod** utility to enable a module:

```
sudo a2enmod auth_mysql
sudo /etc/init.d/apache2 restart
```

Similarly, **a2dismod** will disable a module:

```
sudo a2dismod auth_mysql
sudo /etc/init.d/apache2 restart
```

10.1.3. HTTPS Configuration

The **mod_ssl** module adds an important feature to the Apache2 server - the ability to encrypt communications. Thus, when your browser is communicating using SSL, the https:// prefix is used at the beginning of the Uniform Resource Locator (URL) in the browser navigation bar.

The **mod_ssl** module is available in **apache2-common** package. Execute the following command from a terminal prompt to enable the **mod_ssl** module:

```
sudo a2enmod ssl
```

There is a default HTTPS configuration file in /etc/apache2/sites-available/default-ssl. In order for **Apache2** to provide HTTPS, a *certificate* and *key* file are also needed. The default HTTPS configuration will use a certificate and key generated by the **ssl-cert** package. They are good for testing, but the auto-generated certificate and key should be replaced by a certificate specific to the site or server. For information on generating a key and obtaining a certificate see the Section 8.5, *Certificates*

To configure **Apache2** for HTTPS, enter the following:

```
sudo a2ensite default-ssl
```

 Note

The directories `/etc/ssl/certs` and `/etc/ssl/private` are the default locations. If you install the certificate and key in another directory make sure to change *SSLCertificateFile* and *SSLCertificateKeyFile* appropriately.

With Apache2 now configured for HTTPS, restart the service to enable the new settings:

```
sudo /etc/init.d/apache2 restart
```

 Note

Depending on how you obtained your certificate you may need to enter a passphrase when **Apache2** starts.

You can access the secure server pages by typing https://your_hostname/url/ in your browser address bar.

10.1.4. References

- *Apache2 Documentation*[6] contains in depth information on Apache2 configuration directives. Also, see the **apache2-doc** package for the official Apache2 docs.

- See the *Mod SSL Documentation*[7] site for more SSL related information.

- O'Reilly's *Apache Cookbook*[8] is a good resource for accomplishing specific Apache2 configurations.

- For Ubuntu specific Apache2 questions, ask in the *#ubuntu-server* IRC channel on *freenode.net*[9].

- Usually integrated with PHP and MySQL the *Apache MySQL PHP Ubuntu Wiki*[10] page is a good resource.

---

[6] *http://httpd.apache.org/docs/2.2/*

[7] *http://www.modssl.org/docs/*

[8] *http://oreilly.com/catalog/9780596001919/*

[9] *http://freenode.net/*

[10] *https://help.ubuntu.com/community/ApacheMySQLPHP*

10.2. PHP5 - Scripting Language

PHP is a general-purpose scripting language suited for Web development. The PHP script can be embedded into HTML. This section explains how to install and configure PHP5 in Ubuntu System with Apache2 and MySQL.

This section assumes you have installed and configured Apache 2 Web Server and MySQL Database Server. You can refer to Apache 2 section and MySQL sections in this document to install and configure Apache 2 and MySQL respectively.

10.2.1. Installation

The PHP5 is available in Ubuntu Linux.

- To install PHP5 you can enter the following command in the terminal prompt:

```
sudo apt-get install php5 libapache2-mod-php5
```

You can run PHP5 scripts from command line. To run PHP5 scripts from command line you should install **php5-cli** package. To install **php5-cli** you can enter the following command in the terminal prompt:

```
sudo apt-get install php5-cli
```

You can also execute PHP5 scripts without installing PHP5 Apache module. To accomplish this, you should install **php5-cgi** package. You can run the following command in a terminal prompt to install **php5-cgi** package:

```
sudo apt-get install php5-cgi
```

To use **MySQL** with PHP5 you should install **php5-mysql** package. To install **php5-mysql** you can enter the following command in the terminal prompt:

```
sudo apt-get install php5-mysql
```

Similarly, to use **PostgreSQL** with PHP5 you should install **php5-pgsql** package. To install **php5-pgsql** you can enter the following command in the terminal prompt:

```
sudo apt-get install php5-pgsql
```

10.2.2. Configuration

Once you install PHP5, you can run PHP5 scripts from your web browser. If you have installed **php5-cli** package, you can run PHP5 scripts from your command prompt.

By default, the Apache2 Web server is configured to run PHP5 scripts. In other words, the PHP5 module is enabled in Apache2 Web server automatically when you install the module. Please verify if the files /etc/apache2/mods-enabled/php5.conf and /etc/apache2/mods-enabled/php5.load exist. If they do not exists, you can enable the module using **a2enmod** command.

Once you install PHP5 related packages and enabled PHP5 Apache 2 module, you should restart Apache2 Web server to run PHP5 scripts. You can run the following command at a terminal prompt to restart your web server:

```
sudo /etc/init.d/apache2 restart
```

10.2.3. Testing

To verify your installation, you can run following PHP5 phpinfo script:

```
<?php
phpinfo();
?>
```

You can save the content in a file `phpinfo.php` and place it under **DocumentRoot** directory of Apache2 Web server. When point your browser to `http://hostname/phpinfo.php`, it would display values of various PHP5 configuration parameters.

10.2.4. References

- For more in depth information see *php.net*[11] documentation.
- There are a plethora of books on PHP. Two good books from O'Reilly are *Learning PHP 5*[12] and the *PHP Cook Book*[13].
- Also, see the *Apache MySQL PHP Ubuntu Wiki*[14] page for more information.

10.3. Squid - Proxy Server

Squid is a full-featured web proxy cache server application which provides proxy and cache services for Hyper Text Transport Protocol (HTTP), File Transfer Protocol (FTP), and other popular network protocols. Squid can implement caching and proxying of Secure Sockets Layer (SSL) requests and caching of Domain Name Server (DNS) lookups, and perform transparent caching. Squid also supports a wide variety of caching protocols, such as Internet Cache Protocol, (ICP) the Hyper Text Caching Protocol, (HTCP) the Cache Array Routing Protocol (CARP), and the Web Cache Coordination Protocol. (WCCP)

The Squid proxy cache server is an excellent solution to a variety of proxy and caching server needs, and scales from the branch office to enterprise level networks while providing extensive, granular access control mechanisms and monitoring of critical parameters via the Simple Network Management Protocol (SNMP). When selecting a computer system for use

---

[11] *http://www.php.net/docs.php*
[12] *http://oreilly.com/catalog/9780596005603/*
[13] *http://oreilly.com/catalog/9781565926813/*
[14] *https://help.ubuntu.com/community/ApacheMySQLPHP*

as a dedicated Squid proxy, or caching servers, ensure your system is configured with a large amount of physical memory, as Squid maintains an in-memory cache for increased performance.

10.3.1. Installation

At a terminal prompt, enter the following command to install the Squid server:

```
sudo apt-get install squid
```

10.3.2. Configuration

Squid is configured by editing the directives contained within the `/etc/squid/squid.conf` configuration file. The following examples illustrate some of the directives which may be modified to affect the behavior of the Squid server. For more in-depth configuration of Squid, see the References section.

 Tip

Prior to editing the configuration file, you should make a copy of the original file and protect it from writing so you will have the original settings as a reference, and to re-use as necessary.

Copy the `/etc/squid/squid.conf` file and protect it from writing with the following commands entered at a terminal prompt:

```
sudo cp /etc/squid/squid.conf /etc/squid/squid.conf.original
sudo chmod a-w /etc/squid/squid.conf.original
```

- To set your Squid server to listen on TCP port 8888 instead of the default TCP port 3128, change the http_port directive as such:

```
http_port 8888
```

- Change the visible_hostname directive in order to give the Squid server a specific hostname. This hostname does not necessarily need to be the computer's hostname. In this example it is set to *weezie*

```
visible_hostname weezie
```

- Using Squid's access control, you may configure use of Internet services proxied by Squid to be available only users with certain Internet Protocol (IP) addresses. For example, we will illustrate access by users of the 192.168.42.0/24 subnetwork only:

  Add the following to the **bottom** of the ACL section of your `/etc/squid/squid.conf` file:

```
acl fortytwo_network src 192.168.42.0/24
```

  Then, add the following to the **top** of the http_access section of your `/etc/squid/squid.conf` file:

```
http_access allow fortytwo_network
```

- Using the excellent access control features of Squid, you may configure use of Internet services proxied by Squid to be available only during normal business hours. For example, we'll illustrate access by employees of a business which is operating between 9:00AM and 5:00PM, Monday through Friday, and which uses the 10.1.42.0/42 subnetwork:

  Add the following to the **bottom** of the ACL section of your `/etc/squid/squid.conf` file:

  ```
  acl biz_network src 10.1.42.0/24
  acl biz_hours time M T W T F 9:00-17:00
  ```

  Then, add the following to the **top** of the http_access section of your `/etc/squid/squid.conf` file:

  ```
  http_access allow biz_network biz_hours
  ```

 Note

After making changes to the `/etc/squid/squid.conf` file, save the file and restart the **squid** server application to effect the changes using the following command entered at a terminal prompt:

```
sudo /etc/init.d/squid restart
```

10.3.3. References

- Squid Website[15]
- *Ubuntu Wiki Squid*[16] page

10.4. Ruby on Rails

Ruby on Rails is an open source web framework for developing database backed web applications. It is optimized for sustainable productivity of the programmer since it lets the programmer to write code by favouring convention over configuration.

10.4.1. Installation

Before installing **Rails** you should install **Apache** and **MySQL**. To install the **Apache** package, please refer to the Section 10.1, *HTTPD - Apache2 Web Server*. For instructions on installing **MySQL** refer to the Section 11.1, *MySQL*.

---

[15] *http://www.squid-cache.org/*
[16] *https://help.ubuntu.com/community/Squid*

Once you have **Apache** and **MySQL** packages installed, you are ready to install **Ruby on Rails** package.

To install the **Ruby** base packages and **Ruby on Rails**, you can enter the following command in the terminal prompt:

```
sudo apt-get install rails
```

10.4.2. Configuration

Modify the `/etc/apache2/sites-available/default` configuration file to setup your domains.

The first thing to change is the *DocumentRoot* directive:

```
DocumentRoot /path/to/rails/application/public
```

Next, change the <Directory "/path/to/rails/application/public"> directive:

```
<Directory "/path/to/rails/application/public">
        Options Indexes FollowSymLinks MultiViews ExecCGI
        AllowOverride All
        Order allow,deny
        allow from all
        AddHandler cgi-script .cgi
</Directory>
```

You should also enable the **mod_rewrite** module for Apache. To enable **mod_rewrite** module, please enter the following command in a terminal prompt:

```
sudo a2enmod rewrite
```

Finally you will need to change the ownership of the `/path/to/rails/application/public` and `/path/to/rails/application/tmp` directories to the user used to run the **Apache** process:

```
sudo chown -R www-data:www-data /path/to/rails/application/public
sudo chown -R www-data:www-data /path/to/rails/application/tmp
```

That's it! Now you have your Server ready for your **Ruby on Rails** applications.

10.4.3. References

- See the *Ruby on Rails*[17] website for more information.
- Also *Agile Development with Rails*[18] is a great resource.
- Another place for more information is the *Ruby on Rails Ubuntu Wiki*[19] page.

---

[17] *http://rubyonrails.org/*
[18] *http://pragprog.com/titles/rails3/agile-web-development-with-rails-third-edition*
[19] *https://help.ubuntu.com/community/RubyOnRails*

10.5. Apache Tomcat

Apache Tomcat is a web container that allows you to serve Java Servlets and JSP (Java Server Pages) web applications.

The Tomcat 6.0 packages in Ubuntu support two different ways of running Tomcat. You can install them as a classic unique system-wide instance, that will be started at boot time will run as the tomcat6 unprivileged user. But you can also deploy private instances that will run with your own user rights, and that you should start and stop by yourself. This second way is particularly useful in a development server context where multiple users need to test on their own private Tomcat instances.

10.5.1. System-wide installation

To install the Tomcat server, you can enter the following command in the terminal prompt:

```
sudo apt-get install tomcat6
```

This will install a Tomcat server with just a default ROOT webapp that displays a minimal "It works" page by default.

10.5.2. Configuration

Tomcat configuration files can be found in /etc/tomcat6. Only a few common configuration tweaks will be described here, please see *Tomcat 6.0 documentation*[20] for more.

10.5.2.1. Changing default ports

By default Tomcat 6.0 runs a HTTP connector on port 8080 and an AJP connector on port 8009. You might want to change those default ports to avoid conflict with another server on the system. This is done by changing the following lines in /etc/tomcat6/server.xml:

```
<Connector port="8080" protocol="HTTP/1.1"
           connectionTimeout="20000"
           redirectPort="8443" />
...
<Connector port="8009" protocol="AJP/1.3" redirectPort="8443" />
```

10.5.2.2. Changing JVM used

By default Tomcat will run preferably with OpenJDK-6, then try Sun's JVM, then try some other JVMs. If you have various JVMs installed, you can set which should be used by setting JAVA_HOME in /etc/default/tomcat6:

```
JAVA_HOME=/usr/lib/jvm/java-6-sun
```

---

[20] *http://tomcat.apache.org/tomcat-6.0-doc/index.html*

10.5.2.3. Declaring users and roles

Usernames, passwords and roles (groups) can be defined centrally in a Servlet container. In Tomcat 6.0 this is done in the `/etc/tomcat6/tomcat-users.xml` file:

```
<role rolename="admin"/>
<user username="tomcat" password="s3cret" roles="admin"/>
```

10.5.3. Using Tomcat standard webapps

Tomcat is shipped with webapps that you can install for documentation, administration or demo purposes.

10.5.3.1. Tomcat documentation

The **tomcat6-docs** package contains Tomcat 6.0 documentation, packaged as a webapp that you can access by default at http://yourserver:8080/docs. You can install it by entering the following command in the terminal prompt:

```
sudo apt-get install tomcat6-docs
```

10.5.3.2. Tomcat administration webapps

The **tomcat6-admin** package contains two webapps that can be used to administer the Tomcat server using a web interface. You can install them by entering the following command in the terminal prompt:

```
sudo apt-get install tomcat6-admin
```

The first one is the *manager* webapp, which you can access by default at *http://yourserver:8080/manager/html*. It is primarily used to get server status and restart webapps.

Note

Access to the *manager* application is protected by default: you need to define a user with the role "manager" in `/etc/tomcat6/tomcat-users.xml` before you can access it.

The second one is the *host-manager* webapp, which you can access by default at *http://yourserver:8080/host-manager/html*. It can be used to create virtual hosts dynamically.

Note

Access to the *host-manager* application is also protected by default: you need to define a user with the role "admin" in `/etc/tomcat6/tomcat-users.xml` before you can access it.

For security reasons, the tomcat6 user cannot write to the `/etc/tomcat6` directory by default. Some features in these admin webapps (application deployment, virtual host creation) need write access to that directory. If you want to use these features execute the following, to give users in the tomcat6 group the necessary rights:

```
sudo chgrp -R tomcat6 /etc/tomcat6
sudo chmod -R g+w /etc/tomcat6
```

10.5.3.3. Tomcat examples webapps

The **tomcat6-examples** package contains two webapps that can be used to test or demonstrate Servlets and JSP features, which you can access them by default at http://yourserver:8080/examples. You can install them by entering the following command in the terminal prompt:

```
sudo apt-get install tomcat6-examples
```

10.5.4. Using private instances

Tomcat is heavily used in development and testing scenarios where using a single system-wide instance doesn't meet the requirements of multiple users on a single system. The Tomcat 6.0 packages in Ubuntu come with tools to help deploy your own user-oriented instances, allowing every user on a system to run (without root rights) separate private instances while still using the system-installed libraries.

 Note

> It is possible to run the system-wide instance and the private instances in parallel, as long as they do not use the same TCP ports.

10.5.4.1. Installing private instance support

You can install everything necessary to run private instances by entering the following command in the terminal prompt:

```
sudo apt-get install tomcat6-user
```

10.5.4.2. Creating a private instance

You can create a private instance directory by entering the following command in the terminal prompt:

```
tomcat6-instance-create my-instance
```

This will create a new `my-instance` directory with all the necessary subdirectories and scripts. You can for example install your common libraries in the `lib/` subdirectory and deploy your webapps in the `webapps/` subdirectory. No webapps are deployed by default.

10.5.4.3. Configuring your private instance

You will find the classic Tomcat configuration files for your private instance in the `conf/` subdirectory. You should for example certainly edit the `conf/server.xml` file to change the default ports used by your private Tomcat instance to avoid conflict with other instances that might be running.

10.5.4.4. Starting/stopping your private instance

You can start your private instance by entering the following command in the terminal prompt (supposing your instance is located in the `my-instance` directory):

```
my-instance/bin/startup.sh
```

 Note

> You should check the `logs/` subdirectory for any error. If you have a
> *java.net.BindException: Address already in use<null>:8080* error, it means that the port
> you're using is already taken and that you should change it.

You can stop your instance by entering the following command in the terminal prompt (supposing your instance is located in the `my-instance` directory):

```
my-instance/bin/shutdown.sh
```

10.5.5. References

* See the *Apache Tomcat*[21] website for more information.
* *Tomcat: The Definitive Guide*[22] is a good resource for building web applications with Tomcat.
* For additional books see the *Tomcat Books*[23] list page.
* Also, see the*Ubuntu Wiki Apache Tomcat*[24] page.

---

[21] *http://tomcat.apache.org/*
[22] *http://oreilly.com/catalog/9780596003180/*
[23] *http://wiki.apache.org/tomcat/Tomcat/Books*
[24] *https://help.ubuntu.com/community/ApacheTomcat5*

Chapter 11.
Databases

Ubuntu provides two popular database servers. They are:

- **MySQL™**
- **PostgreSQL**

They are available in the main repository. This section explains how to install and configure these database servers.

11.1. MySQL

MySQL is a fast, multi-threaded, multi-user, and robust SQL database server. It is intended for mission-critical, heavy-load production systems as well as for embedding into mass-deployed software.

11.1.1. Installation

To install MySQL, run the following command from a terminal prompt:

```
sudo apt-get install mysql-server
```

During the installation process you will be prompted to enter a password for the **MySQL** root user.

Once the installation is complete, the MySQL server should be started automatically. You can run the following command from a terminal prompt to check whether the MySQL server is running:

```
sudo netstat -tap | grep mysql
```

When you run this command, you should see the following line or something similar:

```
tcp        0      0 localhost:mysql         *:*                    LISTEN     2556/mysqld
```

If the server is not running correctly, you can type the following command to start it:

```
sudo /etc/init.d/mysql restart
```

11.1.2. Configuration

You can edit the `/etc/mysql/my.cnf` file to configure the basic settings -- log file, port number, etc. For example, to configure **MySQL** to listen for connections from network hosts, change the *bind-address* directive to the server's IP address:

```
bind-address            = 192.168.0.5
```

 Note

Replace 192.168.0.5 with the appropriate address.

After making a change to `/etc/mysql/my.cnf` the **mysql** daemon will need to be restarted:

```
sudo /etc/init.d/mysql restart
```

If you would like to change the **MySQL** *root* password, in a terminal enter:

```
sudo dpkg-reconfigure mysql-server-5.1
```

The **mysql** daemon will be stopped, and you will be prompted to enter a new password.

11.1.3. Resources

- See the *MySQL Home Page*[1] for more information.
- The *MySQL Handbook* is also available in the **mysql-doc-5.0** package. To install the package enter the following in a terminal:

  ```
  sudo apt-get install mysql-doc-5.0
  ```

  The documentation is in HTML format, to view them enter **file:///usr/share/doc/mysql-doc-5.0/refman-5.0-en.html-chapter/index.html** in your browser's address bar.
- For general SQL information see *Using SQL Special Edition*[2] by Rafe Colburn.
- The *Apache MySQL PHP Ubuntu Wiki*[3] page also has useful information.

11.2. PostgreSQL

PostgreSQL is an object-relational database system that has the features of traditional commercial database systems with enhancements to be found in next-generation DBMS systems.

11.2.1. Installation

To install PostgreSQL, run the following command in the command prompt:

---

[1] *http://www.mysql.com/*
[2] *http://www.informit.com/store/product.aspx?isbn=0768664128*
[3] *https://help.ubuntu.com/community/ApacheMySQLPHP*

```
sudo apt-get install postgresql
```

Once the installation is complete, you should configure the PostgreSQL server based on your needs, although the default configuration is viable.

11.2.2. Configuration

By default, connection via TCP/IP is disabled. PostgreSQL supports multiple client authentication methods. By default, IDENT authentication method is used for **postgres** and local users. Please refer *the PostgreSQL Administrator's Guide*[4].

The following discussion assumes that you wish to enable TCP/IP connections and use the MD5 method for client authentication. PostgreSQL configuration files are stored in the `/etc/postgresql/<version>/main` directory. For example, if you install PostgreSQL 8.4, the configuration files are stored in the `/etc/postgresql/8.4/main` directory.

 Tip

> To configure *ident* authentication, add entries to the `/etc/postgresql/8.4/main/pg_ident.conf` file.

To enable TCP/IP connections, edit the file `/etc/postgresql/8.4/main/postgresql.conf`

Locate the line *#listen_addresses = 'localhost'* and change it to:

```
listen_addresses = 'localhost'
```

 Note

> To allow other computers to connect to your **PostgreSQL** server replace 'localhost' with the *IP Address* of your server.

You may also edit all other parameters, if you know what you are doing! For details, refer to the configuration file or to the PostgreSQL documentation.

Now that we can connect to our **PostgreSQL** server, the next step is to set a password for the *postgres* user. Run the following command at a terminal prompt to connect to the default PostgreSQL template database:

```
sudo -u postgres psql template1
```

The above command connects to PostgreSQL database *template1* as user *postgres*. Once you connect to the PostgreSQL server, you will be at a SQL prompt. You can run the following SQL command at the **psql** prompt to configure the password for the user postgres.

```
ALTER USER postgres with encrypted password 'your_password';
```

---

[4] *http://www.postgresql.org/docs/8.4/static/admin.html*

After configuring the password, edit the file `/etc/postgresql/8.4/main/pg_hba.conf` to use *MD5* authentication with the *postgres* user:

```
local   all           postgres                          md5
```

Finally, you should restart the **PostgreSQL** service to initialize the new configuration. From a terminal prompt enter the following to restart **PostgreSQL**:

```
sudo /etc/init.d/postgresql-8.4 restart
```

Warning

The above configuration is not complete by any means. Please refer *the PostgreSQL Administrator's Guide*[5] to configure more parameters.

11.2.3. Resources

- As mentioned above the *Administrator's Guide*[6] is an excellent resource. The guide is also available in the **postgresql-doc-8.4** package. Execute the following in a terminal to install the package:

  ```
  sudo apt-get install postgresql-doc-8.4
  ```

  To view the guide enter **file:///usr/share/doc/postgresql-doc-8.4/html/index.html** into the address bar of your browser.

- For general SQL information see *Using SQL Special Edition*[7] by Rafe Colburn.

- Also, see the *PostgreSQL Ubuntu Wiki*[8] page for more information.

---

[5] *http://www.postgresql.org/docs/8.4/static/admin.html*

[6] *http://www.postgresql.org/docs/8.4/static/admin.html*

[7] *http://www.informit.com/store/product.aspx?isbn=0768664128*

[8] *https://help.ubuntu.com/community/PostgreSQL*

Chapter 12.
LAMP Applications

12.1. Overview

LAMP installations (Linux + Apache + MySQL + PHP) are a popular setup for Ubuntu servers. There is a plethora of Open Source applications written using the LAMP application stack. Some popular LAMP applications are Wiki's, Content Management Systems, and Management Software such as phpMyAdmin.

One advantage of LAMP is the substantial flexibility for different database, web server, and scripting languages. Popular substitutes for MySQL include PostgreSQL and SQLite. Python, Perl, and Ruby are also frequently used instead of PHP.

The traditional way to install most *LAMP* applications is:

- Download an archive containing the application source files.
- Unpack the archive, usually in a directory accessible to a web server.
- Depending on where the source was extracted, configure a web server to serve the files.
- Configure the application to connect to the database.
- Run a script, or browse to a page of the application, to install the database needed by the application.
- Once the steps above, or similar steps, are completed you are ready to begin using the application.

A disadvantage of using this approach is that the application files are not placed in the file system in a standard way, which can cause confusion as to where the application is installed. Another larger disadvantage is updating the application. When a new version is released, the same process used to install the application is needed to apply updates.

Fortunately, a number of *LAMP* applications are already packaged for Ubuntu, and are available for installation in the same way as non-LAMP applications. Depending on the application some extra configuration and setup steps may be needed, however.

This section covers howto install and configure the Wiki applications **MoinMoin**, **MediaWiki**, and the MySQL management application **phpMyAdmin**.

Note

A Wiki is a website that allows the visitors to easily add, remove and modify available content easily. The ease of interaction and operation makes Wiki an effective tool for mass collaborative authoring. The term Wiki is also referred to the collaborative software.

12.2. Moin Moin

MoinMoin is a Wiki engine implemented in Python, based on the PikiPiki Wiki engine, and licensed under the GNU GPL.

12.2.1. Installation

To install **MoinMoin**, run the following command in the command prompt:

```
sudo apt-get install python-moinmoin
```

You should also install **apache2** web server. For installing **apache2** web server, please refer to the section called *"Installation"* sub-section in the Section 10.1, *HTTPD - Apache2 Web Server* section.

12.2.2. Configuration

For configuring your first Wiki application, please run the following set of commands. Let us assume that you are creating a Wiki named *mywiki*:

```
cd /usr/share/moin
sudo mkdir mywiki
sudo cp -R data mywiki
sudo cp -R underlay mywiki
sudo cp server/moin.cgi mywiki
sudo chown -R www-data.www-data mywiki
sudo chmod -R ug+rwX mywiki
sudo chmod -R o-rwX mywiki
```

Now you should configure **MoinMoin** to find your new Wiki *mywiki*. To configure **MoinMoin**, open /etc/moin/mywiki.py file and change the following line:

```
data_dir = '/org/mywiki/data'
```

to

```
data_dir = '/usr/share/moin/mywiki/data'
```

Also, below the *data_dir* option add the *data_underlay_dir*:

```
data_underlay_dir='/usr/share/moin/mywiki/underlay'
```

Note

If the `/etc/moin/mywiki.py` file does not exists, you should copy `/etc/moin/moinmaster.py` file to `/etc/moin/mywiki.py` file and do the above mentioned change.

 Note

If you have named your Wiki as *my_wiki_name* you should insert a line "("my_wiki_name", r".*")" in `/etc/moin/farmconfig.py` file after the line "("mywiki", r".*")".

Once you have configured **MoinMoin** to find your first Wiki application *mywiki*, you should configure **apache2** and make it ready for your Wiki application.

You should add the following lines in `/etc/apache2/sites-available/default` file inside the "<VirtualHost *>" tag:

```
### moin
  ScriptAlias /mywiki "/usr/share/moin/mywiki/moin.cgi"
  alias /moin_static184 "/usr/share/moin/htdocs"
  <Directory /usr/share/moin/htdocs>
  Order allow,deny
  allow from all
  </Directory>
### end moin
```

 Note

Adjust the "*moin_static184*" in the *alias* line above, to the **moinmoin** version installed.

Once you configure the **apache2** web server and make it ready for your Wiki application, you should restart it. You can run the following command to restart the **apache2** web server:

```
sudo /etc/init.d/apache2 restart
```

12.2.3. Verification

You can verify the Wiki application and see if it works by pointing your web browser to the following URL:

```
http://localhost/mywiki
```

For more details, please refer to the *MoinMoin*[1] web site.

12.2.4. References

- For more information see the *moinmoin Wiki*[2].

---

[1] *http://moinmo.in/*

- Also, see the *Ubuntu Wiki MoinMoin*[3] page.

12.3. MediaWiki

MediaWiki is an web based Wiki software written in the PHP language. It can either use **MySQL** or **PostgreSQL** Database Management System.

12.3.1. Installation

Before installing **MediaWiki** you should also install **Apache2**, the **PHP5** scripting language and Database a Management System. **MySQL** or **PostgreSQL** are the most common, choose one depending on your need. Please refer to those sections in this manual for installation instructions.

To install **MediaWiki**, run the following command in the command prompt:

```
sudo apt-get install mediawiki php5-gd
```

For additional **MediaWiki** functionality see the **mediawiki-extensions** package.

12.3.2. Configuration

The Apache configuration file `mediawiki.conf` for MediaWiki is installed in `/etc/apache2/conf.d/` directory. You should uncomment the following line in this file to access MediaWiki application.

```
# Alias /mediawiki /var/lib/mediawiki
```

After you uncomment the above line, restart Apache server and access MediaWiki using the following url:

http://localhost/mediawiki/config/index.php

Tip

Please read the "Checking environment..." section in this page. You should be able to fix many issues by carefully reading this section.

Once the configuration is complete, you should copy the `LocalSettings.php` file to `/etc/mediawiki` directory:

```
sudo mv /var/lib/mediawiki/config/LocalSettings.php /etc/mediawiki/
```

You may also want to edit `/etc/mediawiki/LocalSettings.php` adjusting:

```
ini_set( 'memory_limit', '64M' );
```

---

[2] *http://moinmo.in/*
[3] *https://help.ubuntu.com/community/MoinMoin*

12.3.3. Extensions

The extensions add new features and enhancements for the MediaWiki application. The extensions give wiki administrators and end users the ability to customize MediaWiki to their requirements.

You can download MediaWiki extensions as an archive file or checkout from the Subversion repository. You should copy it to `/var/lib/mediawiki/extensions` directory. You should also add the following line at the end of file: `/etc/mediawiki/LocalSettings.php`.

```
require_once "$IP/extensions/ExtentionName/ExtentionName.php";
```

12.3.4. References

- For more details, please refer to the *MediaWiki*[4] web site.
- The *MediaWiki Administrators' Tutorial Guide*[5] contains a wealth of information for new MediaWiki administrators.
- Also, the *Ubuntu Wiki MediaWiki*[6] page is a good resource.

12.4. phpMyAdmin

phpMyAdmin is a LAMP application specifically written for administering **MySQL** servers. Written in **PHP**, and accessed through a web browser, phpMyAdmin provides a graphical interface for database administration tasks.

12.4.1. Installation

Before installing **phpMyAdmin** you will need access to a **MySQL** database either on the same host as that phpMyAdmin is installed on, or on a host accessible over the network. For more information see the Section 11.1, *MySQL*. From a terminal prompt enter:

```
sudo apt-get install phpmyadmin
```

At the prompt choose which web server to be configured for **phpMyAdmin**. The rest of this section will use **Apache2** for the web server.

In a browser go to *http://servername/phpmyadmin*, replacing serveranme with the server's actual hostname. At the login, page enter *root* for the *username*, or another **MySQL** user if you any setup, and enter the **MySQL** user's password.

Once logged in you can reset the *root* password if needed, create users, create/destroy databases and tables, etc.

---

[4] *http://www.mediawiki.org/*
[5] *http://www.packtpub.com/Mediawiki/book*
[6] *https://help.ubuntu.com/community/MediaWiki*

12.4.2. Configuration

The configuration files for **phpMyAdmin** are located in `/etc/phpmyadmin`. The main configuration file is `/etc/phpmyadmin/config.inc.php`. This file contains configuration options that apply globally to **phpMyAdmin**.

To use **phpMyAdmin** to administer a MySQL database hosted on another server, adjust the following in `/etc/phpmyadmin/config.inc.php`:

```
$cfg['Servers'][$i]['host'] = 'db_server';
```

Note

Replace db_server with the actual remote database server name or IP address. Also, be sure that the **phpMyAdmin** host has permissions to access the remote database.

Once configured, log out of **phpMyAdmin** and back in, and you should be accessing the new server.

The `config.header.inc.php` and `config.footer.inc.php` files are used to add a HTML header and footer to **phpMyAdmin**.

Another important configuration file is `/etc/phpmyadmin/apache.conf`, this file is symlinked to `/etc/apache2/conf.d/phpmyadmin.conf`, and is used to configure **Apache2** to serve the **phpMyAdmin** site. The file contains directives for loading **PHP**, directory permissions, etc. For more information on configuring **Apache2** see Section 10.1, *HTTPD - Apache2 Web Server*.

12.4.3. References

- The **phpMyAdmin** documentation comes installed with the package and can be accessed from the *phpMyAdmin Documentation* link (a question mark with a box around it) under the phpMyAdmin logo. The official docs can also be access on the *phpMyAdmin*[7] site.
- Also, *Mastering phpMyAdmin*[8] is a great resource.
- A third resource is the *phpMyAdmin Ubuntu Wiki*[9] page.

---

[7] *http://www.phpmyadmin.net/home_page/docs.php*
[8] *http://www.packtpub.com/phpmyadmin-3rd-edition/book*
[9] *https://help.ubuntu.com/community/phpMyAdmin*

Chapter 13.
File Servers

If you have more than one computer on a single network. At some point you will probably need to share files between them. In this section we cover installing and configuring FTP, NFS, and CUPS.

13.1. FTP Server

File Transfer Protocol (FTP) is a TCP protocol for uploading and downloading files between computers. FTP works on a client/server model. The server component is called an *FTP daemon*. It continuously listens for FTP requests from remote clients. When a request is received, it manages the login and sets up the connection. For the duration of the session it executes any of commands sent by the FTP client.

Access to an FTP server can be managed in two ways:

- Anonymous
- Authenticated

In the Anonymous mode, remote clients can access the FTP server by using the default user account called "anonymous" or "ftp" and sending an email address as the password. In the Authenticated mode a user must have an account and a password. User access to the FTP server directories and files is dependent on the permissions defined for the account used at login. As a general rule, the FTP daemon will hide the root directory of the FTP server and change it to the FTP Home directory. This hides the rest of the file system from remote sessions.

13.1.1. vsftpd - FTP Server Installation

vsftpd is an FTP daemon available in Ubuntu. It is easy to install, set up, and maintain. To install **vsftpd** you can run the following command:

```
sudo apt-get install vsftpd
```

13.1.2. Anonymous FTP Configuration

By default **vsftpd** is *not* configured to only allow anonymous download. If you wish to enable anonymous download edit /etc/vsftpd.conf changing:

```
anonymous_enable=Yes
```

During installation a *ftp* user is created with a home directory of `/srv/ftp`. This is the default FTP directory.

If you wish to change this location, to `/srv/files/ftp` for example, simply create a directory in another location and change the *ftp* user's home directory:

```
sudo mkdir /srv/files/ftp
sudo usermod -d /srv/files/ftp ftp
```

After making the change restart **vsftpd**:

```
sudo restart vsftpd
```

Finally, copy any files and directories you would like to make available through anonymous FTP to `/srv/files/ftp`, or `/srv/ftp` if you wish to use the default.

13.1.3. User Authenticated FTP Configuration

By default **vsftpd** is configured to authenticate system users and allow them to download files. If you want users to be able to upload files, edit `/etc/vsftpd.conf`:

```
write_enable=YES
```

Now restart **vsftpd**:

```
sudo restart vsftpd
```

Now when system users login to FTP they will start in their *home* directories where they can download, upload, create directories, etc.

Similarly, by default, the anonymous users are not allowed to upload files to FTP server. To change this setting, you should uncomment the following line, and restart **vsftpd**:

```
anon_upload_enable=YES
```

 Warning

Enabling anonymous FTP upload can be an extreme security risk. It is best to not enable anonymous upload on servers accessed directly from the Internet.

The configuration file consists of many configuration parameters. The information about each parameter is available in the configuration file. Alternatively, you can refer to the man page, **man 5 vsftpd.conf** for details of each parameter.

13.1.4. Securing FTP

There are options in `/etc/vsftpd.conf` to help make **vsftpd** more secure. For example users can be limited to their home directories by uncommenting:

```
chroot_local_user=YES
```

You can also limit a specific list of users to just their home directories:

```
chroot_list_enable=YES
chroot_list_file=/etc/vsftpd.chroot_list
```

After uncommenting the above options, create a /etc/vsftpd.chroot_list containing a list of users one per line. Then restart **vsftpd**:

```
sudo restart vsftpd
```

Also, the /etc/ftpusers file is a list of users that are *disallowed* FTP access. The default list includes root, daemon, nobody, etc. To disable FTP access for additional users simply add them to the list.

FTP can also be encrypted using *FTPS*. Different from *SFTP*, *FTPS* is FTP over Secure Socket Layer (SSL). *SFTP* is a FTP like session over an encrypted *SSH* connection. A major difference is that users of SFTP need to have a *shell* account on the system, instead of a *nologin* shell. Providing all users with a shell may not be ideal for some environments, such as a shared web host.

To configure *FTPS*, edit /etc/vsftpd.conf and at the bottom add:

```
ssl_enable=Yes
```

Also, notice the certificate and key related options:

```
rsa_cert_file=/etc/ssl/certs/ssl-cert-snakeoil.pem
rsa_private_key_file=/etc/ssl/private/ssl-cert-snakeoil.key
```

By default these options are set the certificate and key provided by the **ssl-cert** package. In a production environment these should be replaced with a certificate and key generated for the specific host. For more information on certificates see Section 8.5, *Certificates*.

Now restart **vsftpd**, and non-anonymous users will be forced to use *FTPS*:

```
sudo restart vsftpd
```

To allow users with a shell of /usr/sbin/nologin access to FTP, but have no shell access, edit /etc/shells adding the *nologin* shell:

```
# /etc/shells: valid login shells
/bin/csh
/bin/sh
/usr/bin/es
/usr/bin/ksh
/bin/ksh
/usr/bin/rc
/usr/bin/tcsh
/bin/tcsh
/usr/bin/esh
/bin/dash
/bin/bash
```

```
/bin/rbash
/usr/bin/screen
/usr/sbin/nologin
```

This is necessary because, by default **vsftpd** uses PAM for authentication, and the `/etc/pam.d/vsftpd` configuration file contains:

```
auth       required        pam_shells.so
```

The *shells* PAM module restricts access to shells listed in the `/etc/shells` file.

Most popular FTP clients can be configured connect using FTPS. The **lftp** command line FTP client has the ability to use FTPS as well.

13.1.5. References

- See the *vsftpd website*[1] for more information.

- For detailed `/etc/vsftpd.conf` options see the *vsftpd.conf man page*[2].

- The CodeGurus article *FTPS vs. SFTP: What to Choose*[3] has useful information contrasting FTPS and SFTP.

- Also, for more information see the *Ubuntu Wiki vsftpd*[4] page.

13.2. Network File System (NFS)

NFS allows a system to share directories and files with others over a network. By using NFS, users and programs can access files on remote systems almost as if they were local files.

Some of the most notable benefits that NFS can provide are:

- Local workstations use less disk space because commonly used data can be stored on a single machine and still remain accessible to others over the network.

- There is no need for users to have separate home directories on every network machine. Home directories could be set up on the NFS server and made available throughout the network.

- Storage devices such as floppy disks, CDROM drives, and USB Thumb drives can be used by other machines on the network. This may reduce the number of removable media drives throughout the network.

---

[1] *http://vsftpd.beasts.org/vsftpd_conf.html*

[2] *http://manpages.ubuntu.com/manpages/natty/en/man5/vsftpd.conf.5.html*

[3] *http://www.codeguru.com/csharp/.net/net_general/internet/article.php/c14329*

[4] *https://help.ubuntu.com/community/vsftpd*

13.2.1. Installation

At a terminal prompt enter the following command to install the NFS Server:

```
sudo apt-get install nfs-kernel-server
```

13.2.2. Configuration

You can configure the directories to be exported by adding them to the `/etc/exports` file. For example:

```
/ubuntu   *(ro,sync,no_root_squash)
/home     *(rw,sync,no_root_squash)
```

You can replace * with one of the hostname formats. Make the hostname declaration as specific as possible so unwanted systems cannot access the NFS mount.

To start the NFS server, you can run the following command at a terminal prompt:

```
sudo /etc/init.d/nfs-kernel-server start
```

13.2.3. NFS Client Configuration

Use the **mount** command to mount a shared NFS directory from another machine, by typing a command line similar to the following at a terminal prompt:

```
sudo mount example.hostname.com:/ubuntu /local/ubuntu
```

 Warning

> The mount point directory `/local/ubuntu` **must exist. There should be no files or subdirectories in the** `/local/ubuntu` **directory.**

An alternate way to mount an NFS share from another machine is to add a line to the `/etc/fstab` file. The line must state the hostname of the NFS server, the directory on the server being exported, and the directory on the local machine where the NFS share is to be mounted.

The general syntax for the line in `/etc/fstab` file is as follows:

```
example.hostname.com:/ubuntu /local/ubuntu nfs rsize=8192,wsize=8192,timeo=14,intr
```

If you have trouble mounting an NFS share, make sure the **nfs-common** package is installed on your client. To install **nfs-common** enter the following command at the terminal prompt:

```
sudo apt-get install nfs-common
```

13.2.4. References

- *Linux NFS faq*[5]
- *Ubuntu Wiki NFS Howto*[6]

---

[5] *http://nfs.sourceforge.net/*

13.3. CUPS - Print Server

The primary mechanism for Ubuntu printing and print services is the **Common UNIX Printing System** (CUPS). This printing system is a freely available, portable printing layer which has become the new standard for printing in most Linux distributions.

CUPS manages print jobs and queues and provides network printing using the standard Internet Printing Protocol (IPP), while offering support for a very large range of printers, from dot-matrix to laser and many in between. CUPS also supports PostScript Printer Description (PPD) and auto-detection of network printers, and features a simple web-based configuration and administration tool.

13.3.1. Installation

To install CUPS on your Ubuntu computer, simply use **sudo** with the **apt-get** command and give the packages to install as the first parameter. A complete CUPS install has many package dependencies, but they may all be specified on the same command line. Enter the following at a terminal prompt to install CUPS:

```
sudo apt-get install cups
```

Upon authenticating with your user password, the packages should be downloaded and installed without error. Upon the conclusion of installation, the CUPS server will be started automatically.

For troubleshooting purposes, you can access CUPS server errors via the error log file at: `/var/log/cups/error_log`. If the error log does not show enough information to troubleshoot any problems you encounter, the verbosity of the CUPS log can be increased by changing the **LogLevel** directive in the configuration file (discussed below) to "debug" or even "debug2", which logs everything, from the default of "info". If you make this change, remember to change it back once you've solved your problem, to prevent the log file from becoming overly large.

13.3.2. Configuration

The Common UNIX Printing System server's behavior is configured through the directives contained in the file `/etc/cups/cupsd.conf`. The CUPS configuration file follows the same syntax as the primary configuration file for the Apache HTTP server, so users familiar with editing Apache's configuration file should feel at ease when editing the CUPS configuration file. Some examples of settings you may wish to change initially will be presented here.

---

[6] *https://help.ubuntu.com/community/NFSv4Howto*

Tip

Prior to editing the configuration file, you should make a copy of the original file and protect it from writing, so you will have the original settings as a reference, and to reuse as necessary.

Copy the `/etc/cups/cupsd.conf` file and protect it from writing with the following commands, issued at a terminal prompt:

```
sudo cp /etc/cups/cupsd.conf /etc/cups/cupsd.conf.original
sudo chmod a-w /etc/cups/cupsd.conf.original
```

- **ServerAdmin**: To configure the email address of the designated administrator of the CUPS server, simply edit the `/etc/cups/cupsd.conf` configuration file with your preferred text editor, and modify the ServerAdmin line accordingly. For example, if you are the Administrator for the CUPS server, and your e-mail address is 'bjoy@somebigco.com', then you would modify the ServerAdmin line to appear as such:

```
ServerAdmin bjoy@somebigco.com
```

- **Listen**: By default on Ubuntu, the CUPS server installation listens only on the loopback interface at IP address *127.0.0.1*. In order to instruct the CUPS server to listen on an actual network adapter's IP address, you must specify either a hostname, the IP address, or optionally, an IP address/port pairing via the addition of a Listen directive. For example, if your CUPS server resides on a local network at the IP address 192.168.10.250 and you'd like to make it accessible to the other systems on this subnetwork, you would edit the `/etc/cups/cupsd.conf` and add a Listen directive, as such:

```
Listen 127.0.0.1:631            # existing loopback Listen
Listen /var/run/cups/cups.sock # existing socket Listen
Listen 192.168.10.250:631       # Listen on the LAN interface, Port 631 (IPP)
```

In the example above, you may comment out or remove the reference to the Loopback address (127.0.0.1) if you do not wish **cupsd** to listen on that interface, but would rather have it only listen on the Ethernet interfaces of the Local Area Network (LAN). To enable listening for all network interfaces for which a certain hostname is bound, including the Loopback, you could create a Listen entry for the hostname *socrates* as such:

```
Listen socrates:631  # Listen on all interfaces for the hostname 'socrates'
```

or by omitting the Listen directive and using *Port* instead, as in:

```
Port 631  # Listen on port 631 on all interfaces
```

For more examples of configuration directives in the CUPS server configuration file, view the associated system manual page by entering the following command at a terminal prompt:

```
man cupsd.conf
```

 Note

Whenever you make changes to the `/etc/cups/cupsd.conf` configuration file, you'll need to restart the CUPS server by typing the following command at a terminal prompt:

```
sudo /etc/init.d/cups restart
```

13.3.3. Web Interface

 Tip

CUPS can be configured and monitored using a web interface, which by default is available at *http://localhost:631/admin*. The web interface can be used to perform all printer management tasks.

In order to perform administrative tasks via the web interface, you must either have the root account enabled on your server, or authenticate as a user in the lpadmin group. For security reasons, CUPS won't authenticate a user that doesn't have a password.

To add a user to the lpadmin group, run at the terminal prompt:

```
sudo usermod -aG lpadmin username
```

Further documentation is available in the Documentation/Help tab of the web interface.

13.3.4. References

- *CUPS Website*[7]
- *Ubuntu Wiki CUPS page*[8]

---

[7] *http://www.cups.org/*
[8] *https://help.ubuntu.com/community/cups*

Chapter 14.
Email Services

The process of getting an email from one person to another over a network or the Internet involves many systems working together. Each of these systems must be correctly configured for the process to work. The sender uses a *Mail User Agent* (MUA), or email client, to send the message through one or more *Mail Transfer Agents* (MTA), the last of which will hand it off to a *Mail Delivery Agent* (MDA) for delivery to the recipient's mailbox, from which it will be retrieved by the recipient's email client, usually via a POP3 or IMAP server.

14.1. Postfix

Postfix is the default Mail Transfer Agent (MTA) in Ubuntu. It attempts to be fast and easy to administer and secure. It is compatible with the MTA **sendmail**. This section explains how to install and configure **postfix**. It also explains how to set it up as an SMTP server using a secure connection (for sending emails securely).

 Note

> This guide does not cover setting up Postfix *Virtual Domains*, for information on Virtual Domains and other advanced configurations see the Section 14.1.7.3, *References*.

14.1.1. Installation

To install **postfix** run the following command:

```
sudo apt-get install postfix
```

Simply press return when the installation process asks questions, the configuration will be done in greater detail in the next stage.

14.1.2. Basic Configuration

To configure **postfix**, run the following command:

```
sudo dpkg-reconfigure postfix
```

The user interface will be displayed. On each screen, select the following values:

- Internet Site
- mail.example.com
- steve
- mail.example.com, localhost.localdomain, localhost
- No
- 127.0.0.0/8 [::ffff:127.0.0.0]/104 [::1]/128 192.168.0.0/24
- 0
- +
- all

Note

Replace mail.example.com with the domain for which you'll accept email, 192.168.0.0/24 with the actual network and class range of your mail server, and steve with the appropriate username.

Now is a good time to decide which mailbox format you want to use. By default Postfix will use **mbox** for the mailbox format. Rather than editing the configuration file directly, you can use the **postconf** command to configure all **postfix** parameters. The configuration parameters will be stored in /etc/postfix/main.cf file. Later if you wish to re-configure a particular parameter, you can either run the command or change it manually in the file.

To configure the mailbox format for **Maildir:**

```
sudo postconf -e 'home_mailbox = Maildir/'
```

Note

This will place new mail in /home/username/Maildir so you will need to configure your Mail Delivery Agent (MDA) to use the same path.

14.1.3. SMTP Authentication

SMTP-AUTH allows a client to identify itself through an authentication mechanism (SASL). Transport Layer Security (TLS) should be used to encrypt the authentication process. Once authenticated the SMTP server will allow the client to relay mail.

1. Configure Postfix for SMTP-AUTH using SASL (Dovecot SASL):

```
sudo postconf -e 'smtpd_sasl_type = dovecot'
sudo postconf -e 'smtpd_sasl_path = private/auth-client'
sudo postconf -e 'smtpd_sasl_local_domain ='
sudo postconf -e 'smtpd_sasl_security_options = noanonymous'
```

```
sudo postconf -e 'broken_sasl_auth_clients = yes'
sudo postconf -e 'smtpd_sasl_auth_enable = yes'
sudo postconf -e 'smtpd_recipient_restrictions =
       permit_sasl_authenticated,permit_mynetworks,reject_unauth_destination'
sudo postconf -e 'inet_interfaces = all'
```

Note

The *smtpd_sasl_path* configuration is a path relative to the Postfix queue directory.

2. Next, obtain a digital certificate for TLS. See Section 8.5, *Certificates* for details. This example also uses a Certificate Authority (CA). For information on generating a CA certificate see the Section 8.5.5, *Certification Authority*.

Note

You can get the digital certificate from a certificate authority. But unlike web clients, SMTP clients rarely complain about "self-signed certificates", so alternatively, you can create the certificate yourself. Refer to the Section 8.5.3, *Creating a Self-Signed Certificate* for more details.

3. Once you have a certificate, configure Postfix to provide TLS encryption for both incoming and outgoing mail:

```
sudo postconf -e 'smtpd_tls_auth_only = no'
sudo postconf -e 'smtp_tls_security_level = may'
sudo postconf -e 'smtpd_tls_security_level = may'
sudo postconf -e 'smtp_tls_note_starttls_offer = yes'
sudo postconf -e 'smtpd_tls_key_file = /etc/ssl/private/server.key'
sudo postconf -e 'smtpd_tls_cert_file = /etc/ssl/certs/server.crt'
sudo postconf -e 'smtpd_tls_loglevel = 1'
sudo postconf -e 'smtpd_tls_received_header = yes'
sudo postconf -e 'smtpd_tls_session_cache_timeout = 3600s'
sudo postconf -e 'tls_random_source = dev:/dev/urandom'
sudo postconf -e 'myhostname = mail.example.com'
```

4. If you are using your own *Certificate Authority* to sign the certificate enter:

```
sudo postconf -e 'smtpd_tls_CAfile = /etc/ssl/certs/cacert.pem'
```

Again, for more details about certificates see Section 8.5, *Certificates*.

Note

After running all the commands, **Postfix** is configured for SMTP-AUTH and a self-signed certificate has been created for TLS encryption.

Now, the file /etc/postfix/main.cf should look like *this*[1].

---

[1] *https://help.ubuntu.com/9.10/serverguide/sample/postfix_configuration*

The postfix initial configuration is complete. Run the following command to restart the postfix daemon:

```
sudo /etc/init.d/postfix restart
```

Postfix supports SMTP-AUTH as defined in *RFC2554*[2]. It is based on *SASL*[3]. However it is still necessary to set up SASL authentication before you can use SMTP-AUTH.

14.1.4. Configuring SASL

Postfix supports two SASL implementations Cyrus SASL and Dovecot SASL. To enable Dovecot SASL the **dovecot-common** package will need to be installed. From a terminal prompt enter the following:

```
sudo apt-get install dovecot-common
```

Next you will need to edit /etc/dovecot/dovecot.conf. In the *auth default* section uncomment the *socket listen* option and change the following:

```
socket listen {
    #master {
        # Master socket provides access to userdb information. It's typically
        # used to give Dovecot's local delivery agent access to userdb so it
        # can find mailbox locations.
        #path = /var/run/dovecot/auth-master
        #mode = 0600
        # Default user/group is the one who started dovecot-auth (root)
        #user =
        #group =
    #}
    client {
        # The client socket is generally safe to export to everyone. Typical use
        # is to export it to your SMTP server so it can do SMTP AUTH lookups
        # using it.
        path = /var/spool/postfix/private/auth-client
        mode = 0660
        user = postfix
        group = postfix
    }
}
```

In order to let **Outlook** clients use SMTP-AUTH, in the *auth default* section of /etc/dovecot/dovecot.conf add "*login*":

```
mechanisms = plain login
```

Once you have **Dovecot** configured restart it with:

```
sudo /etc/init.d/dovecot restart
```

---

[2] *http://www.ietf.org/rfc/rfc2554.txt*
[3] *http://www.ietf.org/rfc/rfc2222.txt*

14.1.5. Postfix-Dovecot

Another option for configuring **Postfix** for SMTP-AUTH is using the **dovecot-postfix** package. This package will install **Dovecot** and configure **Postfix** to use it for both SASL authentication and as a Mail Delivery Agent (MDA). The package also configures **Dovecot** for IMAP, IMAPS, POP3, and POP3S.

 Note

> You may or may not want to run IMAP, IMAPS, POP3, or POP3S on your mail server. For example, if you are configuring your server to be a mail gateway, spam/virus filter, etc. If this is the case it may be easier to use the above commands to configure Postfix for SMTP-AUTH.

To install the package, from a terminal prompt enter:

```
sudo apt-get install dovecot-postfix
```

You should now have a working mail server, but there are a few options that you may wish to further customize. For example, the package uses the certificate and key from the **ssl-cert** package, and in a production environment you should use a certificate and key generated for the host. See Section 8.5, *Certificates* for more details.

Once you have a customized certificate and key for the host, change the following options in `/etc/postfix/main.cf`:

```
smtpd_tls_cert_file = /etc/ssl/certs/ssl-mail.pem
smtpd_tls_key_file = /etc/ssl/private/ssl-mail.key
```

Then restart Postfix:

```
sudo /etc/init.d/postfix restart
```

14.1.6. Testing

SMTP-AUTH configuration is complete. Now it is time to test the setup.

To see if SMTP-AUTH and TLS work properly, run the following command:

```
telnet mail.example.com 25
```

After you have established the connection to the postfix mail server, type:

```
ehlo mail.example.com
```

If you see the following lines among others, then everything is working perfectly. Type **quit** to exit.

```
250-STARTTLS
250-AUTH LOGIN PLAIN
250-AUTH=LOGIN PLAIN
250 8BITMIME
```

14.1.7. Troubleshooting

This section introduces some common ways to determine the cause if problems arise.

14.1.7.1. Escaping chroot

The Ubuntu **postfix** package will by default install into a *chroot* environment for security reasons. This can add greater complexity when troubleshooting problems.

To turn off the chroot operation locate for the following line in the /etc/postfix/master.cf configuration file:

```
smtp      inet  n      -      -      -      -      smtpd
```

and modify it as follows:

```
smtp      inet  n      -      n      -      -      smtpd
```

You will then need to restart Postfix to use the new configuration. From a terminal prompt enter:

```
sudo /etc/init.d/postfix restart
```

14.1.7.2. Log Files

Postfix sends all log messages to /var/log/mail.log. However error and warning messages can sometimes get lost in the normal log output so they are also logged to /var/log/mail.err and /var/log/mail.warn respectively.

To see messages entered into the logs in real time you can use the **tail -f** command:

```
tail -f /var/log/mail.err
```

The amount of detail that is recorded in the logs can be increased. Below are some configuration options for increasing the log level for some of the areas covered above.

- To increase *TLS* activity logging set the *smtpd_tls_loglevel* option to a value from 1 to 4.
  ```
  sudo postconf -e 'smtpd_tls_loglevel = 4'
  ```
- If you are having trouble sending or receiving mail from a specific domain you can add the domain to the *debug_peer_list* parameter.
  ```
  sudo postconf -e 'debug_peer_list = problem.domain'
  ```
- You can increase the verbosity of any **Postfix** daemon process by editing the /etc/postfix/master.cf and adding a *-v* after the entry. For example edit the *smtp* entry:
  ```
  smtp      unix  -      -      -      -      -      smtp -v
  ```

Note

It is important to note that after making one of the logging changes above the **Postfix** process will need to be reloaded in order to recognize the new configuration: **sudo /etc/init.d/postfix reload**

- To increase the amount of information logged when troubleshooting *SASL* issues you can set the following options in `/etc/dovecot/dovecot.conf`

```
auth_debug=yes
auth_debug_passwords=yes
```

Note

Just like **Postfix** if you change a **Dovecot** configuration the process will need to be reloaded: **sudo /etc/init.d/dovecot reload**.

Note

Some of the options above can drastically increase the amount of information sent to the log files. Remember to return the log level back to normal after you have corrected the problem. Then reload the appropriate daemon for the new configuration to take affect.

14.1.7.3. References

Administering a **Postfix** server can be a very complicated task. At some point you may need to turn to the Ubuntu community for more experienced help.

A great place to ask for **Postfix** assistance, and get involved with the Ubuntu Server community, is the *#ubuntu-server* IRC channel on *freenode*[4]. You can also post a message to one of the *Web Forums*[5].

For in depth **Postfix** information Ubuntu developers highly recommend: *The Book of Postfix*[6].

Finally, the *Postfix*[7] website also has great documentation on all the different configuration options available.

Also, the *Ubuntu Wiki Postifx*[8] page has more information.

---

[4] *http://freenode.net/*

[5] *http://www.ubuntu.com/support/community/webforums*

[6] *http://www.postfix-book.com/*

[7] *http://www.postfix.org/documentation.html*

[8] *https://help.ubuntu.com/community/Postfix*

14.2. Exim4

Exim4 is another Message Transfer Agent (MTA) developed at the University of Cambridge for use on Unix systems connected to the Internet. Exim can be installed in place of **sendmail**, although the configuration of **exim** is quite different to that of **sendmail**.

14.2.1. Installation

To install **exim4**, run the following command:

```
sudo apt-get install exim4
```

14.2.2. Configuration

To configure **Exim4**, run the following command:

```
sudo dpkg-reconfigure exim4-config
```

The user interface will be displayed. The user interface lets you configure many parameters. For example, In **Exim4** the configuration files are split among multiple files. If you wish to have them in one file you can configure accordingly in this user interface.

All the parameters you configure in the user interface are stored in /etc/exim4/update-exim4.conf.conf file. If you wish to re-configure, either you re-run the configuration wizard or manually edit this file using your favorite editor. Once you configure, you can run the following command to generate the master configuration file:

```
sudo update-exim4.conf
```

The master configuration file, is generated and it is stored in /var/lib/exim4/config.autogenerated.

Warning

At any time, you should not edit the master configuration file, /var/lib/exim4/config.autogenerated manually. It is updated automatically every time you run **update-exim4.conf**

You can run the following command to start **Exim4** daemon.

```
sudo /etc/init.d/exim4 start
```

14.2.3. SMTP Authentication

This section covers configuring Exim4 to use SMTP-AUTH with TLS and SASL.

The first step is to create a certificate for use with TLS. Enter the following into a terminal prompt:

```
sudo /usr/share/doc/exim4-base/examples/exim-gencert
```

Now Exim4 needs to be configured for TLS by editing
`/etc/exim4/conf.d/main/03_exim4-config_tlsoptions` add the following:

```
MAIN_TLS_ENABLE = yes
```

Next you need to configure **Exim4** to use the **saslauthd** for authentication. Edit
`/etc/exim4/conf.d/auth/30_exim4-config_examples` and uncomment the
plain_saslauthd_server and *login_saslauthd_server* sections:

```
plain_saslauthd_server:
   driver = plaintext
   public_name = PLAIN
   server_condition = ${if saslauthd{{$auth2}{$auth3}}{1}{0}}
   server_set_id = $auth2
   server_prompts = :
   .ifndef AUTH_SERVER_ALLOW_NOTLS_PASSWORDS
   server_advertise_condition = ${if eq{$tls_cipher}{}{}{*}}
   .endif
#
login_saslauthd_server:
   driver = plaintext
   public_name = LOGIN
   server_prompts = "Username:: : Password::"
   # don't send system passwords over unencrypted connections
   server_condition = ${if saslauthd{{$auth1}{$auth2}}{1}{0}}
   server_set_id = $auth1
   .ifndef AUTH_SERVER_ALLOW_NOTLS_PASSWORDS
   server_advertise_condition = ${if eq{$tls_cipher}{}{}{*}}
   .endif
```

Finally, update the Exim4 configuration and restart the service:

```
sudo update-exim4.conf
sudo /etc/init.d/exim4 restart
```

14.2.4. Configuring SASL

This section provides details on configuring the saslauthd to provide authentication for
Exim4.

The first step is to install the sasl2-bin package. From a terminal prompt enter the following:

```
sudo apt-get install sasl2-bin
```

To configure saslauthd edit the /etc/default/saslauthd configuration file and set
START=no to:

```
START=yes
```

Next the *Debian-exim* user needs to be part of the *sasl* group in order for Exim4 to use the
saslauthd service:

```
sudo adduser Debian-exim sasl
```

Now start the **saslauthd** service:

```
sudo /etc/init.d/saslauthd start
```

Exim4 is now configured with SMTP-AUTH using TLS and SASL authentication.

14.2.5. References

- See *exim.org*[9] for more information.
- There is also an *Exim4 Book*[10] available.
- Another resource is the *Exim4 Ubuntu Wiki*[11] page.

14.3. Dovecot Server

Dovecot is a Mail Delivery Agent, written with security primarily in mind. It supports the major mailbox formats: mbox or Maildir. This section explain how to set it up as an imap or pop3 server.

14.3.1. Installation

To install **dovecot**, run the following command in the command prompt:

```
sudo apt-get install dovecot-imapd dovecot-pop3d
```

14.3.2. Configuration

To configure **dovecot**, you can edit the file /etc/dovecot/dovecot.conf. You can choose the protocol you use. It could be pop3, pop3s (pop3 secure), imap and imaps (imap secure). A description of these protocols is beyond the scope of this guide. For further information, refer to the Wikipedia articles on *POP3*[12] and *IMAP*[13].

IMAPS and POP3S are more secure that the simple IMAP and POP3 because they use SSL encryption to connect. Once you have chosen the protocol, amend the following line in the file /etc/dovecot/dovecot.conf:

```
protocols = pop3 pop3s imap imaps
```

Next, choose the mailbox you would like to use. **Dovecot** supports **maildir** and **mbox** formats. These are the most commonly used mailbox formats. They both have their own benefits and are discussed on *the Dovecot web site*[14].

---

[9] *http://www.exim.org/*
[10] *http://www.uit.co.uk/content/exim-smtp-mail-server*
[11] *https://help.ubuntu.com/community/Exim4*
[12] *http://en.wikipedia.org/wiki/POP3*
[13] *http://en.wikipedia.org/wiki/Internet_Message_Access_Protocol*
[14] *http://wiki.dovecot.org/MailboxFormat*

Once you have chosen your mailbox type, edit the file `/etc/dovecot/dovecot.conf` and change the following line:

```
mail_location = maildir:~/Maildir # (for maildir)
or
mail_location = mbox:~/mail:INBOX=/var/spool/mail/%u # (for mbox)
```

 Note

> You should configure your Mail Transport Agent (MTA) to transfer the incoming mail to this type of mailbox if it is different from the one you have configured.

Once you have configured dovecot, restart the **dovecot** daemon in order to test your setup:

```
sudo /etc/init.d/dovecot restart
```

If you have enabled imap, or pop3, you can also try to log in with the commands **telnet localhost pop3** or **telnet localhost imap2**. If you see something like the following, the installation has been successful:

```
bhuvan@rainbow:~$ telnet localhost pop3
Trying 127.0.0.1...
Connected to localhost.localdomain.
Escape character is '^]'.
+OK Dovecot ready.
```

14.3.3. Dovecot SSL Configuration

To configure **dovecot** to use SSL, you can edit the file `/etc/dovecot/dovecot.conf` and amend following lines:

```
ssl_cert_file = /etc/ssl/certs/ssl-cert-snakeoil.pem
ssl_key_file = /etc/ssl/private/ssl-cert-snakeoil.key
ssl_disable = no
disable_plaintext_auth = no
```

You can get the SSL certificate from a Certificate Issuing Authority or you can create self signed SSL certificate. The latter is a good option for email, because SMTP clients rarely complain about "self-signed certificates". Please refer to the Section 8.5, *Certificates* for details about how to create self signed SSL certificate. Once you create the certificate, you will have a key file and a certificate file. Please copy them to the location pointed in the `/etc/dovecot/dovecot.conf` configuration file.

14.3.4. Firewall Configuration for an Email Server

To access your mail server from another computer, you must configure your firewall to allow connections to the server on the necessary ports.

- IMAP - 143
- IMAPS - 993

- POP3 - 110
- POP3S - 995

14.3.5. References

- See the *Dovecot website*[15] for more information.
- Also, the *Dovecot Ubuntu Wiki*[16] page has more details.

14.4. Mailman

Mailman is an open source program for managing electronic mail discussions and e-newsletter lists. Many open source mailing lists (including all the *Ubuntu mailing lists*[17]) use Mailman as their mailing list software. It is powerful and easy to install and maintain.

14.4.1. Installation

Mailman provides a web interface for the administrators and users, using an external mail server to send and receive emails. It works perfectly with the following mail servers:

- **Postfix**
- **Exim**
- **Sendmail**
- **Qmail**

We will see how to install and configure Mailman with, the Apache web server, and either the Postfix or Exim mail server. If you wish to install Mailman with a different mail server, please refer to the references section.

 Note

> You only need to install one mail server and **Postfix** is the default Ubuntu Mail Transfer Agent.

14.4.1.1. Apache2

To install apache2 you refer to the Section 10.1.1, *Installation* for details.

14.4.1.2. Postfix

For instructions on installing and configuring Postfix refer to the Section 14.1, *Postfix*.

---

[15] *http://www.dovecot.org/*
[16] *https://help.ubuntu.com/community/Dovecot*
[17] *http://lists.ubuntu.com/*

14.4.1.3. Exim4

To install Exim4 refer to the Section 14.2, *Exim4*.

Once exim4 is installed, the configuration files are stored in the `/etc/exim4` directory. In Ubuntu, by default, the exim4 configuration files are split across different files. You can change this behavior by changing the following variable in the `/etc/exim4/update-exim4.conf` file:

```
dc_use_split_config='true'
```

14.4.1.4. Mailman

To install **Mailman**, run following command at a terminal prompt:

```
sudo apt-get install mailman
```

It copies the installation files in **/var/lib/mailman** directory. It installs the CGI scripts in **/usr/lib/cgi-bin/mailman** directory. It creates *list* linux user. It creates the *list* linux group. The mailman process will be owned by this user.

14.4.2. Configuration

This section assumes you have successfully installed **mailman**, **apache2**, and **postfix** or **exim4**. Now you just need to configure them.

14.4.2.1. Apache2

An example Apache configuration file comes with **Mailman** and is placed in `/etc/mailman/apache.conf`. In order for Apache to use the config file it needs to be copied to `/etc/apache2/sites-available`:

```
sudo cp /etc/mailman/apache.conf /etc/apache2/sites-available/mailman.conf
```

This will setup a new Apache *VirtualHost* for the Mailman administration site. Now enable the new configuration and restart Apache:

```
sudo a2ensite mailman.conf
sudo /etc/init.d/apache2 restart
```

Mailman uses apache2 to render its CGI scripts. The mailman CGI scripts are installed in the **/usr/lib/cgi-bin/mailman** directory. So, the mailman url will be http://hostname/cgi-bin/mailman/. You can make changes to the `/etc/apache2/sites-available/mailman.conf` file if you wish to change this behavior.

14.4.2.2. Postfix

For **Postfix** integration, we will associate the domain lists.example.com with the mailing lists. Please replace *lists.example.com* with the domain of your choosing.

You can use the postconf command to add the necessary configuration to
`/etc/postfix/main.cf`:

```
sudo postconf -e 'relay_domains = lists.example.com'
sudo postconf -e 'transport_maps = hash:/etc/postfix/transport'
sudo postconf -e 'mailman_destination_recipient_limit = 1'
```

In `/etc/postfix/master.cf` double check that you have the following transport:

```
mailman   unix   -      n      n      -      -      pipe
  flags=FR user=list argv=/usr/lib/mailman/bin/postfix-to-mailman.py
  ${nexthop} ${user}
```

It calls the *postfix-to-mailman.py* script when a mail is delivered to a list.

Associate the domain lists.example.com to the Mailman transport with the transport map.
Edit the file `/etc/postfix/transport`:

```
lists.example.com        mailman:
```

Now have **Postfix** build the transport map by entering the following from a terminal
prompt:

```
sudo postmap -v /etc/postfix/transport
```

Then restart Postfix to enable the new configurations:

```
sudo /etc/init.d/postfix restart
```

14.4.2.3. Exim4

Once Exim4 is installed, you can start the Exim server using the following command from a
terminal prompt:

```
sudo /etc/init.d/exim4 start
```

In order to make mailman work with Exim4, you need to configure Exim4. As mentioned
earlier, by default, Exim4 uses multiple configuration files of different types. For details,
please refer to the *Exim*[18] web site. To run mailman, we should add new a configuration file
to the following configuration types:

- Main
- Transport
- Router

Exim creates a master configuration file by sorting all these mini configuration files. So, the
order of these configuration files is very important.

---

[18] *http://www.exim.org/*

14.4.2.4. Main

All the configuration files belonging to the main type are stored in the
/etc/exim4/conf.d/main/ directory. You can add the following content to a new file,
named 04_exim4-config_mailman:

```
# start
# Home dir for your Mailman installation -- aka Mailman's prefix
# directory.
# On Ubuntu this should be "/var/lib/mailman"
# This is normally the same as ~mailman
MM_HOME=/var/lib/mailman
#
# User and group for Mailman, should match your --with-mail-gid
# switch to Mailman's configure script.  Value is normally "mailman"
MM_UID=list
MM_GID=list
#
# Domains that your lists are in - colon separated list
# you may wish to add these into local_domains as well
domainlist mm_domains=hostname.com
#
# -=-=-=-=-=-=-=-=-=-=-=-=-=-=-=-=-=-=-=-=-=-=-=-=-=-=-=-=-=-=-=-=
#
# These values are derived from the ones above and should not need
# editing unless you have munged your mailman installation
#
# The path of the Mailman mail wrapper script
MM_WRAP=MM_HOME/mail/mailman
#
# The path of the list config file (used as a required file when
# verifying list addresses)
MM_LISTCHK=MM_HOME/lists/${lc::$local_part}/config.pck
# end
```

14.4.2.5. Transport

All the configuration files belonging to transport type are stored in the
/etc/exim4/conf.d/transport/ directory. You can add the following content to a new
file named 40_exim4-config_mailman:

```
  mailman_transport:
    driver = pipe
    command = MM_WRAP \
               '${if def:local_part_suffix \
                    {${sg{$local_part_suffix}{-(\\w+)(\\+.*)?}{\$1}}} \
                    {post}}' \
               $local_part
    current_directory = MM_HOME
    home_directory = MM_HOME
    user = MM_UID
    group = MM_GID
```

14.4.2.6. Router

All the configuration files belonging to router type are stored in the `/etc/exim4/conf.d/router/` directory. You can add the following content in to a new file named `101_exim4-config_mailman`:

```
mailman_router:
  driver = accept
  require_files = MM_HOME/lists/$local_part/config.pck
  local_part_suffix_optional
  local_part_suffix = -bounces : -bounces+* : \
                      -confirm+* : -join : -leave : \
                      -owner : -request : -admin
  transport = mailman_transport
```

 Warning

The order of main and transport configuration files can be in any order. But, the order of router configuration files must be the same. This particular file must appear before the **200_exim4-config_primary** file. These two configuration files contain same type of information. The first file takes the precedence. For more details, please refer to the references section.

14.4.2.7. Mailman

Once mailman is installed, you can run it using the following command:

```
sudo /etc/init.d/mailman start
```

Once mailman is installed, you should create the default mailing list. Run the following command to create the mailing list:

```
sudo /usr/sbin/newlist mailman
  Enter the email address of the person running the list: bhuvan at ubuntu.com
  Initial mailman password:
  To finish creating your mailing list, you must edit your /etc/aliases (or
  equivalent) file by adding the following lines, and possibly running the
  `newaliases' program:

## mailman mailing list
mailman:              "|/var/lib/mailman/mail/mailman post mailman"
mailman-admin:        "|/var/lib/mailman/mail/mailman admin mailman"
mailman-bounces:      "|/var/lib/mailman/mail/mailman bounces mailman"
mailman-confirm:      "|/var/lib/mailman/mail/mailman confirm mailman"
mailman-join:         "|/var/lib/mailman/mail/mailman join mailman"
mailman-leave:        "|/var/lib/mailman/mail/mailman leave mailman"
mailman-owner:        "|/var/lib/mailman/mail/mailman owner mailman"
mailman-request:      "|/var/lib/mailman/mail/mailman request mailman"
mailman-subscribe:    "|/var/lib/mailman/mail/mailman subscribe mailman"
mailman-unsubscribe:  "|/var/lib/mailman/mail/mailman unsubscribe mailman"

  Hit enter to notify mailman owner...

#
```

We have configured either Postfix or Exim4 to recognize all emails from mailman. So, it is not mandatory to make any new entries in /etc/aliases. If you have made any changes to the configuration files, please ensure that you restart those services before continuing to next section.

 Note

> The Exim4 does not use the above aliases to forward mails to Mailman, as it uses a *discover* approach. To suppress the aliases while creating the list, you can add *MTA=None* line in Mailman configuration file, /etc/mailman/mm_cfg.py.

14.4.3. Administration

We assume you have a default installation. The mailman cgi scripts are still in the **/usr/lib/cgi-bin/mailman/** directory. Mailman provides a web based administration facility. To access this page, point your browser to the next url: *http://hostname/cgi-bin/mailman/admin*

The default mailing list, *mailman*, will appear in this screen. If you click the mailing list name, it will ask for your authentication password. If you enter the correct password, you will be able to change administrative settings of this mailing list. You can create a new mailing list using the command line utility (**/usr/sbin/newlist**). Alternatively, you can create a new mailing list using the web interface.

14.4.4. Users

Mailman provides a web based interface for users. To access this page, point your browser to the following url: *http://hostname/cgi-bin/mailman/listinfo*

The default mailing list, *mailman*, will appear in this screen. If you click the mailing list name, it will display the subscription form. You can enter your email address, name (optional), and password to subscribe. An email invitation will be sent to you. You can follow the instructions in the email to subscribe.

14.4.5. References

- *GNU Mailman - Installation Manual*[19]

- *HOWTO - Using Exim 4 and Mailman 2.1 together*[20]

- Also, see the *Mailman Ubuntu Wiki*[21] page.

---

[19] *http://www.list.org/mailman-install/index.html*
[20] *http://www.exim.org/howto/mailman21.html*
[21] *https://help.ubuntu.com/community/Mailman*

14.5. Mail Filtering

One of the largest issues with email today is the problem of Unsolicited Bulk Email (UBE). Also known as SPAM, such messages may also carry viruses and other forms of malware. According to some reports these messages make up the bulk of all email traffic on the Internet.

This section will cover integrating **Amavisd-new**, **Spamassassin**, and **ClamAV** with the **Postfix** Mail Transport Agent (MTA). **Postfix** can also check email validity by passing it through external content filters. These filters can sometimes determine if a message is spam without needing to process it with more resource intensive applications. Two common filters are **opendkim** and **python-policyd-spf**.

- **Amavisd-new** is a wrapper program that can call any number of content filtering programs for spam detection, antivirus, etc.
- **Spamassassin** uses a variety of mechanisms to filter email based on the message content.
- **ClamAV** is an open source antivirus application.
- **opendkim** implements a Sendmail Mail Filter (Milter) for the DomainKeys Identified Mail (DKIM) standard.
- **python-policyd-spf** enables Sender Policy Framework (SPF) checking with **Postfix**.

This is how the pieces fit together:

- An email message is accepted by **Postfix**.
- The message is passed through any external filters **opendkim** and **python-policyd-spf** in this case.
- **Amavisd-new** then processes the message.
- **ClamAV** is used to scan the message. If the message contains a virus **Postfix** will reject the message.
- Clean messages will then be analyzed by **Spamassassin** to find out if the message is spam. **Spamassassin** will then add X-Header lines allowing **Amavisd-new** to further manipulate the message.

For example, if a message has a Spam score of over fifty the message could be automatically dropped from the queue without the recipient ever having to be bothered. Another, way to handle flagged messages is to deliver them to the Mail User Agent (MUA) allowing the user to deal with the message as they see fit.

14.5.1. Installation

See the Section 14.1, *Postfix* for instructions on installing and configuring Postfix.

To install the rest of the applications enter the following from a terminal prompt:

```
sudo apt-get install amavisd-new spamassassin clamav-daemon
sudo apt-get install opendkim python-policyd-spf
```

There are some optional packages that integrate with **Spamassassin** for better spam detection:

```
sudo apt-get install pyzor razor
```

Along with the main filtering applications compression utilities are needed to process some email attachments:

```
sudo apt-get install arj cabextract cpio lha nomarch pax rar unrar unzip zip
```

 Note

> If some packages are not found, check that the *multiverse* repository is enabled in `/etc/apt/sources.list`
>
> If you make changes to the file, be sure to run **sudo apt-get update** before trying to install again.

14.5.2. Configuration

Now configure everything to work together and filter email.

14.5.2.1. ClamAV

The default behaviour of **ClamAV** will fit our needs. For more ClamAV configuration options, check the configuration files in `/etc/clamav`.

Add the *clamav* user to the *amavis* group in order for **Amavisd-new** to have the appropriate access to scan files:

```
sudo adduser clamav amavis
```

14.5.2.2. Spamassassin

Spamassassin automatically detects optional components and will use them if they are present. This means that there is no need to configure **pyzor** and **razor**.

Edit `/etc/default/spamassassin` to activate the **Spamassassin** daemon. Change *ENABLED=0* to:

```
ENABLED=1
```

Now start the daemon:

```
sudo /etc/init.d/spamassassin start
```

14.5.2.3. Amavisd-new

First activate spam and antivirus detection in **Amavisd-new** by editing
`/etc/amavis/conf.d/15-content_filter_mode`:

```
use strict;

# You can modify this file to re-enable SPAM checking through spamassassin
# and to re-enable antivirus checking.

#
# Default antivirus checking mode
# Uncomment the two lines below to enable it
#

@bypass_virus_checks_maps = (
    \%bypass_virus_checks, \@bypass_virus_checks_acl, \$bypass_virus_checks_re);


#
# Default SPAM checking mode
# Uncomment the two lines below to enable it
#

@bypass_spam_checks_maps = (
    \%bypass_spam_checks, \@bypass_spam_checks_acl, \$bypass_spam_checks_re);

1;   # insure a defined return
```

Bouncing spam can be a bad idea as the return address is often faked. Consider editing
`/etc/amavis/conf.d/20-debian_defaults` to set *$final_spam_destiny* to D_DISCARD
rather than D_BOUNCE, as follows:

```
$final_spam_destiny        = D_DISCARD;
```

Additionally, you may want to adjust the following options to flag more messages as spam:

```
$sa_tag_level_deflt = -999;  # add spam info headers if at, or above that level
$sa_tag2_level_deflt = 6.0;  # add 'spam detected' headers at that level
$sa_kill_level_deflt = 21.0; # triggers spam evasive actions
$sa_dsn_cutoff_level = 4;    # spam level beyond which a DSN is not sent
```

If the server's *hostname* is different from the domain's MX record you may need to manually
set the *$myhostname* option. Also, if the server receives mail for multiple domains the
@local_domains_acl option will need to be customized. Edit the `/etc/amavis/conf.d/50-user` file:

```
$myhostname = 'mail.example.com';
@local_domains_acl = ("example.com", "example.org");
```

After configuration **Amavisd-new** needs to be restarted:

```
sudo /etc/init.d/amavis restart
```

14.5.2.3.1 DKIM Whitelist

Amavisd-new can be configured to automatically *Whitelist* addresses from domains with valid Domain Keys. There are some pre-configured domains in the `/etc/amavis/conf.d/40-policy_banks`.

There are multiple ways to configure the Whitelist for a domain:

- *'example.com' => 'WHITELIST'*,: will whitelist any address from the "example.com" domain.
- *'.example.com' => 'WHITELIST'*,: will whitelist any address from any *subdomains* of "example.com" that have a valid signature.
- *'.example.com/@example.com' => 'WHITELIST'*,: will whitelist subdomains of "example.com" that use the signature of example.com the parent domain.
- *'./@example.com' => 'WHITELIST'*,: adds addresses that have a valid signature from "example.com". This is usually used for discussion groups that sign their messages.

A domain can also have multiple Whitelist configurations. After editing the file, restart **amavisd-new**:

```
sudo /etc/init.d/amavis restart
```

 Note

> In this context, once a domain has been added to the Whitelist the message will not receive any anti-virus or spam filtering. This may or may not be the intended behavior you wish for a domain.

14.5.2.4. Postfix

For **Postfix** integration, enter the following from a terminal prompt:

```
sudo postconf -e 'content_filter = smtp-amavis:[127.0.0.1]:10024'
```

Next edit `/etc/postfix/master.cf` and add the following to the end of the file:

```
smtp-amavis      unix    -       -       -       -       2       smtp
        -o smtp_data_done_timeout=1200
        -o smtp_send_xforward_command=yes
        -o disable_dns_lookups=yes
        -o max_use=20

127.0.0.1:10025 inet    n       -       -       -       -       smtpd
        -o content_filter=
        -o local_recipient_maps=
        -o relay_recipient_maps=
        -o smtpd_restriction_classes=
        -o smtpd_delay_reject=no
        -o smtpd_client_restrictions=permit_mynetworks,reject
        -o smtpd_helo_restrictions=
        -o smtpd_sender_restrictions=
```

```
        -o smtpd_recipient_restrictions=permit_mynetworks,reject
        -o smtpd_data_restrictions=reject_unauth_pipelining
        -o smtpd_end_of_data_restrictions=
        -o mynetworks=127.0.0.0/8
        -o smtpd_error_sleep_time=0
        -o smtpd_soft_error_limit=1001
        -o smtpd_hard_error_limit=1000
        -o smtpd_client_connection_count_limit=0
        -o smtpd_client_connection_rate_limit=0
        -o
receive_override_options=no_header_body_checks,no_unknown_recipient_checks
```

Also add the following two lines immediately below the "*pickup*" transport service:

```
        -o content_filter=
        -o receive_override_options=no_header_body_checks
```

This will prevent messages that are generated to report on spam from being classified as spam.

Now restart **Postfix**:

```
sudo /etc/init.d/postfix restart
```

Content filtering with spam and virus detection is now enabled.

14.5.2.5. Amavisd-new and Spamassassin

When integrating **Amavisd-new** with **Spamassassin**, if you choose to disable the bayes filtering by editing /etc/spamassassin/local.cf and use **cron** to update the nightly rules, the result can cause a situation where a large amount of error messages are sent to the *amavis* user via the amavisd-new **cron** job.

There are several ways to handle this situation:

- Configure your MDA to filter messages you do not wish to see.
- Change /usr/sbin/amavisd-new-cronjob to check for *use_bayes 0*. For example, edit /usr/sbin/amavisd-new-cronjob and add the following to the top before the *test* statements:
  ```
  egrep -q "^[ \t]*use_bayes[ \t]*0" /etc/spamassassin/local.cf && exit 0
  ```

14.5.3. Testing

First, test that the **Amavisd-new** SMTP is listening:

```
telnet localhost 10024
Trying 127.0.0.1...
Connected to localhost.
Escape character is '^]'.
220 [127.0.0.1] ESMTP amavisd-new service ready
^]
```

In the Header of messages that go through the content filter you should see:

```
X-Spam-Level:
X-Virus-Scanned: Debian amavisd-new at example.com
X-Spam-Status: No, hits=-2.3 tagged_above=-1000.0 required=5.0 tests=AWL, BAYES_00
X-Spam-Level:
```

 Note

> Your output will vary, but the important thing is that there are *X-Virus-Scanned* and *X-Spam-Status* entries.

14.5.4. Troubleshooting

The best way to figure out why something is going wrong is to check the log files.

- For instructions on **Postfix** logging see the Section 14.1.7, *Troubleshooting*.
- **Amavisd-new** uses **Syslog** to send messages to /var/log/mail.log. The amount of detail can be increased by adding the *$log_level* option to /etc/amavis/conf.d/50-user, and setting the value from 1 to 5.
  ```
  $log_level = 2;
  ```

 Note

> When the **Amavisd-new** log output is increased **Spamassassin** log output is also increased.

- The **ClamAV** log level can be increased by editing /etc/clamav/clamd.conf and setting the following option:
  ```
  LogVerbose true
  ```
  By default **ClamAV** will send log messages to /var/log/clamav/clamav.log.

 Note

> After changing an applications log settings remember to restart the service for the new settings to take affect. Also, once the issue you are troubleshooting is resolved it is a good idea to change the log settings back to normal.

14.5.5. References

For more information on filtering mail see the following links:

- *Amavisd-new Documentation*[22]
- *ClamAV Documentation*[23] and *ClamAV Wiki*[24]

---

[22] *http://www.ijs.si/software/amavisd/amavisd-new-docs.html*
[23] *http://www.clamav.org/doc/latest/html/*

- *Spamassassin Wiki*[25]
- *Pyzor Homepage*[26]
- *Razor Homepage*[27]
- *DKIM.org*[28]
- *Postfix Amavis New*[29]

Also, feel free to ask questions in the *#ubuntu-server* IRC channel on *freenode*[30].

[24] *http://wiki.clamav.net/Main/WebHome*

[25] *http://wiki.apache.org/spamassassin/*

[26] *http://pyzor.sourceforge.net/*

[27] *http://razor.sourceforge.net/*

[28] *http://dkim.org/*

[29] *https://help.ubuntu.com/community/PostfixAmavisNew*

[30] *http://freenode.net/*

Chapter 15.
Chat Applications

15.1. Overview

In this section, we will discuss how to install and configure a IRC server, **ircd-irc2**. We will also discuss how to install and configure Jabber, an instance messaging server.

15.2. IRC Server

The Ubuntu repository has many Internet Relay Chat servers. This section explains how to install and configure the original IRC server **ircd-irc2**.

15.2.1. Installation

To install **ircd-irc2**, run the following command in the command prompt:

```
sudo apt-get install ircd-irc2
```

The configuration files are stored in /etc/ircd directory. The documents are available in /usr/share/doc/ircd-irc2 directory.

15.2.2. Configuration

The IRC settings can be done in the configuration file /etc/ircd/ircd.conf. You can set the IRC host name in this file by editing the following line:

```
M:irc.localhost::Debian ircd default configuration::000A
```

Please make sure you add DNS aliases for the IRC host name. For instance, if you set irc.livecipher.com as IRC host name, please make sure irc.livecipher.com is resolvable in your Domain Name Server. The IRC host name should not be same as the host name.

The IRC admin details can be configured by editing the following line:

```
A:Organization, IRC dept.:Daemon <ircd@example.irc.org>:Client Server::IRCnet:
```

You should add specific lines to configure the list of IRC ports to listen on, to configure Operator credentials, to configure client authentication, etc. For details, please refer to the example configuration file /usr/share/doc/ircd-irc2/ircd.conf.example.gz.

The IRC banner to be displayed in the IRC client, when the user connects to the server can be set in /etc/ircd/ircd.motd file.

After making necessary changes to the configuration file, you can restart the IRC server using following command:

```
sudo /etc/init.d/ircd-irc2 restart
```

15.2.3. References

You may also be interested to take a look at other IRC servers available in Ubuntu Repository. It includes, **ircd-ircu** and **ircd-hybrid**.

- Refer to *IRCD FAQ*[1] for more details about the IRC Server.

- Also, the *Ubuntu Wiki IRCD*[2] page has more information.

15.3. Jabber Instant Messaging Server

Jabber a popular instant message protocol is based on XMPP, an open standard for instant messaging, and used by many popular applications. This section covers setting up a *Jabberd* 2 server on a local LAN. This configuration can also be adapted to providing messaging services to users over the Internet.

15.3.1. Installation

To install **jabberd2**, in a terminal enter:

```
sudo apt-get install jabberd2
```

15.3.2. Configuration

A couple of XML configuration files will be used to configure **jabberd2** for *Berkely DB* user authentication. This is a very simple form of authentication. However, **jabberd2** can be configured to use LDAP, MySQL, PostgreSQL, etc for for user authentication.

First, edit /etc/jabberd2/sm.xml changing:

```
<id>jabber.example.com</id>
```

Note

Replace *jabber.example.com* with the hostname, or other id, of your server.

Now in the <storage> section change the <driver> to:

```
<driver>db</driver>
```

---

[1] *http://www.irc.org/tech_docs/ircnet/faq.html*
[2] *https://help.ubuntu.com/community/ircd*

Next, edit `/etc/jabberd2/c2s.xml` in the *<local>* section change:

```
<id>jabber.example.com</id>
```

And in the <authreg> section adjust the <module> section to:

```
<module>db</module>
```

Finally, restart **jabberd2** to enable the new settings:

```
sudo /etc/init.d/jabberd2 restart
```

You should now be able to connect to the server using a Jabber client like **Pidgin** for example.

 Note

The advantage of using Berkeley DB for user data is that after being configured no additional maintenance is required. If you need more control over user accounts and credentials another authentication method is recommended.

15.3.3. References

- The *Jabberd2 Web Site*[3] contains more details on configuring **Jabberd2**.

- For more authentication options see the *Jabberd2 Install Guide*[4].

- Also, the *Setting Up Jabber Server Ubuntu Wiki*[5] page has more information.

---

[3] *http://codex.xiaoka.com/wiki/jabberd2:start*

[4] *http://www.jabberdoc.org/*

[5] *https://help.ubuntu.com/community/SettingUpJabberServer*

Chapter 16.
Version Control System

Version control is the art of managing changes to information. It has long been a critical tool for programmers, who typically spend their time making small changes to software and then undoing those changes the next day. But the usefulness of version control software extends far beyond the bounds of the software development world. Anywhere you can find people using computers to manage information that changes often, there is room for version control.

16.1. Bazaar

Bazaar is a new version control system sponsored by Canonical, the commercial company behind Ubuntu. Unlike Subversion and CVS that only support a central repository model, Bazaar also supports *distributed version control*, giving people the ability to collaborate more efficiently. In particular, Bazaar is designed to maximize the level of community participation in open source projects.

16.1.1. Installation

At a terminal prompt, enter the following command to install **bzr**:

```
sudo apt-get install bzr
```

16.1.2. Configuration

To introduce yourself to **bzr**, use the *whoami* command like this:

```
$ bzr whoami 'Joe Doe <joe.doe@gmail.com>'
```

16.1.3. Learning Bazaar

Bazaar comes with bundled documentation installed into **/usr/share/doc/bzr/html** by default. The tutorial is a good place to start. The **bzr** command also comes with built-in help:

```
$ bzr help
```

To learn more about the *foo* command:

```
$ bzr help foo
```

16.1.4. Launchpad Integration

While highly useful as a stand-alone system, Bazaar has good, optional integration with *Launchpad*[1], the collaborative development system used by Canonical and the broader open source community to manage and extend Ubuntu itself. For information on how Bazaar can be used with Launchpad to collaborate on open source projects, see *http://bazaar-vcs.org/LaunchpadIntegration*.

16.2. Subversion

Subversion is an open source version control system. Using Subversion, you can record the history of source files and documents. It manages files and directories over time. A tree of files is placed into a central repository. The repository is much like an ordinary file server, except that it remembers every change ever made to files and directories.

16.2.1. Installation

To access Subversion repository using the HTTP protocol, you must install and configure a web server. Apache2 is proven to work with Subversion. Please refer to the HTTP subsection in the Apache2 section to install and configure Apache2. To access the Subversion repository using the HTTPS protocol, you must install and configure a digital certificate in your Apache 2 web server. Please refer to the HTTPS subsection in the Apache2 section to install and configure the digital certificate.

To install Subversion, run the following command from a terminal prompt:

```
sudo apt-get install subversion libapache2-svn
```

16.2.2. Server Configuration

This step assumes you have installed above mentioned packages on your system. This section explains how to create a Subversion repository and access the project.

16.2.2.1. Create Subversion Repository

The Subversion repository can be created using the following command from a terminal prompt:

```
svnadmin create /path/to/repos/project
```

16.2.2.2. Importing Files

Once you create the repository you can *import* files into the repository. To import a directory, enter the following from a terminal prompt:

```
svn import /path/to/import/directory file:///path/to/repos/project
```

---

[1] *https://launchpad.net/*

16.2.3. Access Methods

Subversion repositories can be accessed (checked out) through many different methods --on local disk, or through various network protocols. A repository location, however, is always a URL. The table describes how different URL schemes map to the available access methods.

Schema	Access Method
file://	direct repository access (on local disk)
http://	Access via WebDAV protocol to Subversion-aware Apache2 web server
https://	Same as http://, but with SSL encryption
svn://	Access via custom protocol to an svnserve server
svn+ssh://	Same as svn://, but through an SSH tunnel

Table 16.1. Access Methods

In this section, we will see how to configure Subversion for all these access methods. Here, we cover the basics. For more advanced usage details, refer to the *svn book*[2].

16.2.3.1. Direct repository access (file://)

This is the simplest of all access methods. It does not require any Subversion server process to be running. This access method is used to access Subversion from the same machine. The syntax of the command, entered at a terminal prompt, is as follows:

```
svn co file:///path/to/repos/project
```

or

```
svn co file://localhost/path/to/repos/project
```

 Note

> If you do not specify the hostname, there are three forward slashes (///) -- two for the protocol (file, in this case) plus the leading slash in the path. If you specify the hostname, you must use two forward slashes (//).

The repository permissions depend on filesystem permissions. If the user has read/write permission, he can checkout from and commit to the repository.

16.2.3.2. Access via WebDAV protocol (http://)

To access the Subversion repository via WebDAV protocol, you must configure your Apache 2 web server. Add the following snippet between the *<VirtualHost>* and

---

[2] *http://svnbook.red-bean.com/*

</VirtualHost> elements in `/etc/apache2/sites-available/default`, or another
VirtualHost file:

```
<Location /svn>
  DAV svn
  SVNPath /home/svn
  AuthType Basic
  AuthName "Your repository name"
  AuthUserFile /etc/subversion/passwd
  Require valid-user
</Location>
```

Note

The above configuration snippet assumes that Subversion repositories are created
under `/home/svn/` directory using **svnadmin** command. They can be accessible
using *http://hostname/svn/repos_name* url.

To import or commit files to your Subversion repository over HTTP, the repository should
be owned by the HTTP user. In Ubuntu systems, normally the HTTP user is **www-data**. To
change the ownership of the repository files enter the following command from terminal
prompt:

```
sudo chown -R www-data:www-data /path/to/repos
```

Note

By changing the ownership of repository as **www-data** you will not be able to
import or commit files into the repository by running **svn import file:///** command as
any user other than **www-data**.

Next, you must create the `/etc/subversion/passwd` file that will contain user
authentication details. To create a file issue the following command at a command prompt
(which will create the file and add the first user):

```
sudo htpasswd -c /etc/subversion/passwd user_name
```

To add additional users omit the "*-c*" option as this option replaces the old file. Instead use
this form:

```
sudo htpasswd /etc/subversion/passwd user_name
```

This command will prompt you to enter the password. Once you enter the password, the
user is added. Now, to access the repository you can run the following command:

```
              svn co http://servername/svn
```

Warning

The password is transmitted as plain text. If you are worried about password snoo-
ping, you are advised to use SSL encryption. For details, please refer next section.

16.2.3.3. Access via WebDAV protocol with SSL encryption (https://)

Accessing Subversion repository via WebDAV protocol with SSL encryption (https://) is similar to http:// except that you must install and configure the digital certificate in your Apache2 web server. To use SSL with Subversion add the above Apache2 configuration to `/etc/apache2/sites-available/default-ssl`. For more information on setting up Apache2 with SSL see the Section 10.1.3, *HTTPS Configuration*.

You can install a digital certificate issued by a signing authority. Alternatively, you can install your own self-signed certificate.

This step assumes you have installed and configured a digital certificate in your Apache 2 web server. Now, to access the Subversion repository, please refer to the above section! The access methods are exactly the same, except the protocol. You must use https:// to access the Subversion repository.

16.2.3.4. Access via custom protocol (svn://)

Once the Subversion repository is created, you can configure the access control. You can edit the `/path/to/repos/project/conf/svnserve.conf` file to configure the access control. For example, to set up authentication, you can uncomment the following lines in the configuration file:

```
# [general]
# password-db = passwd
```

After uncommenting the above lines, you can maintain the user list in the passwd file. So, edit the file `passwd` in the same directory and add the new user. The syntax is as follows:

```
username = password
```

For more details, please refer to the file.

Now, to access Subversion via the svn:// custom protocol, either from the same machine or a different machine, you can run svnserver using svnserve command. The syntax is as follows:

```
$ svnserve -d --foreground -r /path/to/repos
# -d -- daemon mode
# --foreground -- run in foreground (useful for debugging)
# -r -- root of directory to serve

For more usage details, please refer to:
$ svnserve --help
```

Once you run this command, Subversion starts listening on default port (3690). To access the project repository, you must run the following command from a terminal prompt:

```
svn co svn://hostname/project project --username user_name
```

Based on server configuration, it prompts for password. Once you are authenticated, it checks out the code from Subversion repository. To synchronize the project repository with the local copy, you can run the **update** sub-command. The syntax of the command, entered at a terminal prompt, is as follows:

```
cd project_dir ; svn update
```

For more details about using each Subversion sub-command, you can refer to the manual. For example, to learn more about the co (checkout) command, please run the following command from a terminal prompt:

```
                    svn co help
```

16.2.3.5. Access via custom protocol with SSL encryption (svn+ssh://)

The configuration and server process is same as in the svn:// method. For details, please refer to the above section. This step assumes you have followed the above step and started the Subversion server using **svnserve** command.

It is also assumed that the ssh server is running on that machine and that it is allowing incoming connections. To confirm, please try to login to that machine using ssh. If you can login, everything is perfect. If you cannot login, please address it before continuing further.

The svn+ssh:// protocol is used to access the Subversion repository using SSL encryption. The data transfer is encrypted using this method. To access the project repository (for example with a checkout), you must use the following command syntax:

```
svn co svn+ssh://hostname/var/svn/repos/project
```

 Note

> You must use the full path (/path/to/repos/project) to access the Subversion repository using this access method.

Based on server configuration, it prompts for password. You must enter the password you use to login via ssh. Once you are authenticated, it checks out the code from the Subversion repository.

16.3. CVS Server

CVS is a version control system. You can use it to record the history of source files.

16.3.1. Installation

To install **CVS**, run the following command from a terminal prompt:

```
sudo apt-get install cvs
```

After you install **cvs**, you should install **xinetd** to start/stop the cvs server. At the prompt, enter the following command to install **xinetd**:

```
sudo apt-get install xinetd
```

16.3.2. Configuration

Once you install cvs, the repository will be automatically initialized. By default, the repository resides under the **/srv/cvs** directory. You can change this path by running following command:

```
cvs -d /your/new/cvs/repo init
```

Once the initial repository is set up, you can configure **xinetd** to start the CVS server. You can copy the following lines to the /etc/xinetd.d/cvspserver file.

```
service cvspserver
{
    port = 2401
    socket_type = stream
    protocol = tcp
    user = root
    wait = no
    type = UNLISTED
    server = /usr/bin/cvs
    server_args = -f --allow-root /srv/cvs pserver
    disable = no
}
```

Note

Be sure to edit the repository if you have changed the default repository (**/srv/cvs**) directory.

Once you have configured **xinetd** you can start the cvs server by running following command:

```
sudo /etc/init.d/xinetd restart
```

You can confirm that the CVS server is running by issuing the following command:

```
sudo netstat -tap | grep cvs
```

When you run this command, you should see the following line or something similar:

```
tcp        0      0 *:cvspserver            *:* LISTEN
```

From here you can continue to add users, add new projects, and manage the CVS server.

Warning

CVS allows the user to add users independently of the underlying OS installation. Probably the easiest way is to use the Linux Users for CVS, although it has potential security issues. Please refer to the CVS manual for details.

16.3.3. Add Projects

This section explains how to add new project to the CVS repository. Create the directory and add necessary document and source files to the directory. Now, run the following command to add this project to CVS repository:

```
cd your/project
cvs -d :pserver:username@hostname.com: /srv/cvs import -m "Importing my project to
CVS repository" . new_project start
```

Tip

You can use the CVSROOT environment variable to store the CVS root directory. Once you export the CVSROOT environment variable, you can avoid using -d option in the above cvs command.

The string *new_project* is a vendor tag, and *start* is a release tag. They serve no purpose in this context, but since CVS requires them, they must be present.

Warning

When you add a new project, the CVS user you use must have write access to the CVS repository (**/srv/cvs**). By default, the **src** group has write access to the CVS repository. So, you can add the user to this group, and he can then add and manage projects in the CVS repository.

16.4. References

- *Bazaar Home Page*[3]
- *Launchpad*[4]
- *Subversion Home Page*[5]
- *Subversion Book*[6]
- *CVS Manual*[7]
- *Easy Bazaar Ubuntu Wiki*[8] page
- *Ubuntu Wiki Subversion*[9] page

---

[3] *http://bazaar-vcs.org/*
[4] *https://launchpad.net/*
[5] *http://subversion.tigris.org/*
[6] *http://svnbook.red-bean.com/*
[7] *http://ximbiot.com/cvs/manual/cvs-1.11.21/cvs_toc.html*
[8] *https://help.ubuntu.com/community/EasyBazaar*
[9] *https://help.ubuntu.com/community/Subversion*

Chapter 17.
Windows Networking

Computer networks are often comprised of diverse systems, and while operating a network made up entirely of Ubuntu desktop and server computers would certainly be fun, some network environments must consist of both Ubuntu and Microsoft® Windows® systems working together in harmony. This section of the Ubuntu Server Guide introduces principles and tools used in configuring your Ubuntu Server for sharing network resources with Windows computers.

17.1. Introduction

Successfully networking your Ubuntu system with Windows clients involves providing and integrating with services common to Windows environments. Such services assist the sharing of data and information about the computers and users involved in the network, and may be classified under three major categories of functionality:

- **File and Printer Sharing Services**. Using the Server Message Block (SMB) protocol to facilitate the sharing of files, folders, volumes, and the sharing of printers throughout the network.
- **Directory Services**. Sharing vital information about the computers and users of the network with such technologies as the Lightweight Directory Access Protocol (LDAP) and Microsoft Active Directory®.
- **Authentication and Access**. Establishing the identity of a computer or user of the network and determining the information the computer or user is authorized to access using such principles and technologies as file permissions, group policies, and the Kerberos authentication service.

Fortunately, your Ubuntu system may provide all such facilities to Windows clients and share network resources among them. One of the principal pieces of software your Ubuntu system includes for Windows networking is the Samba suite of SMB server applications and tools.

This section of the Ubuntu Server Guide will introduce some of the common Samba use cases, and how to install and configure the necessary packages. Additional detailed documentation and information on Samba can be found on the *Samba website*[1].

---

[1] *http://www.samba.org/*

17.2. Samba File Server

One of the most common ways to network Ubuntu and Windows computers is to configure Samba as a File Server. This section covers setting up a **Samba** server to share files with Windows clients.

The server will be configured to share files with any client on the network without prompting for a password. If your environment requires stricter Access Controls see the Section 17.4, *Securing a Samba File and Print Server*.

17.2.1. Installation

The first step is to install the **samba** package. From a terminal prompt enter:

```
sudo apt-get install samba
```

That's all there is to it; you are now ready to configure Samba to share files.

17.2.2. Configuration

The main Samba configuration file is located in /etc/samba/smb.conf. The default configuration file has a significant amount of comments in order to document various configuration directives.

Note

Not all the available options are included in the default configuration file. See the smb.conf **man** page or the *Samba HOWTO Collection*[2] for more details.

1. First, edit the following key/value pairs in the *[global]* section of /etc/samba/smb.conf:

   ```
   workgroup = EXAMPLE
   ...
   security = user
   ```

   The *security* parameter is farther down in the [global] section, and is commented by default. Also, change *EXAMPLE* to better match your environment.

2. Create a new section at the bottom of the file, or uncomment one of the examples, for the directory to be shared:

   ```
   [share]
       comment = Ubuntu File Server Share
       path = /srv/samba/share
       browsable = yes
       guest ok = yes
       read only = no
       create mask = 0755
   ```

---

[2] *http://samba.org/samba/docs/man/Samba-HOWTO-Collection/*

- *comment:* a short description of the share. Adjust to fit your needs.
- *path:* the path to the directory to share.
- This example uses `/srv/samba/sharename` because, according to the *Filesystem Hierarchy Standard (FHS)*, */srv*[3] is where site-specific data should be served. Technically Samba shares can be placed anywhere on the filesystem as long as the permissions are correct, but adhering to standards is recommended.
- *browsable:* enables Windows clients to browse the shared directory using **Windows Explorer**.
- *guest ok:* allows clients to connect to the share without supplying a password.
- *read only:* determines if the share is read only or if write privileges are granted. Write privileges are allowed only when the value is *no*, as is seen in this example. If the value is *yes*, then access to the share is read only.
- *create mask:* determines the permissions new files will have when created.

3. Now that **Samba** is configured, the directory needs to be created and the permissions changed. From a terminal enter:

```
sudo mkdir -p /srv/samba/share
sudo chown nobody.nogroup /srv/samba/share/
```

Note

The *-p* switch tells mkdir to create the entire directory tree if it doesn't exist.

4. Finally, restart the **samba** services to enable the new configuration:

```
sudo restart smbd
sudo restart nmbd
```

Warning

Once again, the above configuration gives all access to any client on the local network. For a more secure configuration see the Section 17.4, *Securing a Samba File and Print Server*.

From a Windows client you should now be able to browse to the Ubuntu file server and see the shared directory. To check that everything is working try creating a directory from Windows.

To create additional shares simply create new *[dir]* sections in `/etc/samba/smb.conf`, and restart *Samba*. Just make sure that the directory you want to share actually exists and the permissions are correct.

---

[3] *http://www.pathname.com/fhs/pub/fhs-2.3.html#SRVDATAFORSERVICESPROVIDEDBYSYSTEM*

Note

The file share named "*[share]*" and the path /srv/samba/share are just examples. Adjust the share and path names to fit your environment. It is a good idea to name a share after a directory on the file system. Another example would be a share name of *[qa]* with a path of /srv/samba/qa.

17.2.3. Resources

- For in depth Samba configurations see the *Samba HOWTO Collection*[4]
- The guide is also available in *printed format*[5].
- O'Reilly's *Using Samba*[6] is another good reference.
- The *Ubuntu Wiki Samba*[7] page.

17.3. Samba Print Server

Another common use of Samba is to configure it to share printers installed, either locally or over the network, on an Ubuntu server. Similar to the Section 17.2, *Samba File Server* this section will configure Samba to allow any client on the local network to use the installed printers without prompting for a username and password.

For a more secure configuration see the Section 17.4, *Securing a Samba File and Print Server*.

17.3.1. Installation

Before installing and configuring Samba it is best to already have a working **CUPS** installation. See the Section 13.3, *CUPS - Print Server* for details.

To install the **samba** package, from a terminal enter:

```
sudo apt-get install samba
```

17.3.2. Configuration

After installing samba edit /etc/samba/smb.conf. Change the *workgroup* attribute to what is appropriate for your network, and change *security* to share:

```
workgroup = EXAMPLE
...
security = user
```

---

[4] *http://samba.org/samba/docs/man/Samba-HOWTO-Collection/*
[5] *http://www.amazon.com/exec/obidos/tg/detail/-/0131882228*
[6] *http://www.oreilly.com/catalog/9780596007690/*
[7] *https://help.ubuntu.com/community/Samba*

In the *[printers]* section change the *guest ok* option to yes:

```
browsable = yes
guest ok = yes
```

After editing `smb.conf` restart Samba:

```
sudo restart smbd
sudo restart nmbd
```

The default Samba configuration will automatically share any printers installed. Simply install the printer locally on your Windows clients.

17.3.3. Resources

- For in depth Samba configurations see the *Samba HOWTO Collection*[8]
- The guide is also available in *printed format*[9].
- O'Reilly's *Using Samba*[10] is another good reference.
- Also, see the *CUPS Website*[11] for more information on configuring CUPS.
- The *Ubuntu Wiki Samba*[12] page.

17.4. Securing a Samba File and Print Server

17.4.1. Samba Security Modes

There are two security levels available to the Common Internet Filesystem (CIFS) network protocol *user-level* and *share-level*. Samba's *security mode* implementation allows more flexibility, providing four ways of implementing user-level security and one way to implement share-level:

- *security = user:* requires clients to supply a username and password to connect to shares. Samba user accounts are separate from system accounts, but the **libpam-smbpass** package will sync system users and passwords with the Samba user database.
- *security = domain:* this mode allows the Samba server to appear to Windows clients as a Primary Domain Controller (PDC), Backup Domain Controller (BDC), or a Domain Member Server (DMS). See the Section 17.5, *Samba as a Domain Controller* for further information.

---

[8] *http://samba.org/samba/docs/man/Samba-HOWTO-Collection/*
[9] *http://www.amazon.com/exec/obidos/tg/detail/-/0131882228*
[10] *http://www.oreilly.com/catalog/9780596007690/*
[11] *http://www.cups.org/*
[12] *https://help.ubuntu.com/community/Samba*

- *security = ADS:* allows the Samba server to join an Active Directory domain as a native member. See the Section 17.6, *Samba Active Directory Integration* for details.

- *security = server:* this mode is left over from before Samba could become a member server, and due to some security issues should not be used. See the *Server Security*[13] section of the Samba guide for more details.

- *security = share:* allows clients to connect to shares without supplying a username and password.

The security mode you choose will depend on your environment and what you need the Samba server to accomplish.

17.4.2. Security = User

This section will reconfigure the Samba file and print server, from the Section 17.2, *Samba File Server* and the Section 17.3, *Samba Print Server*, to require authentication.

First, install the **libpam-smbpass** package which will sync the system users to the Samba user database:

```
sudo apt-get install libpam-smbpass
```

Note

If you chose the *Samba Server* task during installation **libpam-smbpass** is already installed.

Edit /etc/samba/smb.conf, and in the *[share]* section change:

```
    guest ok = no
```

Finally, restart Samba for the new settings to take effect:

```
sudo restart smbd
sudo restart nmbd
```

Now when connecting to the shared directories or printers you should be prompted for a username and password.

Note

If you choose to map a network drive to the share you can check the "Reconnect at Logon" check box, which will require you to only enter the username and password once, at least until the password changes.

---

[13] *http://samba.org/samba/docs/man/Samba-HOWTO-Collection/ServerType.html#id349531*

17.4.3. Share Security

There are several options available to increase the security for each individual shared directory. Using the *[share]* example, this section will cover some common options.

17.4.3.1. Groups

Groups define a collection of computers or users which have a common level of access to particular network resources and offer a level of granularity in controlling access to such resources. For example, if a group qa is defined and contains the users freda, danika, and rob and a second group support is defined and consists of users danika, jeremy, and vincent then certain network resources configured to allow access by the qa group will subsequently enable access by freda, danika, and rob, but not jeremy or vincent. Since the user danika belongs to both the qa and support groups, she will be able to access resources configured for access by both groups, whereas all other users will have only access to resources explicitly allowing the group they are part of.

By default Samba looks for the local system groups defined in /etc/group to determine which users belong to which groups. For more information on adding and removing users from groups see the Section 8.1.2, *Adding and Deleting Users*.

When defining groups in the Samba configuration file, /etc/samba/smb.conf, the recognized syntax is to preface the group name with an "@" symbol. For example, if you wished to define a group named sysadmin in a certain section of the /etc/samba/smb.conf, you would do so by entering the group name as **@sysadmin**.

17.4.3.2. File Permissions

File Permissions define the explicit rights a computer or user has to a particular directory, file, or set of files. Such permissions may be defined by editing the /etc/samba/smb.conf file and specifying the explicit permissions of a defined file share.

For example, if you have defined a Samba share called *share* and wish to give read-only permissions to the group of users known as qa, but wanted to allow writing to the share by the group called sysadmin and the user named vincent, then you could edit the /etc/samba/smb.conf file, and add the following entries under the *[share]* entry:

```
read list = @qa
write list = @sysadmin, vincent
```

Another possible Samba permission is to declare *administrative* permissions to a particular shared resource. Users having administrative permissions may read, write, or modify any information contained in the resource the user has been given explicit administrative permissions to.

For example, if you wanted to give the user melissa administrative permissions to the share example, you would edit the /etc/samba/smb.conf file, and add the following line under the *[share]* entry:

```
    admin users = melissa
```

After editing /etc/samba/smb.conf, restart Samba for the changes to take effect:

```
sudo restart smbd
sudo restart nmbd
```

Note

> For the *read list* and *write list* to work the Samba security mode must *not* be set to security = share

Now that Samba has been configured to limit which groups have access to the shared directory, the filesystem permissions need to be updated.

Traditional Linux file permissions do not map well to Windows NT Access Control Lists (ACLs). Fortunately POSIX ACLs are available on Ubuntu servers providing more fine grained control. For example, to enable ACLs on /srv an EXT3 filesystem, edit /etc/fstab adding the *acl* option:

```
UUID=66bcdd2e-8861-4fb0-b7e4-e61c569fe17d /srv   ext3    noatime,relatime,acl 0      1
```

Then remount the partition:

```
sudo mount -v -o remount /srv
```

Note

> The above example assumes /srv on a separate partition. If /srv, or wherever you have configured your share path, is part of the / partition a reboot may be required.

To match the Samba configuration above the *sysadmin* group will be given read, write, and execute permissions to /srv/samba/share, the *qa* group will be given read and execute permissions, and the files will be owned by the username *melissa*. Enter the following in a terminal:

```
sudo chown -R melissa /srv/samba/share/
sudo chgrp -R sysadmin /srv/samba/share/
sudo setfacl -R -m g:qa:rx /srv/samba/share/
```

Note

> The **setfacl** command above gives *execute* permissions to all files in the /srv/samba/share directory, which you may or may not want.

Now from a Windows client you should notice the new file permissions are implemented. See the **acl** and **setfacl** man pages for more information on POSIX ACLs.

17.4.4. Samba AppArmor Profile

Ubuntu comes with the **AppArmor** security module, which provides mandatory access controls. The default AppArmor profile for Samba will need to be adapted to your configuration. For more details on using AppArmor see the Section 8.4, *AppArmor*.

There are default AppArmor profiles for `/usr/sbin/smbd` and `/usr/sbin/nmbd`, the Samba daemon binaries, as part of the **apparmor-profiles** packages. To install the package, from a terminal prompt enter:

```
sudo apt-get install apparmor-profiles
```

 Note

This package contains profiles for several other binaries.

By default the profiles for **smbd** and **nmbd** are in *complain* mode allowing Samba to work without modifying the profile, and only logging errors. To place the **smbd** profile into *enforce* mode, and have Samba work as expected, the profile will need to be modified to reflect any directories that are shared.

Edit `/etc/apparmor.d/usr.sbin.smbd` adding information for *[share]* from the file server example:

```
/srv/samba/share/ r,
/srv/samba/share/** rwkix,
```

Now place the profile into *enforce* and reload it:

```
sudo aa-enforce /usr/sbin/smbd
cat /etc/apparmor.d/usr.sbin.smbd | sudo apparmor_parser -r
```

You should now be able to read, write, and execute files in the shared directory as normal, and the **smbd** binary will have access to only the configured files and directories. Be sure to add entries for each directory you configure Samba to share. Also, any errors will be logged to `/var/log/syslog`.

17.4.5. Resources

- For in depth Samba configurations see the *Samba HOWTO Collection*[14]
- The guide is also available in *printed format*[15].
- O'Reilly's *Using Samba*[16] is also a good reference.
- *Chapter 18*[17] of the Samba HOWTO Collection is devoted to security.

---

[14] *http://samba.org/samba/docs/man/Samba-HOWTO-Collection/*
[15] *http://www.amazon.com/exec/obidos/tg/detail/-/0131882228*
[16] *http://www.oreilly.com/catalog/9780596007690/*

- For more information on Samba and ACLs see the *Samba ACLs page*[18].
- The *Ubuntu Wiki Samba*[19] page.

17.5. Samba as a Domain Controller

Although it cannot act as an Active Directory Primary Domain Controller (PDC), a Samba server can be configured to appear as a Windows NT4-style domain controller. A major advantage of this configuration is the ability to centralize user and machine credentials. Samba can also use multiple backends to store the user information.

17.5.1. Primary Domain Controller

This section covers configuring Samba as a Primary Domain Controller (PDC) using the default smbpasswd backend.

1. First, install Samba, and **libpam-smbpass** to sync the user accounts, by entering the following in a terminal prompt:

   ```
   sudo apt-get install samba libpam-smbpass
   ```

2. Next, configure Samba by editing /etc/samba/smb.conf. The *security* mode should be set to user, and the *workgroup* should relate to your organization:

   ```
   workgroup = EXAMPLE
   ...
   security = user
   ```

3. In the commented "Domains" section add or uncomment the following:

   ```
   domain logons = yes
   logon path = \\%N\%U\profile
   logon drive = H:
   logon home = \\%N\%U
   logon script = logon.cmd
   add machine script = sudo /usr/sbin/useradd -N -g machines -c Machine -d
                                             /var/lib/samba -s /bin/false %u
   ```

Note

If you wish to not use *Roaming Profiles* leave the *logon home* and *logon path* options commented.

- *domain logons:* provides the netlogon service causing Samba to act as a domain controller.

---

[17] *http://samba.org/samba/docs/man/Samba-HOWTO-Collection/securing-samba.html*
[18] *http://samba.org/samba/docs/man/Samba-HOWTO-Collection/AccessControls.html#id397568*
[19] *https://help.ubuntu.com/community/Samba*

- *logon path:* places the user's Windows profile into their home directory. It is also possible to configure a *[profiles]* share placing all profiles under a single directory.
- *logon drive:* specifies the home directory local path.
- *logon home:* specifies the home directory location.
- *logon script:* determines the script to be run locally once a user has logged in. The script needs to be placed in the *[netlogon]* share.
- *add machine script:* a script that will automatically create the *Machine Trust Account* needed for a workstation to join the domain.

  In this example the *machines* group will need to be created using the **addgroup** utility see the Section 8.1.2, *Adding and Deleting Users* for details.

4. Uncomment the *[homes]* share to allow the logon home to be mapped:

```
[homes]
   comment = Home Directories
   browseable = no
   read only = no
   create mask = 0700
   directory mask = 0700
   valid users = %S
```

5. When configured as a domain controller a *[netlogon]* share needs to be configured. To enable the share, uncomment:

```
[netlogon]
   comment = Network Logon Service
   path = /srv/samba/netlogon
   guest ok = yes
   read only = yes
   share modes = no
```

Note

The original *netlogon* share path is /home/samba/netlogon, but according to the Filesystem Hierarchy Standard (FHS), */srv*[20] is the correct location for site-specific data provided by the system.

6. Now create the netlogon directory, and an empty (for now) logon.cmd script file:

```
sudo mkdir -p /srv/samba/netlogon
sudo touch /srv/samba/netlogon/logon.cmd
```

You can enter any normal Windows logon script commands in logon.cmd to customize the client's environment.

7. Restart Samba to enable the new domain controller:

---

[20] *http://www.pathname.com/fhs/pub/fhs-2.3.html#SRVDATAFORSERVICESPROVIDEDBYSYSTEM*

```
sudo restart smbd
sudo restart nmbd
```

8. Lastly, there are a few additional commands needed to setup the appropriate rights.

    With *root* being disabled by default, in order to join a workstation to the domain, a system group needs to be mapped to the Windows *Domain Admins* group. Using the **net** utility, from a terminal enter:

```
sudo net groupmap add ntgroup="Domain Admins" unixgroup=sysadmin
                                                    rid=512 type=d
```

 Note

Change sysadmin to whichever group you prefer. Also, the user used to join the domain needs to be a member of the *sysadmin* group, as well as a member of the system *admin* group. The *admin* group allows **sudo** use.

If the user does not have Samba credentials yet, you can add them with the **smbpasswd** utility, change the *sysadmin* username appropriately:

```
sudo smbpasswd -a sysadmin
```

Also, rights need to be explicitly provided to the *Domain Admins* group to allow the *add machine script* (and other admin functions) to work. This is achieved by executing:

```
net rpc rights grant -U sysadmin "EXAMPLE\Domain Admins"
                                        SeMachineAccountPrivilege \
SePrintOperatorPrivilege SeAddUsersPrivilege SeDiskOperatorPrivilege
                                        SeRemoteShutdownPrivilege
```

9. You should now be able to join Windows clients to the Domain in the same manner as joining them to an NT4 domain running on a Windows server.

17.5.2. Backup Domain Controller

With a Primary Domain Controller (PDC) on the network it is best to have a Backup Domain Controller (BDC) as well. This will allow clients to authenticate in case the PDC becomes unavailable.

When configuring Samba as a BDC you need a way to sync account information with the PDC. There are multiple ways of accomplishing this **scp**, **rsync**, or by using **LDAP** as the *passdb backend*.

Using LDAP is the most robust way to sync account information, because both domain controllers can use the same information in real time. However, setting up a LDAP server may be overly complicated for a small number of user and computer accounts. See the Section 6.2, *Samba and LDAP* for details.

1. First, install **samba** and **libpam-smbpass**. From a terminal enter:

```
sudo apt-get install samba libpam-smbpass
```

2. Now, edit `/etc/samba/smb.conf` and uncomment the following in the *[global]*:

```
workgroup = EXAMPLE
...
security = user
```

3. In the commented *Domains* uncomment or add:

```
domain logons = yes
domain master = no
```

4. Make sure a user has rights to read the files in `/var/lib/samba`. For example, to allow users in the *admin* group to **scp** the files, enter:

```
sudo chgrp -R admin /var/lib/samba
```

5. Next, sync the user accounts, using **scp** to copy the `/var/lib/samba` directory from the PDC:

```
sudo scp -r username@pdc:/var/lib/samba /var/lib
```

 Note

Replace *username* with a valid username and *pdc* with the hostname or IP Address of your actual PDC.

6. Finally, restart **samba**:

```
sudo restart smbd
sudo restart nmbd
```

You can test that your Backup Domain controller is working by stopping the Samba daemon on the PDC, then trying to login to a Windows client joined to the domain.

Another thing to keep in mind is if you have configured the *logon home* option as a directory on the PDC, and the PDC becomes unavailable, access to the user's *Home* drive will also be unavailable. For this reason it is best to configure the *logon home* to reside on a separate file server from the PDC and BDC.

17.5.3. Resources

- For in depth Samba configurations see the *Samba HOWTO Collection*[21]
- The guide is also available in *printed format*[22].

---

[21] *http://samba.org/samba/docs/man/Samba-HOWTO-Collection/*
[22] *http://www.amazon.com/exec/obidos/tg/detail/-/0131882228*

- O'Reilly's *Using Samba*[23] is also a good reference.
- *Chapter 4*[24] of the Samba HOWTO Collection explains setting up a Primary Domain Controller.
- *Chapter 5*[25] of the Samba HOWTO Collection explains setting up a Backup Domain Controller.
- The *Ubuntu Wiki Samba*[26] page.

17.6. Samba Active Directory Integration

17.6.1. Accessing a Samba Share

Another, use for Samba is to integrate into an existing Windows network. Once part of an Active Directory domain, Samba can provide file and print services to AD users.

The simplest way to join an AD domain is to use **Likewise-open**. For detailed instructions see the *Likewise Open Installation and Administration Guide*[27].

Once part of the Active Directory domain, enter the following command in the terminal prompt:

```
sudo apt-get install samba smbfs smbclient
```

Next, edit /etc/samba/smb.conf changing:

```
workgroup = EXAMPLE
...
security = ads
realm = EXAMPLE.COM
...
idmap backend = lwopen
idmap uid = 50-9999999999
idmap gid = 50-9999999999
```

Restart **samba** for the new settings to take effect:

```
sudo restart smbd
sudo restart nmbd
```

You should now be able to access any **Samba** shares from a Windows client. However, be sure to give the appropriate AD users or groups access to the share directory. See the Section 17.4, *Securing a Samba File and Print Server* for more details.

---

[23] *http://www.oreilly.com/catalog/9780596007690/*

[24] *http://samba.org/samba/docs/man/Samba-HOWTO-Collection/samba-pdc.html*

[25] *http://us3.samba.org/samba/docs/man/Samba-HOWTO-Collection/samba-bdc.html*

[26] *https://help.ubuntu.com/community/Samba*

[27] *http://www.likewise.com/resources/documentation_library/manuals/open/likewise-open-54-guide.html*

17.6.2. Accessing a Windows Share

Now that the Samba server is part of the Active Directory domain you can access any Windows server shares:

- To mount a Windows file share enter the following in a terminal prompt:

```
mount.cifs //fs01.example.com/share mount_point
```

It is also possible to access shares on computers not part of an AD domain, but a username and password will need to be provided.

- To mount the share during boot place an entry in `/etc/fstab`, for example:

```
//192.168.0.5/share /mnt/windows cifs auto,username=steve,password=secret,rw 0    0
```

- Another way to copy files from a Windows server is to use the **smbclient** utility. To list the files in a Windows share:

```
smbclient //fs01.example.com/share -k -c "ls"
```

- To copy a file from the share, enter:

```
smbclient //fs01.example.com/share -k -c "get file.txt"
```

This will copy the `file.txt` into the current directory.

- And to copy a file to the share:

```
smbclient //fs01.example.com/share -k -c "put /etc/hosts hosts"
```

This will copy the `/etc/hosts` to `//fs01.example.com/share/hosts`.

- The -c option used above allows you to execute the **smbclient** command all at once. This is useful for scripting and minor file operations. To enter the *smb: \>* prompt, a FTP like prompt where you can execute normal file and directory commands, simply execute:

```
smbclient //fs01.example.com/share -k
```

Note

Replace all instances of *fs01.example.com/share*, *//192.168.0.5/share*, *username=steve,password=secret*, and *file.txt* with your server's IP, hostname, share name, file name, and an actual username and password with rights to the share.

17.6.3. Resources

For more **smbclient** options see the man page: **man smbclient**, also available *online*[28].

The **mount.cifs** *man page*[29] is also useful for more detailed information.

The *Ubuntu Wiki Samba*[30] page.

---

[28] *http://manpages.ubuntu.com/manpages/natty/en/man1/smbclient.1.html*

[29] *http://manpages.ubuntu.com/manpages/natty/en/man8/mount.cifs.8.html*

[30] *https://help.ubuntu.com/community/Samba*

Chapter 18.
Backups

There are many ways to backup an Ubuntu installation. The most important thing about backups is to develop a *backup plan* consisting of what to backup, where to back it up to, and how to restore it.

The following sections discuss various ways of accomplishing these tasks.

18.1. Shell Scripts

One of the simplest ways to backup a system is using a *shell script*. For example, a script can be used to configure which directories to backup, and use those directories as arguments to the **tar** utility creating an archive file. The archive file can then be moved or copied to another location. The archive can also be created on a remote file system such as an *NFS* mount.

The **tar** utility creates one archive file out of many files or directories. **tar** can also filter the files through compression utilities reducing the size of the archive file.

18.1.1. Simple Shell Script

The following shell script uses **tar** to create an archive file on a remotely mounted NFS file system. The archive filename is determined using additional command line utilities.

```sh
#!/bin/sh
####################################
#
# Backup to NFS mount script.
#
####################################

# What to backup.
backup_files="/home /var/spool/mail /etc /root /boot /opt"

# Where to backup to.
dest="/mnt/backup"

# Create archive filename.
day=$(date +%A)
hostname=$(hostname -s)
```

```
archive_file="$hostname-$day.tgz"

# Print start status message.
echo "Backing up $backup_files to $dest/$archive_file"
date
echo

# Backup the files using tar.
tar czf $dest/$archive_file $backup_files

# Print end status message.
echo
echo "Backup finished"
date

# Long listing of files in $dest to check file sizes.
ls -lh $dest
```

- *$backup_files:* a variable listing which directories you would like to backup. The list should be customized to fit your needs.
- *$day:* a variable holding the day of the week (Monday, Tuesday, Wednesday, etc). This is used to create an archive file for each day of the week, giving a backup history of seven days. There are other ways to accomplish this including other ways using the **date** utility.
- *$hostname:* variable containing the *short* hostname of the system. Using the hostname in the archive filename gives you the option of placing daily archive files from multiple systems in the same directory.
- *$archive_file:* the full archive filename.
- *$dest:* destination of the archive file. The directory needs to be created and in this case *mounted* before executing the backup script. See the Section 13.2, *Network File System (NFS)* for details using *NFS*.
- *status messages:* optional messages printed to the console using the **echo** utility.
- *tar czf $dest/$archive_file $backup_files:* the **tar** command used to create the archive file.
  - *c:* creates an archive.
  - *z:* filter the archive through the **gzip** utility compressing the archive.
  - *f:* use archive file. Otherwise the **tar** output will be sent to STDOUT.
- *ls -lh $dest:* optional statement prints a *-l* long listing in *-h* human readable format of the destination directory. This is useful for a quick file size check of the archive file. This check should not replace testing the archive file.

This is a simple example of a backup shell script. There are large amount of options that can be included in a backup script. See the Section 18.1.4, *References* for links to resources providing more in depth shell scripting information.

18.1.2. Executing the Script

18.1.2.1. Executing from a Terminal

The simplest way of executing the above backup script is to copy and paste the contents into a file. `backup.sh` for example. Then from a terminal prompt:

```
sudo bash backup.sh
```

This is a great way to test the script to make sure everything works as expected.

18.1.2.2. Executing with cron

The **cron** utility can be used to automate the script execution. The **cron** daemon allows the execution of scripts, or commands, at a specified time and date.

cron is configured through entries in a `crontab` file. `crontab` files are separated into fields:

```
# m h dom mon dow    command
```

- *m:* minute the command executes on between 0 and 59.
- *h:* hour the command executes on between 0 and 23.
- *dom:* day of month the command executes on.
- *mon:* the month the command executes on between 1 and 12.
- *dow:* the day of the week the command executes on between 0 and 7. Sunday may be specified by using 0 or 7, both values are valid.
- *command:* the command to execute.

To add or change entries in a `crontab` file the **crontab -e** command should be used. Also, the contents of a `crontab` file can be viewed using the **crontab -l** command.

To execute the **backup.sh** script listed above using **cron**. Enter the following from a terminal prompt:

```
sudo crontab -e
```

 Note

> Using **sudo** with the **crontab -e** command edits the *root* user's crontab. This is necessary if you are backing up directories only the root user has access to.

Add the following entry to the `crontab` file:

```
# m h dom mon dow    command
0 0 * * * bash /usr/local/bin/backup.sh
```

The **backup.sh** script will now be executed every day at 12:00 am.

Note

The **backup.sh** script will need to be copied to the `/usr/local/bin/` directory in order for this entry to execute properly. The script can reside anywhere on the file system simply change the script path appropriately.

For more in depth **crontab** options see Section 18.1.4, *References*.

18.1.3. Restoring from the Archive

Once an archive has been created it is important to test the archive. The archive can be tested by listing the files it contains, but the best test is to *restore* a file from the archive.

- To see a listing of the archive contents. From a terminal prompt:
  ```
  tar -tzvf /mnt/backup/host-Monday.tgz
  ```

- To restore a file from the archive to a different directory enter:
  ```
  tar -xzvf /mnt/backup/host-Monday.tgz -C /tmp etc/hosts
  ```

  The -C option to **tar** redirects the extracted files to the specified directory. The above example will extract the `/etc/hosts` file to `/tmp/etc/hosts`. **tar** recreates the directory structure that it contains.

  Also, notice the leading "/" is left off the path of the file to restore.

- To restore all files in the archive enter the following:
  ```
  cd /
  sudo tar -xzvf /mnt/backup/host-Monday.tgz
  ```

Note

This will overwrite the files currently on the file system.

18.1.4. References

- For more information on shell scripting see the *Advanced Bash-Scripting Guide*[1]
- The book *Teach Yourself Shell Programming in 24 Hours*[2] is available online and a great resource for shell scripting.
- The *CronHowto Wiki Page*[3] contains details on advanced **cron** options.
- See the *GNU tar Manual*[4] for more **tar** options.

---

[1] *http://tldp.org/LDP/abs/html/*

[2] *http://safari.samspublishing.com/0672323583*

[3] *https://help.ubuntu.com/community/CronHowto*

[4] *http://www.gnu.org/software/tar/manual/index.html*

- The Wikipedia *Backup Rotation Scheme*[5] article contains information on other backup rotation schemes.

- The shell script uses **tar** to create the archive, but there many other command line utilities that can be used. For example:

  - *cpio*[6]: used to copy files to and from archives.

  - *dd*[7]: part of the **coreutils** package. A low level utility that can copy data from one format to another

  - *rsnapshot*[8]: a file system snap shot utility used to create copies of an entire file system.

18.2. Archive Rotation

The shell script in the Section 18.1, *Shell Scripts* only allows for seven different archives. For a server whose data doesn't change often this may be enough. If the server has a large amount of data a more robust rotation scheme should be used.

18.2.1. Rotating NFS Archives

In this section the shell script will be slightly modified to implement a grandfather-father-son rotation scheme (monthly-weekly-daily):

- The rotation will do a *daily* backup Sunday through Friday.

- On Saturday a *weekly* backup is done giving you four weekly backups a month.

- The *monthly* backup is done on the first of the month rotating two monthly backups based on if the month is odd or even.

Here is the new script:

```
#!/bin/bash
####################################
#
# Backup to NFS mount script with
# grandfather-father-son rotation.
#
####################################

# What to backup.
backup_files="/home /var/spool/mail /etc /root /boot /opt"
```

---

[5] *http://en.wikipedia.org/wiki/Backup_rotation_scheme*
[6] *http://www.gnu.org/software/cpio/*
[7] *http://www.gnu.org/software/coreutils/*
[8] *http://www.rsnapshot.org/*

```
# Where to backup to.
dest="/mnt/backup"

# Setup variables for the archive filename.
day=$(date +%A)
hostname=$(hostname -s)

# Find which week of the month 1-4 it is.
day_num=$(date +%d)
if (( $day_num <= 7 )); then
        week_file="$hostname-week1.tgz"
elif (( $day_num > 7 && $day_num <= 14 )); then
        week_file="$hostname-week2.tgz"
elif (( $day_num > 14 && $day_num <= 21 )); then
        week_file="$hostname-week3.tgz"
elif (( $day_num > 21 && $day_num < 32 )); then
        week_file="$hostname-week4.tgz"
fi

# Find if the Month is odd or even.
month_num=$(date +%m)
month=$(expr $month_num % 2)
if [ $month -eq 0 ]; then
        month_file="$hostname-month2.tgz"
else
        month_file="$hostname-month1.tgz"
fi

# Create archive filename.
if [ $day_num == 1 ]; then
  archive_file=$month_file
elif [ $day != "Saturday" ]; then
        archive_file="$hostname-$day.tgz"
else
  archive_file=$week_file
fi

# Print start status message.
echo "Backing up $backup_files to $dest/$archive_file"
date
echo

# Backup the files using tar.
tar czf $dest/$archive_file $backup_files

# Print end status message.
echo
echo "Backup finished"
date

# Long listing of files in $dest to check file sizes.
ls -lh $dest/
```

The script can be executed using the same methods as in the Section 18.1.2, *Executing the Script*.

It is good practice to take backup media off site in case of a disaster. In the shell script example the backup media is another server providing an NFS share. In all likelihood taking the NFS server to another location would not be practical. Depending upon connection speeds it may be an option to copy the archive file over a WAN link to a server in another location.

Another option is to copy the archive file to an external hard drive which can then be taken off site. Since the price of external hard drives continue to decrease it may be cost-effective to use two drives for each archive level. This would allow you to have one external drive attached to the backup server and one in another location.

18.2.2. Tape Drives

A tape drive attached to the server can be used instead of a NFS share. Using a tape drive simplifies archive rotation, and taking the media off site as well.

When using a tape drive the filename portions of the script aren't needed because the date is sent directly to the tape device. Some commands to manipulate the tape are needed. This is accomplished using **mt**, a magnetic tape control utility part of the **cpio** package.

Here is the shell script modified to use a tape drive:

```
#!/bin/bash
####################################
#
# Backup to tape drive script.
#
####################################

# What to backup.
backup_files="/home /var/spool/mail /etc /root /boot /opt"

# Where to backup to.
dest="/dev/st0"

# Print start status message.
echo "Backing up $backup_files to $dest"
date
echo

# Make sure the tape is rewound.
mt -f $dest rewind

# Backup the files using tar.
tar czf $dest $backup_files
```

```
# Rewind and eject the tape.
mt -f $dest rewoffl

# Print end status message.
echo
echo "Backup finished"
date
```

 Note

The default device name for a SCSI tape drive is `/dev/st0`. Use the appropriate device path for your system.

Restoring from a tape drive is basically the same as restoring from a file. Simply rewind the tape and use the device path instead of a file path. For example to restore the `/etc/hosts` file to `/tmp/etc/hosts`:

```
mt -f /dev/st0 rewind
tar -xzf /dev/st0 -C /tmp etc/hosts
```

18.3. Bacula

Bacula is a backup program enabling you to backup, restore, and verify data across your network. There are Bacula clients for Linux, Windows, and Mac OSX. Making it a cross platform network wide solution.

18.3.1. Overview

Bacula is made up of several components and services used to manage which files to backup and where to back them up to:

- **Bacula Director:** a service that controls all backup, restore, verify, and archive operations.
- **Bacula Console:** an application allowing communication with the Director. There are three versions of the Console:
  - Text based command line version.
  - Gnome based GTK+ Graphical User Interface (GUI) interface.
  - wxWidgets GUI interface.
- **Bacula File:** also known as the **Bacula Client** program. This application is installed on machines to be backed up, and is responsible for the data requested by the Director.
- **Bacula Storage:** the programs that perform the storage and recovery of data to the physical media.

- **Bacula Catalog:** is responsible for maintaining the file indexes and volume databases for all files backed up, enabling quick location and restoration of archived files. The Catalog supports three different databases MySQL, PostgreSQL, and SQLite.
- **Bacula Monitor:** allows the monitoring of the Director, File daemons, and Storage daemons. Currently the Monitor is only available as a GTK+ GUI application.

These services and applications can be run on multiple servers and clients, or they can be installed on one machine if backing up a single disk or volume.

18.3.2. Installation

There are multiple packages containing the different **Bacula** components. To install Bacula, from a terminal prompt enter:

```
sudo apt-get install bacula
```

By default installing the **bacula** package will use a **MySQL** database for the Catalog. If you want to use SQLite or PostgreSQL, for the Catalog, install **bacula-director-sqlite3** or **bacula-director-pgsql** respectively.

During the install process you will be asked to supply credentials for the database *administrator* and the *bacula* database *owner*. The database administrator will need to have the appropriate rights to create a database, see the Section 11.1, *MySQL* for more information.

18.3.3. Configuration

Bacula configuration files are formatted based on *resources* comprising of *directives* surrounded by "{}" braces. Each Bacula component has an individual file in the /etc/bacula directory.

The various **Bacula** components must authorize themselves to each other. This is accomplished using the *password* directive. For example, the *Storage* resource password in the /etc/bacula/bacula-dir.conf file must match the *Director* resource password in /etc/bacula/bacula-sd.conf.

By default the backup job named *Client1* is configured to archive the **Bacula** Catalog. If you plan on using the server to backup more than one client you should change the name of this job to something more descriptive. To change the name edit /etc/bacula/bacula-dir.conf:

```
#
# Define the main nightly save backup job
#   By default, this job will back up to disk in
Job {
  Name = "BackupServer"
  JobDefs = "DefaultJob"
```

```
  Write Bootstrap = "/var/lib/bacula/Client1.bsr"
}
```

Note

The example above changes the job name to *BackupServer* matching the machine's host name. Replace "BackupServer" with your appropriate hostname, or other descriptive name.

The *Console* can be used to query the *Director* about jobs, but to use the Console with a *non-root* user, the user needs to be in the *bacula* group. To add a user to the bacula group enter the following from a terminal:

```
sudo adduser $username bacula
```

Note

Replace *$username* with the actual username. Also, if you are adding the current user to the group you should log out and back in for the new permissions to take effect.

18.3.4. Localhost Backup

This section describes how to backup specified directories on a single host to a local tape drive.

- First, the *Storage* device needs to be configured. Edit /etc/bacula/bacula-sd.conf add:

```
Device {
  Name = "Tape Drive"
  Device Type = tape
  Media Type = DDS-4
  Archive Device = /dev/st0
  Hardware end of medium = No;
  AutomaticMount = yes;              # when device opened, read it
  AlwaysOpen = Yes;
  RemovableMedia = yes;
  RandomAccess = no;
  Alert Command = "sh -c 'tapeinfo -f %c | grep TapeAlert'"
}
```

  The example is for a *DDS-4* tape drive. Adjust the Media Type and Archive Device to match your hardware.

  You could also uncomment one of the other examples in the file.

- After editing /etc/bacula/bacula-sd.conf the **Storage** daemon will need to be restarted:

```
sudo /etc/init.d/bacula-sd restart
```

- Now add a *Storage* resource in /etc/bacula/bacula-dir.conf to use the new Device:

```
# Definition of "Tape Drive" storage device
Storage {
  Name = TapeDrive
  # Do not use "localhost" here
  Address = backupserver              # N.B. Use a fully qualified name here
  SDPort = 9103
  Password = "Cv70F6pf1t6pBopT4vQOnigDrR0v3LT3Cgkiyj"
  Device = "Tape Drive"
  Media Type = tape
}
```

The *Address* directive needs to be the Fully Qualified Domain Name (FQDN) of the server. Change *backupserver* to the actual host name.

Also, make sure the *Password* directive matches the password string in `/etc/bacula/bacula-sd.conf`.

- Create a new *FileSet*, which will determine what directories to backup, by adding:

```
# LocalhostBacup FileSet.
FileSet {
  Name = "LocalhostFiles"
  Include {
    Options {
      signature = MD5
      compression=GZIP
    }
    File = /etc
    File = /home
  }
}
```

This *FileSet* will backup the `/etc` and `/home` directories. The *Options* resource directives configure the FileSet to create a MD5 signature for each file backed up, and to compress the files using GZIP.

- Next, create a new *Schedule* for the backup job:

```
# LocalhostBackup Schedule -- Daily.
Schedule {
  Name = "LocalhostDaily"
  Run = Full daily at 00:01
}
```

The job will run every day at 00:01 or 12:01 am. There are many other scheduling options available.

- Finally create the *Job*:

```
# Localhost backup.
Job {
  Name = "LocalhostBackup"
  JobDefs = "DefaultJob"
  Enabled = yes
  Level = Full
  FileSet = "LocalhostFiles"
```

```
    Schedule = "LocalhostDaily"
    Storage = TapeDrive
    Write Bootstrap = "/var/lib/bacula/LocalhostBackup.bsr"
}
```

The job will do a *Full* backup every day to the tape drive.

- Each tape used will need to have a *Label*. If the current tape does not have a label **Bacula** will send an email letting you know. To label a tape using the **Console** enter the following from a terminal:

```
bconsole
```

- At the Bacula Console prompt enter:

```
label
```

- You will then be prompted for the *Storage* resource:

```
 Automatically selected Catalog: MyCatalog
Using Catalog "MyCatalog"
The defined Storage resources are:
     1: File
     2: TapeDrive
Select Storage resource (1-2):2
```

- Enter the new *Volume* name:

```
 Enter new Volume name: Sunday
Defined Pools:
     1: Default
     2: Scratch
```

Replace *Sunday* with the desired label.

- Now, select the *Pool*:

```
Select the Pool (1-2): 1
Connecting to Storage daemon TapeDrive at backupserver:9103 ...
Sending label command for Volume "Sunday" Slot 0 ...
```

Congratulations, you have now configured *Bacula* to backup the localhost to an attached tape drive.

18.3.5. Resources

- For more *Bacula* configuration options refer to the *Bacula User's Manual*[9]
- The *Bacula Home Page*[10] contains the latest Bacula news and developments.
- Also, see the *Bacula Ubuntu Wiki*[11] page.

---

[9] *http://www.bacula.org/en/rel-manual/index.html*
[10] *http://www.bacula.org/*
[11] *https://help.ubuntu.com/community/Bacula*

Chapter 19.
Virtualization

Virtualization is being adopted in many different environments and situations. If you are a developer, virtualization can provide you with a contained environment where you can safely do almost any sort of development safe from messing up your main working environment. If you are a systems administrator, you can use virtualization to more easily separate your services and move them around based on demand.

The default virtualization technology supported in Ubuntu is **KVM**, a technology that takes advantage of virtualization extensions built into Intel and AMD hardware. For hardware without virtualization extensions **Xen** and **Qemu** are popular solutions.

19.1. libvirt

The **libvirt** library is used to interface with different virtualization technologies. Before getting started with **libvirt** it is best to make sure your hardware supports the necessary virtualization extensions for **KVM**. Enter the following from a terminal prompt:

```
kvm-ok
```

A message will be printed informing you if your CPU *does* or *does not* support hardware virtualization.

> **Note**
>
> On most computer whose processor supports virtualization, it is necessary to activate an option in the BIOS to enable it.

19.1.1. Virtual Networking

There are a few different ways to allow a virtual machine access to the external network. The default virtual network configuration is *usermode* networking, which uses the SLIRP protocol and traffic is NATed through the host interface to the outside network.

To enable external hosts to directly access services on virtual machines a *bridge* needs to be configured. This allows the virtual interfaces to connect to the outside network through the physical interface, making them appear as normal hosts to the rest of the network. For information on setting up a bridge see the Section 4.1.4, *Bridging*.

19.1.2. Installation

To install the necessary packages, from a terminal prompt enter:

```
sudo apt-get install kvm libvirt-bin
```

After installing **libvirt-bin**, the user used to manage virtual machines will need to be added to the *libvirtd* group. Doing so will grant the user access to the advanced networking options.

In a terminal enter:

```
sudo adduser $USER libvirtd
```

 Note

If the user chosen is the current user, you will need to log out and back in for the new group membership to take effect.

You are now ready to install a *Guest* operating system. Installing a virtual machine follows the same process as installing the operating system directly on the hardware. You either need a way to automate the installation, or a keyboard and monitor will need to be attached to the physical machine.

In the case of virtual machines a Graphical User Interface (GUI) is analogous to using a physical keyboard and mouse. Instead of installing a GUI the **virt-viewer** application can be used to connect to a virtual machine's console using **VNC**. See the Section 19.1.6, *Virtual Machine Viewer* for more information.

There are several ways to automate the Ubuntu installation process, for example using preseeds, kickstart, etc. Refer to the *Ubuntu Installation Guide* (ISBN-13: 978-1-59682-257-3) for details.

Yet another way to install an Ubuntu virtual machine is to use **ubuntu-vm-builder**. **ubuntu-vm-builder** allows you to setup advanced partitions, execute custom post-install scripts, etc. For details see the Section 19.2, *JeOS and vmbuilder*.

19.1.3. virt-install

virt-install is part of the **virtinst** package. To install it, from a terminal prompt enter:

```
sudo apt-get install virtinst
```

There are several options available when using **virt-install**. For example:

```
sudo virt-install -n web_devel -r 256 \
--disk path=/var/lib/libvirt/images/web_devel.img,size=4 -c jeos.iso --accelerate \
--connect=qemu:///system --vnc \
--noautoconsole -v
```

- *-n web_devel:* the name of the new virtual machine will be *web_devel* in this example.
- *-r 256:* specifies the amount of memory the virtual machine will use in megabytes.
- *-disk path=/var/lib/libvirt/images/web_devel.img,size=4:* indicates the path to the virtual disk which can be a file, partition, or logical volume. In this example a file named `web_devel.img` in the /var/lib/libvirt/images/ directory with a size of 4 gigabytes.
- *-c jeos.iso:* file to be used as a virtual CDROM. The file can be either an ISO file or the path to the host's CDROM device.
- *--accelerate:* enables the kernel's acceleration technologies.
- *--vnc:* exports the guest's virtual console using VNC.
- *--noautoconsole:* will not automatically connect to the virtual machine's console.
- *-v:* creates a fully virtualized guest.

After launching **virt-install** you can connect to the virtual machine's console either locally using a GUI or with the **virt-viewer** utility.

19.1.4. virt-clone

The **virt-clone** application can be used to copy one virtual machine to another. For example:

```
sudo virt-clone -o web_devel -n database_devel -f /path/to/database_devel.img
                                                   --connect=qemu:///system
```

- *-o:* original virtual machine.
- *-n:* name of the new virtual machine.
- *-f:* path to the file, logical volume, or partition to be used by the new virtual machine.
- *--connect:* specifies which hypervisor to connect to.

Also, use *-d* or *--debug* option to help troubleshoot problems with **virt-clone**.

 Note

Replace *web_devel* and *database_devel* with appropriate virtual machine names.

19.1.5. Virtual Machine Management

19.1.5.1. virsh

There are several utilities available to manage virtual machines and **libvirt**. The **virsh** utility can be used from the command line. Some examples:

- To list running virtual machines:
```
virsh -c qemu:///system list
```

- To start a virtual machine:

  ```
  virsh -c qemu:///system start web_devel
  ```

- Similarly, to start a virtual machine at boot:

  ```
  virsh -c qemu:///system autostart web_devel
  ```

- Reboot a virtual machine with:

  ```
  virsh -c qemu:///system reboot web_devel
  ```

- The *state* of virtual machines can be saved to a file in order to be restored later. The following will save the virtual machine state into a file named according to the date:

  ```
  virsh -c qemu:///system save web_devel web_devel-022708.state
  ```

  Once saved the virtual machine will no longer be running.

- A saved virtual machine can be restored using:

  ```
  virsh -c qemu:///system restore web_devel-022708.state
  ```

- To shutdown a virtual machine do:

  ```
  virsh -c qemu:///system shutdown web_devel
  ```

- A CDROM device can be mounted in a virtual machine by entering:

  ```
  virsh -c qemu:///system attach-disk web_devel /dev/cdrom /media/cdrom
  ```

Note

In the above examples replace *web_devel* with the appropriate virtual machine name, and `web_devel-022708.state` with a descriptive file name.

19.1.5.2. Virtual Machine Manager

The **virt-manager** package contains a graphical utility to manage local and remote virtual machines. To install virt-manager enter:

```
sudo apt-get install virt-manager
```

Since **virt-manager** requires a Graphical User Interface (GUI) environment it is recommended to be installed on a workstation or test machine instead of a production server. To connect to the local **libvirt** service enter:

```
virt-manager -c qemu:///system
```

You can connect to the **libvirt** service running on another host by entering the following in a terminal prompt:

```
virt-manager -c qemu+ssh://virtnode1.mydomain.com/system
```

Note

The above example assumes that **SSH** connectivity between the management system and virtnode1.mydomain.com has already been configured, and uses SSH keys for authentication. SSH *keys* are needed because **libvirt** sends the password prompt to another process. For details on configuring **SSH** see the Section 5.1, *OpenSSH Server*.

19.1.6. Virtual Machine Viewer

The **virt-viewer** application allows you to connect to a virtual machine's console. **virt-viewer** does require a Graphical User Interface (GUI) to interface with the virtual machine.

To install **virt-viewer** from a terminal enter:

```
sudo apt-get install virt-viewer
```

Once a virtual machine is installed and running you can connect to the virtual machine's console by using:

```
virt-viewer -c qemu:///system web_devel
```

Similar to **virt-manager**, **virt-viewer** can connect to a remote host using *SSH* with key authentication, as well:

```
virt-viewer -c qemu+ssh://virtnode1.mydomain.com/system web_devel
```

Be sure to replace web_devel with the appropriate virtual machine name.

If configured to use a *bridged* network interface you can also setup **SSH** access to the virtual machine. See the Section 5.1, *OpenSSH Server* and the Section 4.1.4, *Bridging* for more details.

19.1.7. Resources

- See the *KVM*[1] home page for more details.
- For more information on **libvirt** see the *libvirt home page*[2]
- The *Virtual Machine Manager*[3] site has more information on **virt-manager** development.
- Also, stop by the *#ubuntu-virt* IRC channel on *freenode*[4] to discuss virtualization technology in Ubuntu.
- Another good resource is the *Ubuntu Wiki KVM*[5] page.

---

[1] *http://kvm.qumranet.com/kvmwiki*
[2] *http://libvirt.org/*
[3] *http://virt-manager.et.redhat.com/*
[4] *http://freenode.net/*
[5] *https://help.ubuntu.com/community/KVM*

19.2. JeOS and vmbuilder

19.2.1. Introduction

19.2.1.1. What is JeOS

Ubuntu *JeOS* (pronounced "Juice") is an efficient variant of the Ubuntu Server operating system, configured specifically for virtual appliances. No longer available as a CD-ROM ISO for download, but only as an option either:

- While installing from the Server Edition ISO (pressing *F4* on the first screen will allow you to pick "Minimal installation", which is the package selection equivalent to JeOS).
- Or to be built using Ubuntu's vmbuilder, which is described here.

JeOS is a specialized installation of Ubuntu Server Edition with a tuned kernel that only contains the base elements needed to run within a virtualized environment.

Ubuntu JeOS has been tuned to take advantage of key performance technologies in the latest virtualization products from VMware. This combination of reduced size and optimized performance ensures that Ubuntu JeOS Edition delivers a highly efficient use of server resources in large virtual deployments.

Without unnecessary drivers, and only the minimal required packages, ISVs can configure their supporting OS exactly as they require. They have the peace of mind that updates, whether for security or enhancement reasons, will be limited to the bare minimum of what is required in their specific environment. In turn, users deploying virtual appliances built on top of JeOS will have to go through fewer updates and therefore less maintenance than they would have had to with a standard full installation of a server.

19.2.1.2. What is vmbuilder

With vmbuilder, there is no need to download a JeOS ISO anymore. vmbuilder will fetch the various package and build a virtual machine tailored for your needs in about a minute. vmbuilder is a script that automates the process of creating a ready to use Linux based VM. The currently supported hypervisors are KVM and Xen.

You can pass command line options to add extra packages, remove packages, choose which version of Ubuntu, which mirror etc. On recent hardware with plenty of RAM, tmpdir in /dev/shm or using a tmpfs, and a local mirror, you can bootstrap a VM in less than a minute.

First introduced as a shell script in Ubuntu 8.04LTS, **ubuntu-vm-builder** started with little emphasis as a hack to help developers test their new code in a virtual machine without having to restart from scratch each time. As a few Ubuntu administrators started to notice this script, a few of them went on improving it and adapting it for so many use case that Soren Hansen (the author of the script and Ubuntu virtualization specialist, not the golf player) decided to rewrite it from scratch for Intrepid as a python script with a few new design goals:

- Develop it so that it can be reused by other distributions.
- Use a plugin mechanisms for all virtualization interactions so that others can easily add logic for other virtualization environments.
- Provide an easy to maintain web interface as an option to the command line interface.

But the general principles and commands remain the same.

19.2.2. Initial Setup

It is assumed that you have installed and configured **libvirt** and **KVM** locally on the machine you are using. For details on how to perform this, please refer to:

- The Section 19.1, *libvirt*
- The *KVM*[6] Wiki page.

We also assume that you know how to use a text based text editor such as nano or vi. If you have not used any of them before, you can get an overview of the various text editors available by reading the *PowerUsersTextEditors*[7] page. This tutorial has been done on KVM, but the general principle should remain on other virtualization technologies.

19.2.2.1. Install vmbuilder

The name of the package that we need to install is **python-vm-builder**. In a terminal prompt enter:

```
sudo apt-get install python-vm-builder
```

 Note

If you are running Hardy, you can still perform most of this using the older version of the package named **ubuntu-vm-builder**, there are only a few changes to the syntax of the tool.

---

[6] *https://help.ubuntu.com/community/KVM*
[7] *https://help.ubuntu.com/community/PowerUsersTextEditors*

19.2.3. Defining Your Virtual Machine

Defining a virtual machine with Ubuntu's vmbuilder is quite simple, but here are a few thing to consider:

- If you plan on shipping a virtual appliance, do not assume that the end-user will know how to extend disk size to fit their need, so either plan for a large virtual disk to allow for your appliance to grow, or explain fairly well in your documentation how to allocate more space. It might actually be a good idea to store data on some separate external storage.
- Given that RAM is much easier to allocate in a VM, RAM size should be set to whatever you think is a safe minimum for your appliance.

The **vmbuilder** command has 2 main parameters: the *virtualization technology (hypervisor)* and the targeted *distribution*. Optional parameters are quite numerous and can be found using the following command:

```
vmbuilder kvm ubuntu --help
```

19.2.3.1. Base Parameters

As this example is based on **KVM** and Ubuntu 11.04 (Natty Narwhal), and we are likely to rebuild the same virtual machine multiple time, we'll invoke vmbuilder with the following first parameters:

```
sudo vmbuilder kvm ubuntu --suite natty --flavour virtual --arch i386  -o
                                                --libvirt qemu:///system
```

The *--suite* defines the Ubuntu release, the *--flavour* specifies that we want to use the virtual kernel (that's the one used to build a JeOS image), the *--arch* tells that we want to use a 32 bit machine, the *-o* tells vmbuilder to overwrite the previous version of the VM and the *--libvirt* tells to inform the local virtualization environment to add the resulting VM to the list of available machines.

Notes:

- Because of the nature of operations performed by vmbuilder, it needs to have root privilege, hence the use of sudo.
- If your virtual machine needs to use more than 3Gb of ram, you should build a 64 bit machine (--arch amd64).
- Until Ubuntu 8.10, the virtual kernel was only built for 32 bit architecture, so if you want to define an amd64 machine on Hardy, you should use *--flavour* server instead.

19.2.3.2. JeOS Installation Parameters

19.2.3.3. JeOS Networking

19.2.3.4. Assigning a fixed IP address

As a virtual appliance that may be deployed on various very different networks, it is very difficult to know what the actual network will look like. In order to simplify configuration, it is a good idea to take an approach similar to what network hardware vendors usually do, namely assigning an initial fixed IP address to the appliance in a private class network that you will provide in your documentation. An address in the range 192.168.0.0/255 is usually a good choice.

To do this we'll use the following parameters:

- *--ip ADDRESS*: IP address in dotted form (defaults to dhcp if not specified)
- *--hostname NAME*: Set NAME as the hostname of the guest.
- *--mask VALUE*: IP mask in dotted form (default: 255.255.255.0)
- *--net VALUE*: IP net address (default: X.X.X.0)
- *--bcast VALUE*: IP broadcast (default: X.X.X.255)
- *--gw ADDRESS*: Gateway address (default: X.X.X.1)
- *--dns ADDRESS*: Name server address (default: X.X.X.1)

We assume for now that default values are good enough, so the resulting invocation becomes:

```
sudo vmbuilder kvm ubuntu --suite natty --flavour virtual --arch i386
               -o --libvirt qemu:///system --ip 192.168.0.100 --hostname myvm
```

19.2.3.4.1 Bridging

Because our appliance will be likely to need to be accessed by remote hosts, we need to configure libvirt so that the appliance uses bridge networking. To do this add the *--bridge* option to the command:

```
sudo vmbuilder kvm ubuntu --suite natty --flavour virtual --arch i386
        -o --libvirt qemu:///system --ip 192.168.0.100 --hostname myvm --bridge br0
```

 Note

> You will need to have previously setup a bridge interface, see the Section 4.1.4, *Bridging* for more information. Also, if the interface name is different change *br0* to the actual bridge interface.

19.2.3.4.2 Partitioning

Partitioning of the virtual appliance will have to take into consideration what you are planning to do with is. Because most appliances want to have a separate storage for data, having a separate /var would make sense.

In order to do this vmbuilder provides us with --*part*:

```
--part PATH
  Allows you to specify a partition table in a partition file, located at PATH.
  Each line of the partition file should specify
  (root first):
      mountpoint size
  where  size  is  in megabytes. You can have up to 4 virtual disks, a new disk
  starts on a line with '---'.  ie :
      root 1000
      /opt 1000
      swap 256
      ---
      /var 2000
      /log 1500
```

In our case we will define a text file name vmbuilder.partition which will contain the following:

```
root 8000
swap 4000
---
/var 20000
```

Note

Note that as we are using virtual disk images, the actual sizes that we put here are maximum sizes for these volumes.

Our command line now looks like:

```
sudo vmbuilder kvm ubuntu --suite natty --flavour virtual --arch i386 \
-o --libvirt qemu:///system --ip 192.168.0.100 --hostname myvm --part vmbuilder.partition
```

Note

Using a "\" in a command will allow long command strings to wrap to the next line.

19.2.3.5. User and Password

Again setting up a virtual appliance, you will need to provide a default user and password that is generic so that you can include it in your documentation. We will see later on in this tutorial how we will provide some security by defining a script that will be run the first time a user actually logs in the appliance, that will, among other things, ask him to change his password. In this example I will use 'user' as my user name, and 'default' as the password.

To do this we use the following optional parameters:

- *--user USERNAME:* Sets the name of the user to be added. Default: ubuntu.
- *--name FULLNAME:* Sets the full name of the user to be added. Default: Ubuntu.
- *--pass PASSWORD:* Sets the password for the user. Default: ubuntu.

Our resulting command line becomes:

```
sudo vmbuilder kvm ubuntu --suite natty --flavour virtual --arch i386 \
        -o --libvirt qemu:///system --ip 192.168.0.100 --hostname myvm
        --part vmbuilder.partition --user user --name user --pass default
```

19.2.3.6. Installing Required Packages

In this example we will be installing a package **(Limesurvey)** that accesses a **MySQL** database and has a web interface. We will therefore require our OS to provide us with:

- Apache
- PHP
- MySQL
- OpenSSH Server
- Limesurvey (as an example application that we have packaged)

This is done using vmbuilder by specifying the --addpkg option multiple times:

```
--addpkg PKG
  Install PKG into the guest (can be specfied multiple times)
```

However, due to the way vmbuilder operates, packages that have to ask questions to the user during the post install phase are not supported and should instead be installed while interactivity can occur. This is the case of Limesurvey, which we will have to install later, once the user logs in.

Other packages that ask simple debconf question, such as **mysql-server** asking to set a password, the package can be installed immediately, but we will have to reconfigure it the first time the user logs in.

If some packages that we need to install are not in main, we need to enable the additional repositories using --comp and --ppa:

```
--components COMP1,COMP2,...,COMPN
        A comma separated list of distro components to include (e.g. main,universe).
        This defaults to "main"
--ppa=PPA  Add ppa belonging to PPA to the vm's sources.list.
```

Limesurvey not being part of the archive at the moment, we'll specify it's PPA (personal package archive) address so that it is added to the VM /etc/apt/source.list, so we add the following options to the command line:

```
--addpkg apache2 --addpkg apache2-mpm-prefork --addpkg apache2-utils \
--addpkg apache2.2-common --addpkg dbconfig-common --addpkg libapache2-mod-php5 \
--addpkg mysql-client --addpkg php5-cli --addpkg php5-gd --addpkg php5-ldap \
--addpkg php5-mysql --addpkg wwwconfig-common --addpkg mysql-server --ppa nijaba
```

19.2.3.7. Speed Considerations

19.2.3.7.1 Package Caching

When vmbuilder creates builds your system, it has to go fetch each one of the packages that composes it over the network to one of the official repositories, which, depending on your internet connection speed and the load of the mirror, can have a big impact on the actual build time. In order to reduce this, it is recommended to either have a local repository (which can be created using **apt-mirror**) or using a caching proxy such as **apt-proxy**. The later option being much simpler to implement and requiring less disk space, it is the one we will pick in this tutorial. To install it, simply type:

```
sudo apt-get install apt-proxy
```

Once this is complete, your (empty) proxy is ready for use on http://mirroraddress:9999 and will find ubuntu repository under /ubuntu. For vmbuilder to use it, we'll have to use the *--mirror* option:

```
--mirror=URL   Use Ubuntu mirror at URL instead of the default, which
               is http://archive.ubuntu.com/ubuntu for official
               arches and http://ports.ubuntu.com/ubuntu-ports
               otherwise
```

So we add to the command line:

```
--mirror http://mirroraddress:9999/ubuntu
```

 Note

> The mirror address specified here will also be used in the /etc/apt/source.list of the newly created guest, so it is useful to specify here an address that can be resolved by the guest or to plan on reseting this address later on.

19.2.3.7.2 Install a Local Mirror

If we are in a larger environment, it may make sense to setup a local mirror of the Ubuntu repositories. The package apt-mirror provides you with a script that will handle the mirroring for you. You should plan on having about 20 gigabyte of free space per supported release and architecture.

By default, **apt-mirror** uses the configuration file in /etc/apt/mirror.list. As it is set up, it will replicate only the architecture of the local machine. If you would like to support other architectures on your mirror, simply duplicate the lines starting with "deb", replacing the deb keyword by /deb-{arch} where arch can be i386, amd64, etc... For example, on an amd64 machine, to have the i386 archives as well, you will have:

```
deb http://archive.ubuntu.com/ubuntu natty main restricted universe multiverse
/deb-i386 http://archive.ubuntu.com/ubuntu natty main restricted universe multiverse

deb http://archive.ubuntu.com/ubuntu natty-updates main restricted universe multiverse
/deb-i386 http://archive.ubuntu.com/ubuntu natty-updates main restricted universe multiverse

deb http://archive.ubuntu.com/ubuntu/ natty-backports main restricted universe multiverse
/deb-i386 http://archive.ubuntu.com/ubuntu natty-backports main restricted universe
                                                                          multiverse

deb http://security.ubuntu.com/ubuntu natty-security main restricted universe multiverse
/deb-i386 http://security.ubuntu.com/ubuntu natty-security main restricted universe
                                                                          multiverse

deb http://archive.ubuntu.com/ubuntu natty main/debian-installer restricted/debian-installer
                          universe/debian-installer multiverse/debian-installer
/deb-i386 http://archive.ubuntu.com/ubuntu natty main/debian-installer restricted
                    /debian-installer universe/debian-installer multiverse/debian-installer
```

Notice that the source packages are not mirrored as they are seldom used compared to the binaries and they do take a lot more space, but they can be easily added to the list.

Once the mirror has finished replicating (and this can be quite long), you need to configure Apache so that your mirror files (in /var/spool/apt-mirror if you did not change the default), are published by your Apache server. For more information on Apache see Section 10.1, *HTTPD - Apache2 Web Server*.

19.2.4. Package the Application

Two option are available to us:

- The recommended method to do so is to make a *Debian* package. Since this is outside of the scope of this tutorial, we will not perform this here and invite the reader to read the documentation on how to do this in the *Ubuntu Packaging Guide*[8]. In this case it is also a good idea to setup a repository for your package so that updates can be conveniently pulled from it. See the *Debian Administration*[9] article for a tutorial on this.

- Manually install the application under /opt as recommended by the *FHS guidelines*[10].

---

[8] *https://wiki.ubuntu.com/PackagingGuide*
[9] *http://www.debian-administration.org/articles/286*
[10] *http://www.pathname.com/fhs/*

In our case we'll use **Limesurvey** as example web application for which we wish to provide a virtual appliance. As noted before, we've made a version of the package available in a PPA (Personal Package Archive).

19.2.5. Useful Additions

19.2.5.1. Configuring Automatic Updates

To have your system be configured to update itself on a regular basis, we will just install **unattended-upgrades**, so we add the following option to our command line:

```
--addpkg unattended-upgrades
```

As we have put our application package in a PPA, the process will update not only the system, but also the application each time we update the version in the PPA.

19.2.5.2. ACPI Event Handling

For your virtual machine to be able to handle restart and shutdown events it is being sent, it is a good idea to install the acpid package as well. To do this we just add the following option:

```
--addpkg acpid
```

19.2.6. Final Command

Here is the command with all the options discussed above:

```
sudo vmbuilder kvm ubuntu --suite natty --flavour virtual --arch i386 -o \
       --libvirt qemu:///system --ip 192.168.0.100 --hostname myvm \
       --part vmbuilder.partition --user user \
       --name user --pass default --addpkg apache2 --addpkg apache2-mpm-prefork \
       --addpkg apache2-utils --addpkg apache2.2-common --addpkg dbconfig-common \
       --addpkg libapache2-mod-php5 --addpkg mysql-client --addpkg php5-cli \
       --addpkg php5-gd --addpkg php5-ldap --addpkg php5-mysql --addpkg wwwconfig-common \
       --addpkg mysql-server --addpkg unattended-upgrades --addpkg acpid --ppa nijaba \
       --mirror http://mirroraddress:9999/ubuntu
```

19.2.7. Resources

If you are interested in learning more, have questions or suggestions, please contact the Ubuntu Server Team at:

- IRC: #ubuntu-server on freenode
- Mailing list: *ubuntu-server at lists.ubuntu.com*[11]
- Also, see the *JeOSVMBuilder Ubuntu Wiki*[12] page.

---

[11] *https://lists.ubuntu.com/mailman/listinfo/ubuntu-server*

19.3. UEC

19.3.1. Overview

This tutorial covers **UEC** installation from the Ubuntu 11.04 Server Edition CD, and assumes a basic network topology, with a single system serving as the *"all-in-one controller"*, and one or more nodes attached.

From this Tutorial you will learn how to install, configure, register and perform several operations on a basic **UEC** setup that results in a cloud with a one controller *"front-end"* and one or several node(s) for running Virtual Machine (VM) instances. You will also use examples to help get you started using your own private compute cloud.

19.3.2. Prerequisites

To deploy a minimal cloud infrastructure, you'll need at least *two* dedicated systems:

- A front end.
- One or more node(s).

The following are recommendations, rather than fixed requirements. However, our experience in developing this documentation indicated the following suggestions.

19.3.2.1. Front End Requirements

Use the following table for a system that will run one or more of:

- Cloud Controller (CLC)
- Cluster Controller (CC)
- Walrus (the S3-like storage service)
- Storage Controller (SC)

Hardware	Minimum	Suggested	Notes
CPU	1 GHz	2 x 2 GHz	For an *all-in-one* front end, it helps to have at least a dual core processor.
Memory	2 GB	4 GB	The Java web front end benefits from lots of available memory.
Disk	5400 RPM IDE	7200 RPM SATA	Slower disks will work, but will yield much longer instance startup times.

---

[12] *https://help.ubuntu.com/community/JeOSVMBuilder*

Hardware	Minimum	Suggested	Notes
Disk Space	40 GB	200 GB	40GB is only enough space for only a single image, cache, etc., Eucalyptus does not like to run out of disk space.
Networking	100 Mbps	1000 Mbps	Machine images are hundreds of MB, and need to be copied over the network to nodes.

Table 19.1. UEC Front End Requirements

19.3.2.2. Node Requirements

The other system(s) are *nodes*, which will run:

- the Node Controller (NC)

Hardware	Minimum	Suggested	Notes
CPU	VT Extensions	VT, 64-bit, Multicore	64-bit can run both i386, and amd64 instances; by default, Eucalyptus will only run 1 VM per CPU core on a Node.
Memory	1 GB	4 GB	Additional memory means more, and larger guests.
Disk	5400 RPM IDE	7200 RPM SATA or SCSI	Eucalyptus nodes are disk-intensive; I/O wait will likely be the performance bottleneck.
Disk Space	40 GB	100 GB	Images will be cached locally, Eucalyptus does not like to run out of disk space.
Networking	100 Mbps	1000 Mbps	Machine images are hundreds of MB, and need to be copied over the network to nodes.

Table 19.2. UEC Node Requirements

19.3.3. Installing the Cloud/Cluster/Storage/Walrus Front End Server

1. Download the Ubuntu 11.04 Server ISO file, and burn it to a CD.
2. When you boot, select *"Install Ubuntu Enterprise Cloud"*. The installer will detect if any other Eucalyptus components are present.
3. You can then choose which components to install, based on your chosen *topology*[13].
4. When asked whether you want a *"Cluster"* or a *"Node"* install, select *"Cluster"*.
5. It will ask two other cloud-specific questions during the course of the install:

---

[13] *https://help.ubuntu.com/community/UEC/Topologies*

- Name of your cluster.
  - e.g. *cluster1*.
- A range of public IP addresses on the LAN that the cloud can allocate to instances.
  - e.g. *192.168.1.200-192.168.1.249*.

19.3.4. Installing the Node Controller(s)

The node controller install is even simpler. Just make sure that you are connected to the network on which the cloud/cluster controller is already running.

1. Boot from the same ISO on the node(s).

2. When you boot, select *"Install Ubuntu Enterprise Cloud"*.

3. Select *"Install Ubuntu Enterprise Cloud"*.

4. It should detect the Cluster and preselect *"Node"* install for you.

5. Confirm the partitioning scheme.

6. The rest of the installation should proceed uninterrupted; complete the installation and reboot the node.

19.3.5. Register the Node(s)

1. Nodes are the physical systems within **UEC** that actually run the virtual machine instances of the cloud.

   All component registration should be automatic, assuming:

   - Public SSH keys have been exchanged properly.
   - The services are configured properly.
   - The appropriate *uec-component-listener* is running.
   - Verify Registration.

   Steps a to e should only be required if you're using the *UEC/PackageInstall*[14] method. Otherwise, if you are following this guide, these steps should already be completed automatically for you, and therefore you can skip *"a"* to *"e"*.

2. Exchange Public Keys

   The Cloud Controller's *eucalyptus* user needs to have SSH access to the Walrus Controller, Cluster Controller, and Storage Controller as the eucalyptus user.

   Install the Cloud Controller's *eucalyptus* user's public ssh key by:

---

[14] *https://help.ubuntu.com/community/UEC/PackageInstall*

- On the target controller, temporarily set a password for the eucalyptus user:

```
sudo passwd eucalyptus
```

- Then, on the Cloud Controller:

```
sudo -u eucalyptus ssh-copy-id -i ~eucalyptus/.ssh/id_rsa.pub
                                         eucalyptus@<IP_OF_NODE>
```

- You can now remove the password of the eucalyptus account on the target controller, if you wish:

```
sudo passwd -d eucalyptus
```

3. Configuring the Services

On the *Cloud Controller*:

- For the *Cluster Controller* Registration:
  - Define the shell variable CC_NAME in
    `/etc/eucalyptus/eucalyptus-cc.conf`
  - Define the shell variable CC_IP_ADDR in
    `/etc/eucalyptus/eucalyptus-ipaddr.conf`, as a space separated list of one or more IP addresses.

- For the *Walrus Controller* Registration:
  - Define the shell variable WALRUS_IP_ADDR in
    `/etc/eucalyptus/eucalyptus-ipaddr.conf`, as a single IP address.

On the *Cluster Controller*:

- For *Storage Controller* Registration:
  - Define the shell variable CC_NAME in `/etc/eucalyptus/eucalyptus-cc.conf`
  - Define the shell variable SC_IP_ADDR in
    `/etc/eucalyptus/eucalyptus-ipaddr.conf`, as a space separated list of one or more IP addresses.

4. Publish

Now start the publication services.

- *Walrus Controller:*

```
sudo start eucalyptus-walrus-publication
```

- *Cluster Controller:*

```
sudo start eucalyptus-cc-publication
```

- *Storage Controller:*

```
sudo start eucalyptus-sc-publication
```

- *Node Controller:*

```
sudo start eucalyptus-nc-publication
```

5. Start the Listener

On the *Cloud Controller* and the *Cluster Controller(s)*, run:

```
sudo start uec-component-listener
```

6. Verify Registration

```
cat /var/log/eucalyptus/registration.log
2010-04-08 15:46:36-05:00 | 24243 -> Calling node cluster1 node 10.1.1.75
2010-04-08 15:46:36-05:00 | 24243 -> euca_conf --register-nodes returned 0
2010-04-08 15:48:47-05:00 | 25858 -> Calling walrus Walrus 10.1.1.71
2010-04-08 15:48:51-05:00 | 25858 -> euca_conf --register-walrus returned 0
2010-04-08 15:49:04-05:00 | 26237 -> Calling cluster cluster1 10.1.1.71
2010-04-08 15:49:08-05:00 | 26237 -> euca_conf --register-cluster returned 0
2010-04-08 15:49:17-05:00 | 26644 -> Calling storage cluster1 storage
10.1.1.71
2010-04-08 15:49:18-05:00 | 26644 -> euca_conf --register-sc returned 0
```

 Note

The output on your machine will vary from the example above.

19.3.6. Obtain Credentials

After installing and booting the *Cloud Controller*, users of the cloud will need to retrieve their credentials. This can be done either through a web browser, or at the command line.

19.3.6.1. From a Web Browser

1. From your web browser (either remotely or on your Ubuntu server) access the following URL:

```
https://<cloud-controller-ip-address>:8443/
```

 Warning

You must use a secure connection, so make sure you use "https" not "http" in your URL. You will get a security certificate warning. You will have to add an exception to view the page. If you do not accept it you will not be able to view the Eucalyptus configuration page.

2. Use username *'admin'* and password *'admin'* for the first time login (you will be prompted to change your password).

3. Then follow the on-screen instructions to update the admin password and email address.

4. Once the first time configuration process is completed, click the *'credentials'* tab located in the top-left portion of the screen.

5. Click the *'Download Credentials'* button to get your certificates.

6. Save them to ~/.euca.

7. Unzip the downloaded zip file into a safe location (~/.euca).

```
unzip -d ~/.euca mycreds.zip
```

19.3.6.2. From a Command Line

- Alternatively, if you are on the command line of the *Cloud Controller*, you can run:

```
mkdir -p ~/.euca
chmod 700 ~/.euca
cd ~/.euca
sudo euca_conf --get-credentials mycreds.zip
unzip mycreds.zip
ln -s ~/.euca/eucarc ~/.eucarc
cd -
```

19.3.6.3. Extracting and Using Your Credentials

Now you will need to setup EC2 API and AMI tools on your server using X.509 certificates.

1. Install the required cloud user tools:

```
sudo apt-get install euca2ools
```

2. To validate that everything is working correctly, get the local cluster availability details:

```
. ~/.euca/eucarc
euca-describe-availability-zones verbose
AVAILABILITYZONE    myowncloud              192.168.1.1
AVAILABILITYZONE    |- vm types             free / max    cpu    ram    disk
AVAILABILITYZONE    |- m1.small             0004 / 0004    1     128      2
AVAILABILITYZONE    |- c1.medium            0004 / 0004    1     256      5
AVAILABILITYZONE    |- m1.large             0002 / 0002    2     512     10
AVAILABILITYZONE    |- m1.xlarge            0002 / 0002    2    1024     20
AVAILABILITYZONE    |- c1.xlarge            0001 / 0001    4    2048     20
```

 Note

Your output from the above command will vary.

19.3.7. Install an Image from the Store

The following is by far the simplest way to install an image. However, advanced users may be interested in learning how to *Bundle their own image*[15].

---

[15] *https://help.ubuntu.com/community/UEC/BundlingImages*

The simplest way to add an image to **UEC** is to install it from the Image Store on the UEC web interface.

1. Access the web interface at the following URL (Make sure you specify https):

   ```
   https://<cloud-controller-ip-address>:8443/
   ```

2. Enter your login and password (if requested, as you may still be logged in from earlier).

3. Click on the *Store* tab.

4. Browse available images.

5. Click on *install* for the image you want.

Once the image has been downloaded and installed, you can click on *"How to run?"* that will be displayed below the image button to view the command to execute to instantiate (start) this image. The image will also appear on the list given on the *Image* tab.

19.3.8. Run an Image

There are multiple ways to instantiate an image in UEC:

- Use the command line.
- Use one of the UEC compatible management tools such as *Landscape*.
- Use the *ElasticFox*[16] extension to Firefox.

Here we will describe the process from the command line:

1. Before running an instance of your image, you should first create a *keypair* (ssh key) that you can use to log into your instance as root, once it boots. The key is stored, so you will only have to do this once.

   Run the following command:

   ```
   if [ ! -e ~/.euca/mykey.priv ]; then
   mkdir -p -m 700 ~/.euca
       touch ~/.euca/mykey.priv
       chmod 0600 ~/.euca/mykey.priv
       euca-add-keypair mykey > ~/.euca/mykey.priv
   fi
   ```

Note

You can call your key whatever you like (in this example, the key is called '*mykey*'), but remember what it is called. If you forget, you can always run **euca-describe-keypairs** to get a list of created keys stored in the system.

---

[16] *https://help.ubuntu.com/community/UEC/ElasticFox*

---

2. You must also allow access to port 22 in your instances:

```
euca-authorize default -P tcp -p 22 -s 0.0.0.0/0
```

3. Next, you can create instances of your registered image:

```
euca-run-instances $EMI -k mykey -t m1.small
```

 Note

If you receive an error regarding *image_id*, you may find it by viewing Images page or click "*How to Run*" on the *Store* page to see the sample command.

4. The first time you run an instance, the system will be setting up caches for the image from which it will be created. This can often take some time the first time an instance is run given that VM images are usually quite large.

   To monitor the state of your instance, run:

```
watch -n5 euca-describe-instances
```

   In the output, you should see information about the instance, including its state. While first-time caching is being performed, the instance's state will be '*pending*'.

5. When the instance is fully started, the above state will become '*running*'. Look at the IP address assigned to your instance in the output, then connect to it:

```
IPADDR=$(euca-describe-instances | grep $EMI | grep running | tail -n1 |
                                               awk '{print $4}')
ssh -i ~/.euca/mykey.priv ubuntu@$IPADDR
```

6. And when you are done with this instance, exit your SSH connection, then terminate your instance:

```
INSTANCEID=$(euca-describe-instances | grep $EMI | grep running | tail -n1 |
                                                  awk '{print $2}')
euca-terminate-instances $INSTANCEID
```

19.3.8.1. First Boot

The **cloud-init** package provides "first boot" functionality for the Ubuntu UEC images. It is in charge of taking the generic filesystem image that is booting and customizing it for this particular instance. That includes things like:

- Setting the hostname.
- Putting the provided ssh public keys into `~ubuntu/.ssh/authorized_keys`.
- Running a user provided script, or otherwise modifying the image.

Setting hostname and configuring a system so the person who launched it can actually log into it are not terribly interesting. The interesting things that can be done with **cloud-init** are made possible by data provided at launch time called *user-data*[17].

---

[17] *http://developer.amazonwebservices.com/connect/entry.jspa?externalID=1085*

First, install the **cloud-init** package:

```
sudo apt-get install cloud-init
```

If the user-data starts with '#!', then it will be stored and executed as root late in the boot process of the instance's first boot (similar to a traditional 'rc.local' script). Output from the script is directed to the console.

For example, create a file named ud.txt containing:

```
#!/bin/sh
echo ========== Hello World: $(date) ==========
echo "I have been up for $(cut -d\  -f 1 < /proc/uptime) sec"
```

Now start an instance with the *--user-data-file* option:

```
euca-run-instances $EMI -k mykey -t m1.small  --user-data-file=ud.txt
```

Wait now for the system to come up and console to be available. To see the result of the data file commands enter:

```
euca-get-console-output $EMI | grep --after-context=1 Hello
========== Hello World: Mon Mar 29 18:05:05 UTC 2010 ==========
I have been up for 28.26 sec
```

 Note

Your output may vary.

The simple approach shown above gives a great deal of power. The user-data can contain a script in any language where an interpreter already exists in the image (#!/bin/sh, #!/usr/bin/python, #!/usr/bin/perl, #!/usr/bin/awk ...).

For many cases, the user may not be interested in writing a program. For this case, cloud-init provides "*cloud-config*", a configuration based approach towards customization. To utilize the cloud-config syntax, the supplied user-data must start with a '#*cloud-config*'.

For example, create a text file named cloud-config.txt containing:

```
#cloud-config
apt_upgrade: true
apt_sources:
- source: "ppa:ubuntu-server-edgers/server-edgers-apache "

packages:
- build-essential
- pastebinit

runcmd:
- echo ======= Hello World =====
- echo "I have been up for $(cut -d\  -f 1 < /proc/uptime) sec"
Create a new instance:
euca-run-instances $EMI -k mykey -t m1.small --user-data-file=cloud-config.txt
```

Now, when the above system is booted, it will have:

- Added the Apache Edgers PPA.
- Run an upgrade to get all updates available
- Installed the 'build-essential' and 'pastebinit' packages
- Printed a similar message to the script above

 Note

The *Apache Edgers PPA*, in the above example, contains the latest version of Apache from upstream source repositories. Package versions in the PPA are unsupported, and depending on your situation, this may or may not be desirable. See the *Ubuntu Server Edgers*[18] web page for more details.

The '*runcmd*' commands are run at the same point in boot that the '#!' script would run in the previous example. It is present to allow you to get the full power of a scripting language if you need it without abandoning *cloud-config*.

For more information on what kinds of things can be done with **cloud-config**, see *doc/examples*[19] in the source.

19.3.9. More Information

How to use the *Storage Controller*[20]

Controlling eucalyptus services:

- sudo service eucalyptus [start | stop | restart] (on the CLC/CC/SC/Walrus side)
- sudo service eucalyptus-nc [start | stop | restart] (on the Node side)

Locations of some important files:

- *Log files:*
  - /var/log/eucalyptus
- *Configuration files:*
  - /etc/eucalyptus
- *Database:*
  - /var/lib/eucalyptus/db

---

18 *https://launchpad.net/~ubuntu-server-edgers*
19 *http://bazaar.launchpad.net/~cloud-init-dev/cloud-init/trunk/files/head:/doc/examples/*
20 *https://help.ubuntu.com/community/UEC/StorageController*

- *Keys:*
  - /var/lib/eucalyptus
  - /var/lib/eucalyptus/.ssh

 Note

Don't forget to source your `~/.euca/eucarc` before running the client tools.

19.3.10. References

- For information on loading instances see the *Eucalyptus Wiki*[21] page.
- *Eucalyptus Project Site*[22] *(forums, documentation, downloads).*
- *Eucalyptus on Launchpad*[23] *(bugs, code).*
- *Eucalyptus Troubleshooting*[24] *(1.5).*
- *Register your cloud with RightScale*[25].
- You can also find help in the *#ubuntu-virt*, *#eucalyptus*, and *#ubuntu-server* IRC channels on *Freenode*[26].

19.3.11. Glossary

The Ubuntu Enterprise Cloud documentation uses terminology that might be unfamiliar to some readers. This page is intended to provide a glossary of such terms and acronyms.

- *Cloud* - A federated set of physical machines that offer computing resources through virtual machines, provisioned and recollected dynamically.
- *Cloud Controller (CLC)* - Eucalyptus component that provides the web UI (an https server on port 8443), and implements the Amazon EC2 API. There should be only one Cloud Controller in an installation of UEC. This service is provided by the Ubuntu **eucalyptus-cloud** package.
- *Cluster* - A collection of nodes, associated with a Cluster Controller. There can be more than one Cluster in an installation of UEC. Clusters are sometimes physically separate sets of nodes. (e.g. floor1, floor2, floor2).

---

[21] *https://help.ubuntu.com/community/Eucalyptus*

[22] *http://open.eucalyptus.com/*

[23] *https://launchpad.net/eucalyptus/*

[24] *http://open.eucalyptus.com/wiki/EucalyptusTroubleshooting_v1.5*

[25] *http://support.rightscale.com/2._References/02-Cloud_Infrastructures/Eucalyptus/03-Administration_Guide/Register_with_RightScale*

[26] *http://freenode.net/*

- *Cluster Controller (CC)* - Eucalyptus component that manages collections of node resources. This service is provided by the Ubuntu **eucalyptus-cc** package.

- *EBS* - Elastic Block Storage.

- *EC2* - Elastic Compute Cloud. Amazon's pay-by-the-hour, pay-by-the-gigabyte public cloud computing offering.

- *EKI* - Eucalyptus Kernel Image.

- *EMI* - Eucalyptus Machine Image.

- *ERI* - Eucalyptus Ramdisk Image.

- *Eucalyptus* - Elastic Utility Computing Architecture for Linking Your Programs To Useful Systems. An open source project originally from the University of California at Santa Barbara, now supported by Eucalyptus Systems, a Canonical Partner.

- *Front-end* - Physical machine hosting one (or more) of the high level Eucalyptus components (cloud, walrus, storage controller, cluster controller).

- *Node* - A node is a physical machine that's capable of running virtual machines, running a node controller. Within Ubuntu, this generally means that the CPU has VT extensions, and can run the KVM hypervisor.

- *Node Controller (NC)* - Eucalyptus component that runs on nodes which host the virtual machines that comprise the cloud. This service is provided by the Ubuntu package **eucalyptus-nc**.

- *S3* - Simple Storage Service. Amazon's pay-by-the-gigabyte persistent storage solution for EC2.

- *Storage Controller (SC)* - Eucalyptus component that manages dynamic block storage services (EBS). Each 'cluster' in a Eucalyptus installation can have its own Storage Controller. This component is provided by the **eucalyptus-sc** package.

- *UEC* - Ubuntu Enterprise Cloud. Ubuntu's cloud computing solution, based on Eucalyptus.

- *VM* - Virtual Machine.

- *VT* - Virtualization Technology. An optional feature of some modern CPUs, allowing for accelerated virtual machine hosting.

- *Walrus* - Eucalyptus component that implements the Amazon S3 API, used for storing VM images and user storage using S3 bucket put/get abstractions.

Chapter 20.
Clustering

20.1. DRBD

Distributed Replicated Block Device (DRBD) mirrors block devices between multiple hosts. The replication is transparent to other applications on the host systems. Any block device hard disks, partitions, RAID devices, logical volumes, etc can be mirrored.

To get started using **drbd**, first install the necessary packages. From a terminal enter:

```
sudo apt-get install drbd8-utils
```

 Note

> If you are using the *virtual kernel* as part of a virtual machine you will need to manually compile the **drbd** module. It may be easier to install the **linux-server** package inside the virtual machine.

This section covers setting up a **drbd** to replicate a separate /srv partition, with an **ext3** filesystem between two hosts. The partition size is not particularly relevant, but both partitions need to be the same size.

20.1.1. Configuration

The two hosts in this example will be called *drbd01* and *drbd02*. They will need to have name resolution configured either through DNS or the /etc/hosts file. See Chapter 7, *Domain Name Service (DNS)* for details.

- To configure **drbd**, on the first host edit /etc/drbd.conf:

```
global { usage-count no; }
common { syncer { rate 100M; } }
resource r0 {
        protocol C;
        startup {
                wfc-timeout  15;
                degr-wfc-timeout 60;
        }
        net {
                cram-hmac-alg sha1;
```

```
                shared-secret "secret";
        }
        on drbd01 {
                device /dev/drbd0;
                disk /dev/sdb1;
                address 192.168.0.1:7788;
                meta-disk internal;
        }
        on drbd02 {
                device /dev/drbd0;
                disk /dev/sdb1;
                address 192.168.0.2:7788;
                meta-disk internal;

        }
}
```

 Note

There are many other options in /etc/drbd.conf, but for this example their default values are fine.

- Now copy /etc/drbd.conf to the second host:
```
scp /etc/drbd.conf drbd02:~
```

- And, on *drbd02* move the file to /etc:
```
sudo mv drbd.conf /etc/
```

- Now using the **drbdadm** utility initialize the meta data storage. On each server execute:
```
sudo drbdadm create-md r0
```

- Next, on both hosts, start the **drbd** daemon:
```
sudo /etc/init.d/drbd start
```

- Now using the **drbdadm** utility initialize the meta data storage. On each server execute:
```
sudo drbdadm create-md r0
```

- On the *drbd01*, or whichever host you wish to be the primary, enter the following:
```
sudo drbdadm -- --overwrite-data-of-peer primary all
```

- After executing the above command, the data will start syncing with the secondary host. To watch the progress, on *drbd02* enter the following:
```
watch -n1 cat /proc/drbd
```
To stop watching the output press *Ctrl+c*.

- Finally, add a filesystem to /dev/drbd0 and mount it:
```
sudo mkfs.ext3 /dev/drbd0
sudo mount /dev/drbd0 /srv
```

20.1.2. Testing

To test that the data is actually syncing between the hosts copy some files on the *drbd01*, the primary, to /srv:

```
sudo cp -r /etc/default /srv
```

Next, unmount /srv:

```
sudo umount /srv
```

Demote the *primary* server to the *secondary* role:

```
sudo drbdadm secondary r0
```

Now on the *secondary* server *promote* it to the *primary* role:

```
sudo drbdadm primary r0
```

Lastly, mount the partition:

```
sudo mount /dev/drbd0 /srv
```

Using *ls* you should see /srv/default copied from the former *primary* host *drbd01*.

20.1.3. References

- For more information on **DRBD** see the *DRBD web site*[1].
- The *drbd.conf man page*[2] contains details on the options not covered in this guide.
- Also, see the *drbdadm man page*[3].
- The *DRBD Ubuntu Wiki*[4] page also has more information.

---

[1] *http://www.drbd.org/*
[2] *http://manpages.ubuntu.com/manpages/natty/en/man5/drbd.conf.5.html*
[3] *http://manpages.ubuntu.com/manpages/natty/en/man8/drbdadm.8.html*
[4] *https://help.ubuntu.com/community/DRBD*

Chapter 21.
VPN

A Virtual Private Network, or *VPN*, is an encrypted network connection between two or more networks. There are several ways to create a VPN using software as well as dedicated hardware appliances. This chapter will cover installing and configuring **OpenVPN** to create a VPN between two servers.

21.1. OpenVPN

OpenVPN uses Public Key Infrastructure (PKI) to encrypt VPN traffic between nodes. A simple way of setting up a VPN with OpenVPN is to connect the clients through a bridge interface on the VPN server. This guide will assume that one VPN node, the server in this case, has a bridge interface configured. For more information on setting up a bridge see the Section 4.1.4, *Bridging*.

21.1.1. Installation

To install **openvpn** in a terminal enter:

```
sudo apt-get install openvpn
```

21.1.2. Server Certificates

Now that the **openvpn** package is installed, the certificates for the VPN server need to be created.

First, copy the `easy-rsa` directory to `/etc/openvpn`. This will ensure that any changes to the scripts will not be lost when the package is updated. You will also need to adjust permissions in the `easy-rsa` directory to allow the current user permission to create files. From a terminal enter:

```
sudo mkdir /etc/openvpn/easy-rsa/
sudo cp -r /usr/share/doc/openvpn/examples/easy-rsa/2.0/* /etc/openvpn/easy-rsa/
sudo chown -R $USER /etc/openvpn/easy-rsa/
```

Next, edit `/etc/openvpn/easy-rsa/vars` adjusting the following to your environment:

```
export KEY_COUNTRY="US"
export KEY_PROVINCE="NC"
```

```
export KEY_CITY="Winston-Salem"
export KEY_ORG="Example Company"
export KEY_EMAIL="steve@example.com"
```

Enter the following to create the server certificates:

```
cd /etc/openvpn/easy-rsa/
source vars
./clean-all
./build-dh
./pkitool --initca
./pkitool --server server
cd keys
openvpn --genkey --secret ta.key
sudo cp server.crt server.key ca.crt dh1024.pem ta.key /etc/openvpn/
```

21.1.3. Client Certificates

The VPN client will also need a certificate to authenticate itself to the server. To create the certificate, enter the following in a terminal:

```
cd /etc/openvpn/easy-rsa/
source vars
./pkitool hostname
```

 Note

Replace *hostname* with the actual hostname of the machine connecting to the VPN.

Copy the following files to the client:

- /etc/openvpn/ca.crt
- /etc/openvpn/easy-rsa/keys/hostname.crt
- /etc/openvpn/easy-rsa/keys/hostname.key
- /etc/openvpn/ta.key

 Note

Remember to adjust the above file names for your client machine's *hostname*.

It is best to use a secure method to copy the certificate and key files. The **scp** utility is a good choice, but copying the files to removable media then to the client, also works well.

21.2. Configuration

21.2.1. Server Configuration

Now configure the **openvpn** server by creating /etc/openvpn/server.conf from the example file. In a terminal enter:

```
sudo cp /usr/share/doc/openvpn/examples/sample-config-files/server.conf.gz /etc/openvpn/
sudo gzip -d /etc/openvpn/server.conf.gz
```

Edit `/etc/openvpn/server.conf` changing the following options to:

```
local 172.18.100.101
dev tap0
up "/etc/openvpn/up.sh br0"
down "/etc/openvpn/down.sh br0"
;server 10.8.0.0 255.255.255.0
server-bridge 172.18.100.101 255.255.255.0 172.18.100.105 172.18.100.200
push "route 172.18.100.1 255.255.255.0"
push "dhcp-option DNS 172.18.100.20"
push "dhcp-option DOMAIN example.com"
tls-auth ta.key 0 # This file is secret
user nobody
group nogroup
```

- *local*: is the IP address of the bridge interface.
- *server-bridge*: needed when the configuration uses bridging. The *172.18.100.101 255.255.255.0* portion is the bridge interface and mask. The IP range *172.18.100.105 172.18.100.200* is the range of IP addresses that will be assigned to clients.
- *push*: are directives to add networking options for clients.
- *user and group*: configure which user and group the **openvpn** daemon executes as.

Note

Replace all IP addresses and domain names above with those of your network.

Next, create a couple of helper scripts to add the *tap* interface to the bridge. Create `/etc/openvpn/up.sh`:

```
#!/bin/sh

BR=$1
DEV=$2
MTU=$3
/sbin/ifconfig $DEV mtu $MTU promisc up
/usr/sbin/brctl addif $BR $DEV
```

And /etc/openvpn/down.sh:

```
#!/bin/sh

BR=$1
DEV=$2

/usr/sbin/brctl delif $BR $DEV
/sbin/ifconfig $DEV down
```

Then make them executable:

```
sudo chmod 755 /etc/openvpn/down.sh
sudo chmod 755 /etc/openvpn/up.sh
```

After configuring the server, restart **openvpn** by entering:

```
sudo /etc/init.d/openvpn restart
```

21.2.2. Client Configuration

First, install **openvpn** on the client:

```
sudo apt-get install openvpn
```

Then with the server configured and the client certificates copied to the /etc/openvpn/ directory, create a client configuration file by copying the example. In a terminal on the client machine enter:

```
sudo cp /usr/share/doc/openvpn/examples/sample-config-files/client.conf /etc/openvpn
```

Now edit /etc/openvpn/client.conf changing the following options:

```
dev tap
remote vpn.example.com 1194
cert hostname.crt
key hostname.key
tls-auth ta.key 1
```

 Note

Replace *vpn.example.com* with the hostname of your VPN server, and *hostname.** with the actual certificate and key filenames.

Finally, restart **openvpn**:

```
sudo /etc/init.d/openvpn restart
```

You should now be able to connect to the remote LAN through the VPN.

21.3. References

- See the *OpenVPN*[1] website for additional information.
- Also, Pakt's *OpenVPN: Building and Integrating Virtual Private Networks*[2] is a good resource.
- Another source of further information is the *Ubuntu Wiki OpenVPN*[3] page.

---

[1] *http://openvpn.net/*

[2] *http://www.packtpub.com/openvpn/book*

[3] *https://help.ubuntu.com/community/OpenVPN*

Chapter 22.
Other Useful Applications

There are many very useful applications developed by the Ubuntu Server Team, and others that are well integrated with Ubuntu Server Edition, that might not be well known. This chapter will showcase some useful applications that can make administering an Ubuntu server, or many Ubuntu servers, that much easier.

22.1. pam_motd

When logging into an Ubuntu server you may have noticed the informative Message Of The Day (MOTD). This information is obtained and displayed using a couple of packages:

- *landscape-common:* provides the core libraries of **landscape-client**, which can be used to manage systems using the web based *Landscape* application. The package includes the **/usr/bin/landscape-sysinfo** utility which is used to gather the information displayed in the MOTD.

- *update-notifier-common:* is used to automatically update the MOTD via **pam_motd** module.

pam_motd executes the scripts in /etc/update-motd.d in order based on the number prepended to the script. The output of the scripts is written to /var/run/motd, keeping the numerical order, then concatenated with /etc/motd.tail

You can add your own dynamic information to the MOTD. For example, to add local weather information:

- First, install the **weather-util** package:

  ```
  sudo apt-get install weather-util
  ```

- The **weather** utility uses METAR data from the National Oceanic and Atmospheric Administration and forecasts from the National Weather Service. In order to find local information you will need the 4-character ICAO location indicator. This can be determined by browsing to the *National Weather Service*[1] site.

---

[1] *http://www.weather.gov/tg/siteloc.shtml*

Although the National Weather Service is a United States government agency there are weather stations available world wide. However, local weather information for all locations outside the U.S. may not be available.

- Create `/usr/local/bin/local-weather`, a simple shell script to use **weather** with your local ICAO indicator:

```
#!/bin/sh
#
#
# Prints the local weather information for the MOTD.
#
#

# Replace KINT with your local weather station.
# Local stations can be found here: http://www.weather.gov/tg/siteloc.shtml

echo
weather -i KINT
echo
```

- Make the script executable:

```
sudo chmod 755 /usr/local/bin/local-weather
```

- Next, create a symlink to `/etc/update-motd.d/98-local-weather`:

```
sudo ln -s /usr/local/bin/local-weather /etc/update-motd.d/98-local-weather
```

- Finally, exit the server and re-login to view the new MOTD.

You should now be greeted with some useful information, and some information about the local weather that may not be quite so useful. Hopefully the **local-weather** example demonstrates the flexibility of **pam_motd**.

22.2. etckeeper

etckeeper allows the contents of `/etc` be easily stored in Version Control System (VCS) repository. It hooks into **apt** to automatically commit changes to `/etc` when packages are installed or upgraded. Placing `/etc` under version control is considered an industry best practice, and the goal of **etckeeper** is to make this process as painless as possible.

Install **etckeeper** by entering the following in a terminal:

```
sudo apt-get install etckeeper
```

The main configuration file, `/etc/etckeeper/etckeeper.conf`, is fairly simple. The main option is which VCS to use. By default **etckeeper** is configured to use **bzr** for version control. The repository is automatically initialized (and committed for the first time) during package installation. It is possible to undo this by entering the following command:

```
sudo etckeeper uninit
```

By default, etckeeper will commit uncommitted changes made to /etc daily. This can be disabled using the AVOID_DAILY_AUTOCOMMITS configuration option. It will also automatically commit changes before and after package installation. For a more precise tracking of changes, it is recommended to commit your changes manually, together with a commit message, using:

```
sudo etckeeper commit "..Reason for configuration change.."
```

Using the VCS commands you can view log information about files in /etc:

```
sudo bzr log /etc/passwd
```

To demonstrate the integration with the package management system, install **postfix**:

```
sudo apt-get install postfix
```

When the installation is finished, all the **postfix** configuration files should be committed to the repository:

```
Committing to: /etc/
added aliases.db
modified group
modified group-
modified gshadow
modified gshadow-
modified passwd
modified passwd-
added postfix
added resolvconf
added rsyslog.d
modified shadow
modified shadow-
added init.d/postfix
added network/if-down.d/postfix
added network/if-up.d/postfix
added postfix/dynamicmaps.cf
added postfix/main.cf
added postfix/master.cf
added postfix/post-install
added postfix/postfix-files
added postfix/postfix-script
added postfix/sasl
added ppp/ip-down.d
added ppp/ip-down.d/postfix
added ppp/ip-up.d/postfix
added rc0.d/K20postfix
added rc1.d/K20postfix
added rc2.d/S20postfix
added rc3.d/S20postfix
added rc4.d/S20postfix
```

```
added rc5.d/S20postfix
added rc6.d/K20postfix
added resolvconf/update-libc.d
added resolvconf/update-libc.d/postfix
added rsyslog.d/postfix.conf
added ufw/applications.d/postfix
Committed revision 2.
```

For an example of how **etckeeper** tracks manual changes, add new a host to `/etc/hosts`. Using **bzr** you can see which files have been modified:

```
sudo bzr status /etc/
modified:
  hosts
```

Now commit the changes:

```
sudo etckeeper commit "new host"
```

For more information on **bzr** see the Section 16.1, *Bazaar*.

22.3. Byobu

One of the most useful applications for any system administrator is **screen**. It allows the execution of multiple shells in one terminal. To make some of the advanced **screen** features more user friendly, and provide some useful information about the system, the **byobu** package was created.

When executing **byobu** pressing the *F9* key will bring up the **Configuration** menu. This menu will allow you to:

- View the Help menu
- Change Byobu's background color
- Change Byobu's foreground color
- Toggle status notifications
- Change the key binding set
- Change the escape sequence
- Create new windows
- Manage the default windows
- Byobu currently does not launch at login (toggle on)

The *key bindings* determine such things as the escape sequence, new window, change window, etc. There are two key binding sets to choose from *f-keys* and *screen-escape-keys*. If you wish to use the original key bindings choose the *none* set.

byobu provides a menu which displays the Ubuntu release, processor information, memory information, and the time and date. The effect is similar to a desktop menu.

Using the "*Byobu currently does not launch at login (toggle on)*" option will cause **byobu** to be executed any time a terminal is opened. Changes made to **byobu** are on a per user basis, and will not affect other users on the system.

One difference when using byobu is the *scrollback* mode. Press the *F7* key to enter scrollback mode. Scrollback mode allows you to navigate past output using *vi* like commands. Here is a quick list of movement commands:

- *h* - Move the cursor left by one character
- *j* - Move the cursor down by one line
- *k* - Move the cursor up by one line
- *l* - Move the cursor right by one character
- *0* - Move to the beginning of the current line
- *$* - Move to the end of the current line
- *G* - Moves to the specified line (defaults to the end of the buffer)
- */* - Search forward
- *?* - Search backward
- *n* - Moves to the next match, either forward or backword

22.4. References

- See the *update-motd man page*[2] for more options available to **update-motd**.
- The Debian Package of the Day *weather*[3] article has more details about using the **weather**utility.
- See the *etckeeper*[4] site for more details on using **etckeeper**.
- For the latest news and information about **bzr** see the *bzr*[5] web site.
- For more information on **screen** see the *screen web site*[6].
- And the *Ubuntu Wiki screen*[7] page.
- Also, see the **byobu** *project page*[8] for more information.

---

[2] *http://manpages.ubuntu.com/manpages/natty/en/man1/update-motd.1.html*
[3] *http://debaday.debian.net/2007/10/04/weather-check-weather-conditions-and-forecasts-on-the-command-line/*
[4] *http://kitenet.net/~joey/code/etckeeper/*
[5] *http://bazaar-vcs.org/*
[6] *http://www.gnu.org/software/screen/*
[7] *https://help.ubuntu.com/community/Screen*
[8] *https://launchpad.net/byobu*

Appendix A.
Appendix

A.1. Reporting Bugs in Ubuntu Server Edition

While the Ubuntu Project attempts to release software with as few bugs as possible, they do occur. You can help fix these bugs by reporting ones that you find to the project. The Ubuntu Project uses *Launchpad*[1] to track its bug reports. In order to file a bug about Ubuntu Server on Launchpad, you will need to *create an account*[2].

A.1.1. Reporting Bugs With ubuntu-bug

The preferred way to report a bug is with the **ubuntu-bug** command. The ubuntu-bug tool gathers information about the system useful to developers in diagnosing the reported problem that will then be included in the bug report filed on Launchpad. Bug reports in Ubuntu need to be filed against a specific software package, thus the name of the package that the bug occurs in needs to be given to ubuntu-bug:

```
ubuntu-bug PACKAGENAME
```

For example, to file a bug against the openssh-server package, you would do:

```
ubuntu-bug openssh-server
```

You can specify either a binary package or the source package for ubuntu-bug. Again using openssh-server as an example, you could also generate the report against the source package for openssh-server, openssh:

```
ubuntu-bug openssh
```

 Note

> See Chapter 3, *Package Management* for more information about packages in Ubuntu.

---

[1] *https://launchpad.net/*
[2] *https://help.launchpad.net/YourAccount/NewAccount*

The ubuntu-bug command will gather information about the system in question, possibly including information specific to the specified package, and then ask you what you would like to do with collected information:

```
ubuntu-bug postgresql

*** Collecting problem information

The collected information can be sent to the developers to improve the application.
This might take a few minutes.
. . . . . . . . . .

*** Send problem report to the developers?

After the problem report has been sent, please fill out the form in the
automatically opened web browser.

What would you like to do? Your options are:
  S: Send report (1.7 KiB)
  V: View report
  K: Keep report file for sending later or copying to somewhere else
  C: Cancel
Please choose (S/V/K/C):
```

The options available are:

- **Send Report** Selecting Send Report submits the collected information to Launchpad as part of the the process of filing a bug report. You will be given the opportunity to describe the situation that led up to the occurrence of the bug.

```
*** Uploading problem information

The collected information is being sent to the bug tracking system.
This might take a few minutes.
91%

*** To continue, you must visit the following URL:

  https://bugs.launchpad.net/ubuntu/+source/postgresql-
8.4/+filebug/kc6eSnTLnLxF8u0t3e56EukFeqJ?

You can launch a browser now, or copy this URL into a browser on another
computer.

Choices:
  1: Launch a browser now
  C: Cancel
Please choose (1/C):
```

If you choose to start a browser, by default the text based web browser **w3m** will be used to finish filing the bug report. Alternately, you can copy the given URL to a currently running web browser.

- **View Report** Selecting View Report causes the collected information to be displayed to the terminal for review.

```
Package: postgresql 8.4.2-2
PackageArchitecture: all
Tags: natty
ProblemType: Bug
ProcEnviron:
  LANG=en_US.UTF-8
  SHELL=/bin/bash
Uname: Linux 2.6.32-16-server x86_64
Dependencies:
  adduser 3.112ubuntu1
  base-files 5.0.0ubuntu10
  base-passwd 3.5.22
  coreutils 7.4-2ubuntu2
...
```

After viewing the report, you will be brought back to the same menu asking what you would like to do with the report.

- **Keep Report File** Selecting Keep Report File causes the gathered information to be written to a file. This file can then be used to later file a bug report or transferred to a different Ubuntu system for reporting. To submit the report file, simply give it as an argument to the ubuntu-bug command:

```
What would you like to do? Your options are:
  S: Send report (1.7 KiB)
  V: View report
  K: Keep report file for sending later or copying to somewhere else
  C: Cancel
Please choose (S/V/K/C): k
Problem report file: /tmp/apport.postgresql.v4MQas.apport
```

```
ubuntu-bug /tmp/apport.postgresql.v4MQas.apport
```

```
*** Send problem report to the developers?
...
```

- **Cancel** Selecting Cancel causes the collected information to be discarded.

A.1.2. Reporting Application Crashes

The software package that provides the ubuntu-bug utility, **apport**, can be configured to trigger when applications crash. This is disabled by default, as capturing a crash can be resource intensive depending on how much memory the application that crashed was using as apport captures and processes the core dump.

Configuring apport to capture information about crashing applications requires a couple of steps. First, **gdb** needs to be installed; it is not installed by default in Ubuntu Server Edition.

```
sudo apt-get install gdb
```

See Chapter 3, *Package Management* for more information about managing packages in Ubuntu.

Once you have ensured that gdb is installed, open the file `/etc/default/apport` in your text editor, and change the *enabled* setting to be **1** like so:

```
# set this to 0 to disable apport, or to 1 to enable it
# you can temporarily override this with
# sudo service apport start force_start=1
enabled=1

# set maximum core dump file size (default: 209715200 bytes == 200 MB)
maxsize=209715200
```

Once you have completed editing `/etc/default/apport`, start the apport service:

```
sudo start apport
```

After an application crashes, use the **apport-cli** command to search for the existing saved crash report information:

```
apport-cli

*** dash closed unexpectedly on 2010-03-11 at 21:40:59.

If you were not doing anything confidential (entering passwords or other
private information), you can help to improve the application by
reporting
the problem.

What would you like to do? Your options are:
  R: Report Problem...
  I: Cancel and ignore future crashes of this program version
  C: Cancel
Please choose (R/I/C):
```

Selecting *Report Problem* will walk you through similar steps as when using ubuntu-bug. One important difference is that a crash report will be marked as private when filed on Launchpad, meaning that it will be visible to only a limited set of bug triagers. These triagers will review the gathered data for private information before making the bug report publicly visible.

A.1.3. Resources

- See the *Reporting Bugs*[3] Ubuntu wiki page.
- Also, the *Apport*[4] page has some useful information. Though some of it pertains to using a GUI.

---

[3] *https://help.ubuntu.com/community/ReportingBugs*
[4] *https://wiki.ubuntu.com/Apport*

Linbrary™ Advertising Club (LAC)

Linbrary™ Official Docs as a Real Books
http://www.linbrary.com 📚 Linux Library

Linbrary Advertising Club

Fedora Project Official Documentation

http://docs.fedoraproject.org

Version	Title	Edition	ISBN- 10	ISBN- 13
Fedora 14	Fedora 14 Installation Guide	paperback	1-59682-228-7	978-1-59682-228-3
		eBook (pdf)	1-59682-233-3	978-1-59682-233-7
	Fedora 14 User Guide	paperback	1-59682-229-5	978-1-59682-229-0
		eBook (pdf)	1-59682-234-1	978-1-59682-234-4
	Fedora 14 Security Guide	paperback	1-59682-230-9	978-1-59682-230-6
		eBook (pdf)	1-59682-235-X	978-1-59682-235-1
	Fedora 14 Storage Administration Guide	paperback	1-59682-231-7	978-1-59682-231-3
		eBook (pdf)	1-59682-236-8	978-1-59682-236-8
	Fedora 14 Musicians Guide	paperback	1-59682-232-5	978-1-59682-232-0
		eBook (pdf)	1-59682-237-6	978-1-59682-237-5
Fedora 13	Fedora 13 Installation Guide	paperback	1-59682-212-0	978-1-59682-212-2
		eBook (pdf)	1-59682-217-1	978-1-59682-217-7
	Fedora 13 User Guide	paperback	1-59682-213-9	978-1-59682-213-9
		eBook (pdf)	1-59682-218-X	978-1-59682-218-4
	Fedora 13 Security Guide	paperback	1-59682-214-7	978-1-59682-214-6
		eBook (pdf)	1-59682-219-8	978-1-59682-219-1
	Fedora 13 SE Linux User Guide	paperback	1-59682-215-5	978-1-59682-215-3
		eBook (pdf)	1-59682-220-1	978-1-59682-220-7
	Fedora 13 Virtualization Guide	paperback	1-59682-216-3	978-1-59682-216-0
		eBook (pdf)	1-59682-221-X	978-1-59682-221-4

http://www.linbrary.com/fedora/

Linbrary Advertising Club

Fedora Project Official Documentation

http://docs.fedoraproject.org

Version	Title	Edition	ISBN-10	ISBN-13
Fedora 12	Fedora 12 Installation Guide	paperback	1-59682-179-5	978-1-59682-179-8
		eBook (pdf)	1-59682-184-1	978-1-59682-184-2
	Fedora 12 User Guide	paperback	1-59682-180-9	978-1-59682-180-4
		eBook (pdf)	1-59682-185-X	978-1-59682-185-9
	Fedora 12 Security Guide	paperback	1-59682-181-7	978-1-59682-181-1
		eBook (pdf)	1-59682-186-8	978-1-59682-186-6
	Fedora 12 SE Linux User Guide	paperback	1-59682-182-5	978-1-59682-182-8
		eBook (pdf)	1-59682-187-6	978-1-59682-187-3
	Fedora 12 Virtualization Guide	paperback	1-59682-183-3	978-1-59682-183-5
		eBook (pdf)	1-59682-188-4	978-1-59682-188-0
Fedora 11	Fedora 11 Installation Guide	paperback	1-59682-142-6	978-1-59682-142-2
		eBook (pdf)	1-59682-146-9	978-1-59682-146-0
	Fedora 11 User Guide	paperback	1-59682-143-4	978-1-59682-143-9
		eBook (pdf)	1-59682-147-7	978-1-59682-147-7
	Fedora 11 Security Guide	paperback	1-59682-144-2	978-1-59682-144-6
		eBook (pdf)	1-59682-148-5	978-1-59682-148-4
	Fedora 11 SE Linux User Guide	paperback	1-59682-145-0	978-1-59682-145-3
		eBook (pdf)	1-59682-149-3	978-1-59682-149-1
http://www.linbrary.com/fedora/				

Linbrary Advertising Club

PostgreSQL Official Documentation

http://www.postgresq.org/

Version	Title	Edition	ISBN-10	ISBN-13
PostgreSQL 9.0	PostgreSQL 9.0 **Volume I. The SQL Language**	paperback	1-59682-246-5	978-1-59682-246-7
		eBook (pdf)	1-59682-251-1	978-1-59682-251-1
	PostgreSQL 9.0 **Volume II. Server Administration**	paperback	1-59682-247-3	978-1-59682-247-4
		eBook (pdf)	1-59682-252-X	978-1-59682-252-8
	PostgreSQL 9.0 **Volume III. Server Programming**	paperback	1-59682-248-1	978-1-59682-248-1
		eBook (pdf)	1-59682-253-8	978-1-59682-253-5
	PostgreSQL 9.0 **Volume IV. Reference**	paperback	1-59682-249-X	978-1-59682-249-8
		eBook (pdf)	1-59682-254-6	978-1-59682-254-2
	PostgreSQL 9.0 **Volume V. Internals & Appendixes**	paperback	1-59682-250-3	978-1-59682-250-4
		eBook (pdf)	1-59682-255-4	978-1-59682-255-9
PostgreSQL 8.04	PostgreSQL 8.04 **Volume I. The SQL Language**	paperback	1-59682-158-2	978-1-59682-158-3
		eBook (pdf)	1-59682-163-9	978-1-59682-163-7
	PostgreSQL 8.04 **Volume II. Server Administration**	paperback	1-59682-159-0	978-1-59682-159-0
		eBook (pdf)	1-59682-164-7	978-1-59682-164-4
	PostgreSQL 8.04 **Volume III. Server Programming**	paperback	1-59682-160-4	978-1-59682-160-6
		eBook (pdf)	1-59682-165-5	978-1-59682-165-1
	PostgreSQL 8.04 **Volume IV. Reference**	paperback	1-59682-161-2	978-1-59682-161-3
		eBook (pdf)	1-59682-166-3	978-1-59682-166-8
	PostgreSQL 8.04 **Volume V. Internals & Appendixes**	paperback	1-59682-162-0	978-1-59682-162-0
		eBook (pdf)	1-59682-167-1	978-1-59682-167-5

http://www.linbrary.com/postgresql/

Linbrary Advertising Club

CPSIA information can be obtained at www.ICGtesting.com
264769BV00003B/298/P